Library of
Davidson College

# REDEEMING THE SIN: SOCIAL SCIENCE AND LITERATURE

# REDEEMING THE SIN: SOCIAL SCIENCE AND LITERATURE

Audrey Borenstein

1978
Columbia University Press
New York

**Library of Congress Cataloging in Publication Data**

Borenstein, Audrey, 1930–
  Redeeming the sin.

  Bibliography: p.
  Includes index.
  1. Sociology—Methodology.  2. Sociology—
Classification.   3. Literature and society.
4. Humanism—20th century.   5. Creation (Literary,
artistic, etc.)  I. Title.
HM24.B616          301.5          78-9332

ISBN 0-231-04430-5

Columbia University Press
New York    Guildford, Surrey
Copyright © 1978 Columbia University Press
All rights reserved
Printed in the United States of America

*for my husband, Walter,*
*my children, Jeffrey and Shari,*
*and for Professor Robert Bierstedt,*
*first guide in my search for a sociology for humanists*

# CONTENTS

Prefatory Note and Acknowledgments ... ix

Introduction ... xiii

Part One
1  On the Sin of Social Science ... 3
2  On the Search for Reality ... 34

Part Two
3  Satirist and Sociologist: Some Likenesses ... 75
4  On Compassion ... 93

Part Three
5  Witnessing ... 127
6  On the Uses of the Imagination ... 176

Biographical Notes ... 217

Notes ... 231

Bibliography ... 249

Name Index ... 259

Subject Index ... 265

# PREFATORY NOTE AND ACKNOWLEDGMENTS

Those in the world of the social sciences and those in the world of letters have much to say to one another. This is a book about just that. I have elected to write it because I am both a writer and a social scientist, a social scientist by training and a writer by natural inclination, and I want to build a bridge between these worlds. This book, therefore, is a work in humanistic social science and at the same time a literary offering. I have written it as if thinkers from different intellectual disciplines and creative traditions have been having a conversation with one another.

So that social scientists and humanists, literary critics, and writers may acquaint themselves with one another's work, an appendix of brief biographical notes follows the text. Not every name that appears in the text is included in this section. Selection was made not on the basis of eminence or distinction in work but, rather, on the basis of whether or not the work cited is directly related to the topic discussed in one or another of the essays. Owing to the length of the list of names, it was decided that no more than four works by any one author would be included in each entry. Standard biographical sources were consulted for each person and, wherever possible, the English titles of works are given.

The major portion of chapter 1, "On the Sin of Social Science," first appeared in the form of an article entitled "Redeeming the Sin: Humanizing Sociology," in *Antioch Review*, vol. 34, no. 3, May 1976. Grateful acknowledgment is made to the editor of *Antioch Review* for permission to reprint this material. Acknowledgment is also gratefully made to Random House, Inc. and to Faber and Faber Ltd. for permission to reprint the lines from "Under Which Lyre" from *Collected Poems* by W. H. Auden; to Doubleday, Inc. and to Faber and Faber Ltd. for permission to reprint the lines from "The Waking" from *The Collected Poems of Theodore Roethke* by Theodore Roethke; to W. W. Norton and Co., Inc. and to The Hogarth Press Ltd. for permission to reprint the excerpts from Rainer Maria Rilke's letter to Witold von Hulewicz in the *Duino Eleqies* by Rainer Maria Rilke, translated by J. B. Leishman and Stephen Spender; to E. P. Dutton and Co. and to Jonathan Cape Ltd. for permission to reprint the excerpt from *The Book of Imaginary Beings* by Jorge Luis Borges, translated by Norman Thomas di Giovanni in collaboration with the author; to Simon and Schuster and to International Creative Management for permission to reprint selections from *Everything in Its Path: Destruction of Community in the Buffalo Creek Flood*, © 1976 by Kai T. Erikson; to The Viking Press, Inc., and Secker and Warburg Ltd. for permission to reprint selections from *Writers at Work: The Paris Review Interviews*, first series edited by Malcolm Cowley and second series edited by George Plimpton; to Houghton Mifflin Company and to Peter Owen Ltd. for permission to reprint excerpts from *Let Us Now Praise Famous Men* by James Agee and Walker Evans; to Basic Books, Inc., for permission to reprint the lines from " 'Just Sing It Yourself': The American Lyric Tradition" by W. Edson Richmond in *Our Living Traditions: An Introduction to American Folklore*, edited by Tristram Potter Coffin, and to Penguin Books Ltd. for permission to reprint materials from Elizabeth and Tom Burns (eds.), *Sociology of Literature and Drama*.

In June 1976, I was awarded a Creative Writing Fellowship by the National Endowment for the Arts in Literature, to write a book of short stories about the Deep South in the Kennedy years. I completed the book of fiction in the spring of 1977. But I also completed this book of essays during the year 1976–77, when I was still writing under the support of this Creative Writing Fellowship. Therefore, I wish to acknowledge my gratitude to the National Endowment for the Arts in Literature for the support that they gave me from June 1976 to June 1977, during which time I completed both the book of short stories and this book of essays.

For the completion of this book, I am deeply indebted to John D. Moore, editor in chief of Columbia University Press for all the encouragement and assistance he gave me, and for his kindness and good humor, his patience and his wisdom. I wish to express my appreciation to Professors Robert Bierstedt, Rudolf Heberle, Vernon Parenton and the late Donald Taft in sociology, and William Haag in anthropology, for sharing with me, in their classes and in friendship, the pleasures of social science. To my husband, Professor Walter Borenstein, my son Jeffrey and my daughter Shari, my gratitude is given here, for their help in the preparation of the biographical notes and the bibliography, for their loyalty and endurance, and, most of all, for being who they are and what they are.

Audrey Borenstein<br>
June 1977<br>
New Paltz, New York

# INTRODUCTION

In his novel *Magister Ludi (The Bead Game)*, Nobel Laureate Hermann Hesse created an ideal society in which the Castalian Order, an aristocracy of intellectuals, play the *Glasperlenspiel*. This commemoration of the unity of art and science is celebrated by an elite whose mental capacities were purified and enhanced by mathematical and Aristotelian-scholastic exercises, and who had turned away from fame and luxury to embrace a life of contemplation. The Bead Game, which has become a public festival in Hesse's Utopia, was once, in the Age of the Digest, a private exercise. There were intimations of the world-to-come in the Age of the Digest, an age when puzzle games were popular, and *feuilletons*, and lectures—a more sophisticated variation of the *feuilleton*. There were in these articles on myriad subjects, filled with facts and detailed material of topical interest, written—indeed, mass-produced—by writers, journalists, university professors and even poets, intimations of the game that was to achieve a creative synthesis of beauty, truth, and goodness. There were, in a time of uncertainty and despair, those who began to build bridges between the separated worlds of knowledge, between the divided cultures of the sciences and the arts.[1]

Political economy and social anthropology in an earlier day, and, in our own, psychohistory, sociobiology, ethnomycology, multimedia art—perhaps these are intimations of the *Glasperlenspiel*. The resemblance of this time to the Age of the Digest is unmistakable: the films and slides and puzzle games, the lectures and *feuilletons* besiege and bewilder the shaping sensibility. In this age, when knowledge and culture have been dismembered, there are those building bridges—between the arts and intellectual disciplines. These may be predecessors of the masters of the Bead Game.

Given the exotic combinations of arts and sciences created today, the suggestion of a strong relationship between literature and the social sciences is hardly preposterous. Certainly, the discovery of the consonances between them is anything but new. In their introduction to a collection of papers on the sociology of literature and drama, Elizabeth and Tom Burns note that the first explicit effort to treat literature sociologically has been credited to Madame de Staël, and that both Escarpit and Harry Levin have named Taine as the central figure in the conjunction between criticism and sociology.[2] In his recently published work on the novel and social science, Morroe Berger finds many coincidences of observation in fiction and social science. Among these are convergences in the work of Thomas Hardy and Thorstein Veblen, and in the work of George Eliot and Robert Michels, and George Eliot and Robert MacIver. Indeed, it was George Eliot, Berger contends, whose "scientific interests brought her, more than any other novelist, to the point of anticipating the notions and even the language of the social sciences."[3]

Of course, the convergences of works in fiction and in the social sciences are what the sociology of literature, and much literary criticism, are all about. The exchanges between these two worlds are often very lively—though often, too, quite unfriendly. Berger reminds us that the rivalry between poetry and philosophy was remarked long ago by Plato. He also takes note of contemporary thinkers who suggest that literature may be overtaken by social science in the twentieth century. For Max Eastman, humane letters were challenged by the scientific method applied to the study of man, and "this challenge . . . explained the weakness of modern literary criticism, fiction, and poetry. As the natural sciences in the seventeenth century displaced poetry in knowledge of nature, so the psychological and social sciences, including Marxism, were in the twentieth century displacing literature in the knowledge of man."[4] In what Berger interprets as a prelude to the attack made upon science in the 1960s, C. P. Snow delivered a lecture on "The Two Cultures and the Scientific Revolution" at Cambridge. In this lecture, Snow spoke of the absence of communication between scientists and literary intellectuals. He thought that the mutual suspicion between the two was based on dangerous misinterpretations, Berger observes, "and he believed each group to be 'impoverished' by its failure to see the value in the other's approach and achievements. He made a special plea to the literary men to understand the role that the 'scientific revolution' plays in reducing poverty and improving the condition of the world."[5]

Living reality is the source and substance of social science and of fiction. It is therefore inevitable that the fiction writer and the social scientist will meet time and again. Now, it is commonly assumed that the fiction writer enjoys a greater measure of freedom than the other, that he exercises his imaginative powers to the fullest whereas the social scientist must rein in his imagination and abide by the canons of scientific method. Upon closer inspection, however, the exercise of the imagination and the taking of certain liberties are found to enter into the shaping of many a social fact. Social science is an art at least by half. In the "data" gathered in questionnaires and interviews, in case studies, and in statistical tables and charts and graphs, there is "faction," a blend of fiction and fact. In the works of social science, as in fiction, there is verisimilitude.

But the meeting-ground for writers and social scientists is often an arena. In a thoughtful essay on the state of contemporary fiction, Eric Larsen explores matters in such a way as to suggest why this may be so. Larsen inquires into the deeper meaning of the freedom granted the contemporary fiction writer. According to Larsen, the freedom the writer enjoys today is greater than it has been in the past, but this very fact ought to arouse his suspicions. What it may imply is that the traditional relationship between the writer of realistic narrative and his readers has been severed. What is missing today, Larsen contends, is a lively and felt opposition to a writer's work. Realistic narrative "has existed always with a certain critical relationship to established interest of *some* kind," he remarks, "whether personal, social, political or ideological." This relationship has sometimes, as in the case of Jane Austen, been rather subtle. At other times, as in the case of Dickens, it has been "reformist and obvious." But a relationship has existed, nonetheless . . . until recently. The novel, whether an aesthetic or "art" novel, or a work of social realism, was never written in a vacuum. The writer was always conscious of engagement with *some* audience, from whom a crucial response of some sort was expected. This consciousness, in turn, affected the nature of the novel itself. But what has happened, Larsen maintains, is that "established interest no longer feels a threat (not even a threat of recognition or of conscience) from whatever writers might say." Freedom of expression may allow writers to *feel* that their work has some significant relationship to the real world. In truth, however, if there were such a relationship, it would not be expressed either in generosity to the writer, or in benign neglect of his work, but in shame or in anger, or even in repression.[6] Censorship is at least a kind of tribute, a sign that literature is taken seriously. Official society, in granting the writer unlimited freedom, is saying to him, as parents who grant unlimited freedom to their children are saying to them: *Do whatever you like; whatever you do is of no real consequence.*

Sensing a loss of relationship between his art and the forces that shape and drive his society, the writer attempts to connect the two, to find material that will enable him to bring his work out of the void, to bring it to life. But this material has already been claimed by others. How has this come about? Great literary artists appear to have the gift of clairvoyance. They grasp the essentials of the present reality, and, by this, they foresee and foretell. This has been appreciated by literary critics time and again; for example, in an essay on *Robinson Crusoe,* Ian Watt observes that the theoretical formulations of Marx, Weber, and Tawney had been anticipated long before by literary realization: *Robinson Crusoe* depicts the impact of the cash nexus upon *homo economicus.*[7] The writer, as Larsen puts it, is *ahead* of the news; he has been a harbinger of it, and perhaps at times he has even brought it about. "Writing, as a social or emotional barometer, has quivered, risen, fallen or pointed something out before the cruder senses of society at large have found themselves able even to perceive a change in the color of the horizon." Through his art, the writer has caused meaning to be felt or perceived where it was not felt or perceived before.[8] But this the writer finds it ever more difficult to accomplish. The private and the public have become interfused. Therefore, it is ever more difficult for the writer to find private experience to work with that has not "*already* (and perhaps reductively)" been "analyzed, labelled, and made public."[9]

The contemporary writer feels what Larsen refers to as a "panic for material." In a reversal of the process of realistic literary expression that obtained in the past, "The writer no longer scrutinizes privacy and through the alchemy of his art applies what he sees there to the larger world, but he begins to accept 'meanings' that are prepared for him already by that outside world . . . and then applies *them*, like an overlay or a script, to the apparently ungenerative private lives and experiences he moves among." Writing today has come full circle, Larsen maintains, from the manner of the eighteenth century, of depicting the general truth in the particular case. There is one difference, however: "in the 18th century those general truths came from God; here they seem to come from radios and the newspaper."[10]

And from social science, one might add. For, if Larsen is right about this, what the writers today are doing, in order to be published, in order to be noticed, in order to evoke a response, is thinking and writing *not* out of private experience but out of "the official treasury of public 'issues,' " working deductively, from the received opinion of newscasters, journalists and social scientists about the nature of reality, working from generalizations about what is the case to the particular cases that have engaged their attention.

In contemporary society, there is a continuous creation of causes and of social issues. These breed Instant Social Science and Instant Literature. This has not escaped Larsen's attention. He remarks that "A new 'movement' or 'issue' seems invariably to spawn suddenly dozens of works, amounting sometimes almost to new *genres*—on women, ethnicity, the counter-culture, the drug-culture, political protest, corruption, the back-to-the-earth movement, and so on."[11] In these one may recognize the *feuilletons* of Hesse's Age of the Digest. Those who have elected themselves to be the gurus and thus the celebrities of social science and fiction have mastered the technique of crafting a presentation, a blend of social facts and anecdotes that masquerades as culture and art, before vast audiences. Of all this one cannot be too wary, for, Larsen reminds us, "in the drift toward totalitarian social organization private experience is subordinated to public experience" and private thought to public thought. In fully developed totalitarianism, the range and variety of both available experiences and possible responses to life, are diminished:

Subtlety in thought and in the making of distinctions is discouraged, and the organizing of all experiences and of responses to it into a relatively few simplistic, labelled categories is ritually practised. Language is abused, made penurious, and, to whatever extent necessary to keep it from expressing the real vitality in life and thought, crippled.[12]

We may have arrived at this sorry pass some time ago. Our spoken and written language have been debased by self-appointed authorities of social and cultural reality. In their anxiety to be noticed, some writers have caught the fever of what has been aptly called "pseudo-speciation" from journalists and pop social scientists. There is a glibness and a presumptuousness about the social categories bandied about in publications and on television today—"the 50s,"[13] "the Third World," "the mainstream of American society," and about the personae served up from the cauldron of Instant Sociology—"the aged," "women," "the white majority male person." True understanding is ever at peril of being devoured by the sociocultural archetypes assembled by the social technicians that stalk the surfaces of the world. At the same time, the imagination is ever at peril of being swallowed up by the archetypes of interior life. Reality, beckoning to both the fiction writer and the social scientists, is that thin edge, that margin between the two abysses.

Freud, Jones said, was envious of the facility that certain writers have for achieving insights for which he had to labor so arduously.[14] Social insights are probably easier to come by than literary insights, for we are all sidewalk diagnosticians of the ills that beset society. Be that as it may, without knowledge of the social terrain, the writer cannot use his gift much. And, without the ability to express himself clearly, the social scientist is doomed to go on talking to himself. Fiction writers and social scientists drink from the same well. Ideally, their works ought to circulate freely in both worlds.

This has, of course, been known to happen. Michel Foucault opens his preface to *The Order of Things* with the acknowledgment that his work

first arose out of a passage in Borges, out of the laughter that shattered, as I read the passage, all the familiar landmarks of my thought—*our* thought, the thought that bears the stamp of our age and our geography—breaking up all the ordered surfaces and all the planes with which we are accustomed to tame the wild profusion of existing things, and continuing long afterwards to disturb and threaten with collapse our age-old distinction between the Same and the Other.[15]

And, in the remarks made by Saul Bellow to Gordon Lloyd Harper in the *Paris Review* interviews of *Writers at Work*, the work of Max Weber is invoked as Bellow speaks of the attractions that the nineteenth-century Russian writers have for him.[16] Yet, for all that they share, the writer and the social scientist have different paths to follow. There is a tension between them, often even an antagonism. For there is always the territorial imperative, the feeling on the part of the one that the other is trespassing. Thus, in his *Paris Review* interview, Bellow recalled that Herskovits, with whom he had studied African ethnography, rebuked him for writing *Henderson the Rain King*. The subject, Herskovits told Bellow, was far too serious for the "fooling" that *Henderson* seemed to him to represent. Bellow went on to say that he felt that this "fooling" was serious indeed. He suggested here, as he did in a television presentation of excerpts from *Humboldt's Gift* in 1977, that the imagination can be suffocated by literalism, that facts can be the enemy of the literary imagination.[17]

Writers and social scientists alike reach for the truths of their time, for the mentality of the living present. The convergence of the literary with the social scientific imagination is clearly seen in the "nonfiction novel." In his book on this genre and on the "new journalism," John Hollowell devotes a chapter to the vision of Norman Mailer, of "History as a novel, the novel as history." Mailer's three major works of nonfiction, *The Armies of the Night*, *Miami and the Siege of Chicago*, and *Of a Fire on the Moon* tell us, Hollowell says, "more about the American experience during the sixties than have many novelists. His imaginative treatment of the Pentagon march, his convention reports, and finally, his examination of the space effort have treated significant events of the decade." In these books, Hollowell maintains, "Mailer has reaffirmed that reality is mysterious and finally unknowable: to state the facts is to have created a fiction."[18] The "real world" lives in the finest fiction. And the best of works in social science are crafted by those with a lively imagination. It is apparent that any distinctions drawn between the literary and the social scientific imagination are arbitrary. There is much social fact in fiction, much fiction in social fact, as the controversy over Alex Haley's *Roots*—is it history or fiction?—attests.

There are books that defy the librarian's classification systems, that belong, if that is the word, as much to literature as to social science. James Agee and Walker Evans' *Let Us Now Praise Famous Men* is such a work. This book, named by James Carter as his favorite when he was asked this question by a reporter during his campaign for the presidency, has much to offer anthropologists, sociologists, economists and educators, as well as historians, literary critics, and students of photography. It is a work about the Depression, yet more than that; a work about the South, yet more than that; a work about poverty, and yet it transcends any narrowing focus. Books such as this one, and the "interdisciplinary studies" in which they are adopted, may be precursors of the Bead Game. They are a blend of rational analysis with intuitive imagining, which have for so long been kept sternly apart.[19]

The consonances between the two worlds of literature and social science have always fascinated me. Perhaps I hear a somewhat different drummer from sociologists who specialize in the sociology of literature, since I am a writer who happens to have elected to study social science, rather than a social scientist who happens to have elected to study fiction. In my literary endeavors, I learned very early on that I had best forbear wearing the emblem "social scientist" on my sleeve. Indeed, to reveal to the editors of literary journals ("littles") that one is a social scientist will probably have lethal consequences for the chances of having one's fiction published in them. I have found, too, that many social scientists I know look with indulgence upon my having taken the literary veil. They seem to have the attitude toward my fictional works that Herskovits took toward Bellow's *Henderson the Rain King*. There are so many urgent social problems, so many compelling social issues, they imply; making up stories is frivolous, diversionary. One ought to commit oneself, if not to saving the world, at least to making it more intelligible. That this is what many a creative writer is about seems unimaginable to many a social scientist.

The novel, Thomas Hardy remarked, is a series of impressions, not an argument. Of course, he did not speak for every fiction writer; no one could. Still, this comment offers much for social scientists, as well as writers, to reflect upon. In many a work of social science, as in much fiction, there are impressions as well as arguments. Only a social scientist who is a *scientist* with a vengeance would deny the value and the meaning of both. To live in social and cultural reality is to observe continually, and one observes with all one's senses, as well as with the counting mind. Citizens, even scientists, form opinions and make judgments on the bases of their impressions. The scientist, human as anyone else, risks missing what he does not care to see.[20]

Writers, of course, are inclined to be quite frank about what drives them; they are on very familiar terms with their demons. But, probably because social scientists aim to be objective, and endeavor to maintain a substantial psychological and moral distance between themselves and those they study, they remain silent on this subject. While the writer descends into himself, into his private experience in search of truth, the social scientist, ever outward-facing, tends to be suspicious of the connection between his inner life and the outer world. The connection is there, nonetheless: hypotheses and theories, as much as short stories and novels, are spun from the loom of "personal reality." In many truths offered as universal, there is a private truth. In *The Coming Crisis of Western Sociology*, Gouldner writes of these matters. "Every social theory," he maintains, "has both political and personal relevance, which, according to the technical canons of social theory, it is not supposed to have." Therefore, a theory that is presented as such is "purified" of the person and politics that entered into its formulation. But, Gouldner contends, whether he likes the fact or not, whether he is aware of this or not, one who confronts the social world is at the same time confronting himself. This may or may not affect the validity of the theory. It does, however, have bearing "on another legitimate interest: the sources, the motives, and the aims of the sociological quest." According to Gouldner, sociologists must come to terms with two spheres of reality, personal reality and role reality.[21]

In coming to terms with who one is and what one works for, the social scientist (and I am writing of the sociologist and anthropologist in particular, since these are the areas of social science in which I received my education), comes to reflect upon the comedy as well as the tragedy of social and cultural reality. Who misses the absurdity of the world has not been looking deeply or for long. Wherever one looks, one finds puffery and pride, the vanity and hypocrisy, the folly of it all—in human relationships, in "social structures," in "cultural systems." One must be utterly humorless to take it all with deadly seriousness. Perhaps of all the social scientists, the sociologist draws closest to the surveyor's post taken up by the satirist. What they have in common is not only a panoramic sweep of vision, but a moral interest in human relationships, in human affairs. There are exceptions to this, of course; there are always exceptions. But many sociologists want to know about some feature of the social landscape in order to protect and defend it, or to change it.

Whether they are aware of this dimly or keenly, sociologists are deeply engaged with that which they study. It is more than chance that draws a sociologist to the study of a particular social problem or social issue, or of a particular community or social category. The ministerial inclinations, the pastoral bent, the reformer's zeal of many sociologists is so widely recognized as to need no documentation here. By the very choice of an area of specialization, the sociologist makes a statement about what Gouldner calls the "personal realities." One studies the family, and another drug addiction; one is attracted to the ghetto, another to the suburb, one to the issue of capital punishment, and another to the issue of affirmative action.

Compassion is the driving force of many a sociologist's life and work—compassion for those of a particular social class or ethnic group or social category. Indeed, the justification, the rationale, for many studies and for the policies proposed on the basis of their findings, is predicated upon this emotion, about which so little is known, so little written. An inquiry into the nature of compassion reveals the antinomy within the soul of social science, and particularly of sociology. This is the antinomy between the desire to know simply for the sake of knowing, and the desire (or is it the passion?) to know in order to *act*. In the works of social science that are enduring, intellectual and moral commitment are so closely interwoven that the force of an argument often tells one at least as much about the person who advanced it as about the issue itself.

Very like many writers in this way, the social scientists' gift is at the same time their burden, one that releases but at the same time condemns them to a life of thought rather than a life of action. There are those who feel called to wield power, and those who feel called to explore the nature of power. Max Weber, Raymond Aron writes,

belongs to the school of sociologists who are interested in society because of their interest in public affairs and politics itself. There is a breed of sociologists who are nostalgic for political action; Weber, like Machiavelli, is incontestably of this breed. He would have liked to engage in the political contest, to exercise power; he dreamed of being a statesman rather than a party leader—the head of state being, at least in the imagination of outsiders, a man who accedes to the nobility of politics without accepting its servitude. Max Weber was neither a politician nor a statesman, but an advisor to the prince—unheeded, as is so often the case with advisors to the prince.[22]

In the desire to know the world, there is the dream of transforming it, and in the desire to transform the world, there is the dream of knowing it.

These desires and dreams give life to one another. They are the dreams and desires of both writers and of social scientists.

The social sciences are rooted in the humanities. Yet a preoccupation with ideology or methodology draws them ever further from their lifesource. Much that is written in social science today is not even readable; much that is claimed or proposed in its name is, whatever else it may be, not social science. No matter how sophisticated its technology may become, a field of knowledge will wither if its scholars and teachers are wanting in imagination. And the imagination grows restive with any doctrine. The need for the restoration of its link with the humanities may be particularly urgent in the case of sociology, since this of all the social sciences can by its very nature easily become moored in the present moment. Like the gifted writer who may dissipate his talent in the steady manufacture of *feuilletons,* the gifted social scientist may waste himself in pursuing the chimerae of fads and fashions in contemporary life. Both may drown their powers in topicality. One cannot develop a true feeling for one's own time without an understanding of the past. It is the mark of our time that people in America have, as Boorstin perfectly phrases it, "wandered out of history." Boorstin writes of the new price Americans pay for our standard of living, which is our "imprisonment in the present."[23] The responsible social scientist ponders the significance of this; he does not succumb to it himself. Only through the study of the humanities does one fully develop a sense of the past, and through this awareness of the vital connnection between the living and the dead, a true sense of the present.

Ever appreciative of how "anthropology has profited by being born within the scientific tradition," Ruth Benedict expressed the conviction in her essay on "Anthropology and the Humanities" that the humanistic and scientific traditions do not mutually exclude but, rather, complement one another. The neglect of the work of the great humanists, she wrote, has impaired the full realization of method and insight in anthropology.[24] In much the same spirit, E. F. Schumacher, in *Small Is Beautiful,* took the great majority of his colleagues in economics to task for insisting upon the pursuit of an "absurd ideal," that of making economics as precise and as scientific as physics, "as if there were no qualitative difference between mindless atoms and men made in the image of God."[25] There is a view of human nature that is implicit in contemporary economic theory, Schumacher remarked; yet economics is being taught without any appreciation of this. Indeed, he stated that many economists are not aware that a view of human nature is implied by their teachings, and that, if this view changed, their theories would have to change as well. Any subject that fails to make its view of human nature explicit, Schumacher charged, "can hardly be called humanistic."[26] Robert Bierstedt, in his presidential address read at the annual meeting of the Eastern Sociological Society in 1959, reminded his colleagues that Veblen's *The Theory of the Leisure Class*, Sumner's *Folkways*, and Tocqueville's *Democracy in America* were, all three, "quite innocent of the paraphernalia of formal method" and yet each of them "managed to say something of lasting importance about man in society." These writers were great sociologists, Bierstedt remarked, because "they were humanists first, and if they had not been great humanists they could never have become great sociologists."[27]

In this same presidential address, Bierstedt suggested that, while sociology ought to be a science, it ought to be more than that—a bridge between the sciences and the humanities.[28] Today, the walls between the social sciences and the humanities seem very high. Sociologists and anthropologists on the one hand, and fiction writers and literary critics on the other, have much to share. Yet they seldom read one another's work; they have little to do with one another. On any campus, there is not much love lost between social scientists, particularly sociologists, and English professors. In the 1960s, political activism made bedfellows of people from departments that had a tradition of estrangement from if not a hostility toward one another. With its decline in the 1970s, the old enmities are coming to the surface once more. And the financial woes of public and private institutions of higher learning intensify the bitterness of competition for scarce faculty positions and for the sort of impressive enrollments now thought to be necessary for academic survival. Social scientists accuse their colleagues in the humanities of unworldliness, of preoccupation with obscure and trivial concerns, of a shocking lack of acumen about the world in which we live. On their side, professors of literature or philosophy or the fine arts accuse social scientists of functional illiteracy, of intellectual barbarism, of responsibility for the deterioration of academic standards. The charges made on both sides are well founded in some cases.

There are extraordinarily astute professors of English who seem to have little social awareness, little sense of the way things flow in social and cultural reality. On the other hand, there are highly competent social scientists who read the equivalent of penny dreadfuls in their off-hours, who have an idea that literary folk are aesthetes and dilettantes and that literature is no more than the expression of a love of beauty. In the face of this situation, which gives every promise of further deterioration, it is past the time to build a bridge, a bridge between the humanities and the social sciences. Building these small bridges, seedlings of the Bead Game, is a delicate and risky task. One can only undertake it in full appreciation of the wisdom of Georg Simmel's reflection: "Although a bridge connects two banks, it also makes the distance between them measurable."

# REDEEMING THE SIN: SOCIAL SCIENCE AND LITERATURE

# PART ONE

*Thou shalt not answer questionnaires*
*Or quizzes upon World-Affairs,*
    *Nor with compliance*
*Take any test. Thou shalt not sit*
*With statisticians nor commit*
    *A social science.*

—W. H. Auden, "Under Which Lyre,"
*Collected Poems*

# ONE

## On the Sin of Social Science

> *We are all made up of fragments, so shapelessly and strangely assembled that every moment, every piece plays its own game. And there is as much difference between us and ourselves as between us and others.*
> —Montaigne,
> "Of the Inconsistency of Our Actions," *Essays*

Edmund Wilson tells us that Yeats believed that the more a man's mind is on fire, the more creative that mind is, "the less will he look at the outer world or value it for its own sake. It gives him metaphors and examples, and that is all. He is even a little scornful of it . . . ." Perhaps the social scientist's cast of mind was what Yeats condemned so harshly when he remarked that "peering and peeping persons are but hawkers of stolen goods. How else could their noses have grown so ravenous or their eyes so sharp?"[1] Wilson compares Yeats's "A Vision" with the "Guide to Socialism and Capitalism" by "that other great writer from Dublin," George Bernard Shaw. Shaw, Wilson says, "shouldered the whole unwieldly load of contemporary sociology, politics, economics, biology, medicine and journalism, while Yeats, convinced that the world of science and politics was somehow fatal to the poet's vision, as resolutely turned away." The contrast between the angle of vision of the poet and that of the social scientist is brilliantly drawn by Wilson: "While Yeats was editing Blake, Shaw was grappling with Marx." Yeats said that he hated *Arms and the Man*, and revealed that "Shaw appeared to him in a dream in the form of a sewing machine, 'that clicked and shone, but the incredible thing was that the machine smiled, smiled perpetually.'"[2]

The social scientists go on grappling with Marx. And, though they do not shine as brightly as Shaw, nor smile perpetually, they go on clicking, clicking steadily. Perhaps the difference between them and the poets is that they have a different design upon the world. In *Man Made Plain*, Robert Wilson writes that "The poet knows the world in order to feel it intensely. Most men in modern society know the world in order to manipulate it." Not only commerce and popular culture, but the social sciences as well, are directed toward "the instrumental and the extrinsic."[3] In his foreword to Wilson's book, Henry Murray says that the poetic enterprise may be distinguished from the scientific enterprise in that the poet has always "been preoccupied with concrete, emotive presentations of . . . subjective, existential, evaluative truth . . . , knowledge of the *feel* of things," whereas "the social scientist of the new order is preoccupied with abstract . . . , referential presentations of external, . . . objective, . . . non evaluative truth, knowledge of the uninvolving *look* of things." The difference, Murray says, is "between *being* in love . . . and witnessing with cool eyes the *doings* of a lover . . . ."[4]

One does not need to conduct a study in order to discover that, of all social scientists, sociologists may be regarded by the poet as the most sinful. Indeed, sociologists are attacked repeatedly for being antihumanistic; and, of all writers, the poet is the most distant from the sociologist. One might suppose that this is because so many sociologists think of themselves as scientists, who are after a description and analysis of the world of appearances, whereas the poet seeks to see through and under and beyond the surfaces of things. But the matter is not so simple as all that. From the beginning, Peter Berger says, sociology has understood itself to be a science.[5] But from the beginning, too, social scientists—and certainly sociologists among them— have been a part of that which they endeavor to portray. In *The Social Order*, Bierstedt discusses the distinction between the natural sciences, "limited to the use of an *erklärende* (explaining) method" and the social sciences, which may adopt a "*verstehende* (understanding) method," though, he goes on to suggest, this distinction has not always been accepted by American sociologists.[6] Tom and Elizabeth Burns refer to these as two different kinds of methodological strategy. The *verstehende* strategy, associated with the work of Max Weber, envisions human society as an intricate network of interrelated and interdependent meanings. And the *erklärende* strategy, associated with the work of Emile Durkheim, "is more akin to the traditions of the natural sciences, . . . and conceives society, institutions and the social action of individuals as objective facts to be *explained* by the conventional processes of the scientific study of objective reality."[7]

It is the Burnses' contention that, while the two strategies are not mutually exclusive, neither are they fully complementary. For they do not seem to be reconcilable "in some grand, overarching system." Current thinking in sociology "suggests the necessary co-existence of both." Now by the simple device of presuming a dialectical relationship between the two, one might treat the dilemma as though it had been resolved. The idea of a dialectical relationship between the Weberian and Durkheimian strategy, however,

> serves as little more than a life-raft on which it is possible to stand between the clear sky of scientific positivism and the deep waters of post-Kantian phenomenology, and await rescue. We have . . . to regard the relationship as perpetually antithetical. This is no more than to accept the common-sense appreciation, first, of the difference between living our own lives in the world and understanding the world in which we live, and, second, of the business of living, and the attempt to understand the world, being in a necessarily dependent relationship to each other, which is equally common-sense.[8]

The Burnses believe that the dualism between the continuous process of objectification in which living our lives involves us, and our efforts to understand the world in which we live, are given an archetypal model in literature and drama. Following Kermode, the Burnses have distinguished literature, which, they say, "is an attempt to make sense of our lives" from the work of some sociologists and critics, who "attempt to make sense of the ways in which we live our lives."[9]

Whether the relationship between the *verstehende* and *erklärende* perspectives is antithetical or less desperate than that, there are probably few sociologists in the United States in the habit of reading poetry, much less of writing it. Indeed, sociologists are not famous as patrons of *any* of the arts. Gouldner has acknowledged that most of the sociologists whom he knows "seem to have little interest in 'culture' and are rarely in evidence at galleries, concerts, or plays."[10] One suspects that sociologists who regard performances in the theater and concert hall, or the reading of fiction and poetry, or excursions to art galleries and museums as frivolous or diversionary or "elitist," can be easily identified by their uses and abuses of language. But sociologists are not the only culprits; *all* the social scientists stand accused of deformation, mutilation, even outright destruction of our blessèd tongue. Though intentions may (and only *may*) be honorable, the social scientists' offenses to language, were there divine justice in these matters, would have rendered many of them deaf and dumb long ago. Social scientists seem dedicated to the practice, Edwin Newman wrote, of "taking clear ideas and making them opaque."[11] In *Strictly Speaking* (and in its successor, *A Civil Tongue*), Newman gives the entire tribe a verbal drubbing that is richly deserved. One who has the heart to try to penetrate the dense verbiage of many a social scientific report may come to the conclusion that some sociologists and economists, political scientists and psychologists, and even anthropologists and historians (the people in education are, of necessity, though with great reluctance, omitted from this census), are engaged in competition on several fronts at once: Which will be the first to win the title for his discipline of the age's Most Dismal Science? The last to (re-)discover inner life? The first to reach the outer limits of tortured circumlocutions of language in addressing a reasonably clear and simple question?

"Clear writing represents clear thinking," Edward Pessen reminds us all. "It is not a stylistic adornment but an essential proof of the historian's grasp."[12] The writing of many influential books of history, he says, is impenetrable and dull, and the pages filled with equations and tables and graphs. Apparently, some of the "new" historians are adopting certain features of sociology—and some of the worst features, at that. "The subjects of the cliometricians' discussion of slavery," Pessen remarks, "are not human slaves but statistical abstractions." There seems to be an aversion on the part of some "new" historians to what is individual and unique. But, Pessen writes, for the historian, as well as for anyone who endeavors to understand human action, the central subject matter *is* the individual and the unique.[13]

In this article, Pessen makes the telling observation that to dismiss the individual as unique, and therefore not worthy of close study, is more akin to dogma than to scientific empiricism. It well may be that those of an antihumanistic temper who make large claims about being scientific, also happen to be those who dismiss the concern for clear expression as "merely literary" or "belletristic" or "elitist." Of course, not every social scientist is an ideologue. There are those who are infatuated with methodology in the social sciences, just as there are those who are fascinated by technique in the arts. It is apparent just from reading some highly sophisticated statistical treatments of "data" that have been "gathered" in ways very much open to question, that some of them have been written for the sake of having another item to add to one's list of publications, whereas others have been written to support what one wants to believe or to advocate.[14] Social scientists are at least as diverse a lot as priests or judges or writers. There will probably always be those who have a great deal to say, but who lack the time or the inclination or the literary endowment to write more than a fraction of what they have to offer. And there probably will always be those who insist upon inundating the journals with trivia or confusion. "It is the glory of some men to write well," La Bruyère remarked, "and of others not to write at all." Those in search of the truth of the ways in which we live our lives are in desperate need of a divining rod to take to the publications in the "field."

But, as Pessen observes, not all the obscurity is innocent. Committing a social science has meant, for all too many, committing oneself to an ideology, or a patois of ideologies—becoming a true believer who speaks in tongues (though often tied ones) in the classroom. Many social scientists play the missionary, seeking converts to the Faith. In sociology, there are those who hold forth in the classroom as spokesmen and spokeswomen for one or another of the many parts we play in public and in private life: the Woman, the Minority Person, the Homosexual, the Working Class. Jungian psychotherapists speak of "walking around" the dream-narrative of a patient, in order to explore all its possibilities of meaning. This is a felicitous expression. Sociologists, too, are supposed to "walk around" their subject, whether this be work norms in a factory, or a self-criticism session in a drug rehabilitation center. For both psychoanalyst and sociologist, there is supposed to be an effort made to withhold one's private opinions in order to explore the possibilities of perspective and meaning. One stands aside, rather than in one's own light, in order to draw forth the significance of things, in order to shape understanding. Sociologists are not supposed to become partisan to some particular cause or movement or ideology—at the very least, not when they are teaching. In lecturing to his students, Max Weber remarked that there is scarcely a professor who could claim, or who ought to claim, to be a leader either in the vital matters of life or in matters of conduct. The qualities that make for an effective teacher or a good scholar, Weber said, are very different from those necessary for an effective leader in practical life. If one wants to be an activist, there is always the market place, there is always the press, there are always organizations. "But . . . it is somewhat too convenient to demonstrate one's courage in taking a stand where the audience and possible opponents are condemned to silence."[15]

Yet this is precisely what is done in many classrooms; indeed, this has become commonplace since the 1960s. And, though professors of English or history, or mathematics or biology, have been known to use the podium as a pulpit as well, this has become the distinctive style of teaching for many sociologists—a style cultivated all the more since the implementation of "affirmative action." It may be that the very nature of sociology presents temptations for its practitioners that only the most saintly or the most disengaged could resist for very long. However, to understand is not necessarily to forgive. Sociologists do not have the license to absolve students or anyone else from the responsibility for making a conscious and intelligent choice between faiths to be believed, between causes to be served.Knowledge of social and cultural circumstances can ever and only be the beginning of the human adventure.

In an essay on "Literary Fiction and Reality," Frank Kermode cites a passage in Ortega's "History as a System," a paper that contends with many of the the issues to which Sartre has addressed his work. "It is too often forgotten," Ortega wrote, "that man is impossible without imagination, without the capacity to invent for himself a conception of life, to 'ideate' the character he is going to be. Whether he be original or a plagiarist, man is the novelist of himself." Man must choose, Ortega wrote, and is therefore free; but he is free by compulsion (*forced* to be free, in Sartre's phrasing.) And, "To be free means to be lacking in constitutive identity, not to have subscribed to a determined being, to be able to be other than what one was . . . ."[16] Perhaps the denial of this freedom to be the architect of one's own life is at the root of the sociologist's sin. Still, it is one thing to explore the circumstances of a human life, and quite another to argue that they are overwhelming, that an individual has no choice except to surrender to absorption by some social category whose mission is no less than to make history. Many sociologists with an ax to grind merge societally ascribed identity with being. Perhaps it does not occur to them, or they choose to ignore, that all but feral beings have a history and are born into social and cultural circumstances. Nor do they choose to recognize that this, the very understanding of the influences that shape one's view of the world, is the occasion for the birth of freedom.

In Saul Bellow's *Humboldt's Gift*, Charles Citrine reflects upon the category to which common opinion assigns his lady-love, Renata, she who was "as a biologically noble beauty in a false category." Though she wanted to defy and outsmart it, she also collaborated with it. And if there is one historical mission for all of us, Citrine counsels, "it is to break with false categories. Vacate the personae."[17] This is wise counsel, indeed, though a difficult and perilous mission. For the personae of gender and generation, of ethnic and racial, religious and now sexual affiliation, of occupational and economic strata in the social stratification scheme (*system*, yclept) are the very stuff of which our society is said by the sociologists to be made. The personae are real in their consequences, as W. I. Thomas would have put it, for those who play their assigned roles. They have a long and intricate history; and they unfold through time as embodiments of social-historical forces engaged in a struggle for ascendancy. To deny the reality of office, of status or position or sociological *place*, is to deny the reality of the outer world. And it is "no illusion," Henry James reminded us, "no phantasm," this world we inhabit, "no evil dream of a night; we wake up to it again for ever and ever; we can neither forget it nor deny it nor dispense with it."[18]

It is the business of social scientists, and particularly of sociologists, to explore the nature of the personae, to consider the ways in which our lives are expressed through playing our many parts. This is the raison d'être of social science, whose practitioners are cartographers and explorers of the outer world. What shall be done with this understanding, to what uses such knowledge may be applied, is another matter. But the workings of conscious life, of human association, of risk and of choice and of endeavor in this arena called "society," cannot, *will* not be wished away.

Nor can the workings within—the dreaming, the shapes of figures from mythology, the archetypes, the creatures of our imagination and passions, of our wit and our delights, our fears and our anguish—be wished away. Yet, all too often, one eye has been closed for the sake of seeing more clearly with the other. And inner life is thought of, then, as a mere shadow-play of human affairs, of the conflicts between sexes or races, or social classes or generations. In the eyes of the poet, *this* may be the sin—the original sin—of social science.

Sociologists are well aware that most of us do not always hold or express the attitudes, opinions and perspectives that, in theory, flow from our "statuses" in society. Some of them attribute this to the multiplicity of statuses that, like tenants, we occupy now and again in our lives. There are learned treatises in sociology on such matters as "status conflict" and "role conflict" and "situational ethics." Yet time and again, sociologists forget, or choose to forget, that it is only in theory that a woman or a Chicano or a homosexual inherits a history and a web of social circumstances that contribute to the forging of a certain world-view. In theory, but not in experience, one's sociological *place* determines one's mode of consciousness. None of us is always what we make ourselves appear to be, or what we take as social-historical circumstances having "given" or "forced" us to be. There are human faces under the masks of the personae; and each of us in his or her own time wears many masks. As we live out our lives, we move from one social category to another; often, we find ourselves in several at the same time. Yet that which we are eludes all the personae, all the social categories, all the "variables" of age or gender, social class or ethnic affiliation. To be fully human is to vacate the personae, as

Bellow would have it, to outstrip them all: this is the meaning of the examined life.

Age and sex are usually given as examples of the two most clearly "ascribed statuses" in North American society. Yet, even in these two cases, in which identities are societally conferred and socially sustained, it is clear that the statuses are anything but fixed and final. "Everyone is partly their ancestors," Virginia Woolf remarked, "just as everyone is partly man and partly woman." And, in the fullness of time, each of us wends our way upward through the "age-sex pyramid" of the demographers. Just as no young person will remain young for very long, just as every youth carries an "old one" within him, so every elderly person carries somewhere within, the self who was once a child, a youth. There is not, in the way we experience our lives, a purely male or female sex; and every year we live is ghosted by our earlier selves and with intimations of our aging self. Given the epidemic of conversions in contemporary life, the "variables" of "ethnic" and "religious" affiliation hold even less steadily than those of age and sex. Nor, given the uncertainties of the labor market, and the career changes that are sometimes a luxury and at other times a necessity, is occupational identity any less protean.

It is, of course, a fundamental tenet of sociological doctrine that location in the societal structure influences the perspective a person has, that social arrangements, one's fellow human beings, and one's life-chances, all appear one way to a wealthy person and quite another way to one who is poor, one way to a woman and another to a man. One's perspective is certainly influenced by the place where one happens to be standing when looking outward. In Introductory Sociology courses, students often work out a sort of "socio-analysis" of their lives. They consider how their political generation, their religious affiliation, their parents' economic history all influence the ideas they have about justice and beauty and truth, about the human condition and human destiny. They come to appreciate how one's place in the outer world is interwoven with one's thoughts and feelings about things. Those who embrace the Marxist doctrine (perhaps the word "gospel" is more appropriate) conclude that what one feels and thinks to be true, what one apprehends and what one hopes for in life, reflect one's social class position in history and in society. For Marxists, inner life is the image in the mirror. Sociology *is* fundamentally, as C. Wright Mills put it, the fascinating study of how biography intersects with history.[19]

But to deny the autonomy of inner life is to deny what makes us fully and truly human. One does not dream about the masks, the personae puffing and steaming forth from the Aladdin's lamp of the sociologist; one does not dream about the People or Deprived Minorities or the White, Middle-Class, Urban Male. One dreams of wicked witches, or of very particular people. There are archetypes, if Jung is to be believed, and they will appear to us in various guises and work through our thoughts and feelings, wherever and whoever we may happen to be, in history and in society.

Though outer life may be represented as a diagram of links between sociological variables—sex or social class, creed or generation—inner life may not. One is so *many* selves, and so many selves at once, and the rigid model is a mockery of this. Of course, one could dismiss all inner life as an opiate of the people. Indeed, this is a necessary tenet for those who would know the world in order to make an instrument of it. Locating a person in societal space then becomes a form of fortune-telling. Collectivities, social categories, personae, variables are wished or willed into social groups—and, these days, into kinship groups in which sociologically defined compeers are magically transformed into sisters or brothers. The claim that one is the "product" of one's history and social circumstances, however, may be made by those of *any* persuasion—by the executioner, who may say that he cannot help himself any more than could those he executes; by the oppressor as well as by the oppressed, by the torturer as well as by his victim. It is a claim made in "bad faith," in flight from freedom.[20] If sociologists are to understand themselves and others, if they are to explore relationships between human beings and not between robots or variables, they must remain as sensitive to the changing impressions, moods, desires, musings—the humors—of inner life, as to changing fortune . . . and all the more sensitive to the shifting orchestration of inner with outer life.

But the sewing machines go on clicking, the social scientists go on sinning. Diagrams of the interconnections between variables are presented as representations of human experience. The person is dissolved in the persona, the concept is reified, the variables breed shamelessly—the "organization man" or the "Third Force" a generation ago, the "racist," the "sexist," the "ageist," the "Third World," in our own time. And eminent sociologists have spoken repeatedly of the folly of this. Over twenty years ago, in his 1956 presidential address to the American Sociological Association, Herbert Blumer presented a critical examination of variable analysis which, he saw, was becoming the norm of analytical procedure in sociology. The pool of variables, he said, was expanding; there seemed to be no rules governing the selection of variables; and the laxity in choosing them was owing, he thought, to the lack of careful reflection about the problem before undertaking analysis. Blumer also called attention to the absence of truly generic variables, variables that stand for abstract categories. Without these, he said, there can be no empirical science. Blumer enumerated three kinds of variables that are not generic, though they are often taken to be so. One of these he called a "special set of class terms," including "sex" and "age," which, he said, do not function as generic variables. Instead, the variable relations are localized; each has a content given by its particular instance of application. Although Blumer said that these limitations of variable analysis might eventually be overcome, they suggest "the advisability of inquiring more deeply into the interesting and important question of how well variable analysis is suited to the study of human group life in its fuller dimensions."[21]

In the tradition of the *verstehende* approach, Blumer's address reminded us that we act on the basis of the meanings that things have for us, that we wend our way through our lives by defining situations. To understand a "here and now" relation, he said, one must understand the "here and now" context. Variable analysis does not yield this understanding. We do not know what the variables mean; we do not see people as "human beings in their particular world" when we use this approach, and therefore we cannot make sense of the class terms into which we dissolve them. The core of human action, Blumer said, is the process of definition and interpretation that goes on continually in human groups. This process gives human group life a character that is at odds with the premises of variable analysis. For human group life is "a vast interpretative process." And the interpretative process is bypassed by variable analysis.

Nor is this all. Sociologists who work through using the method of variable analysis, also work with factors that have been truncated. Therefore, they conceal or misrepresent what actually obtains in human group life. The empirical reference of a sociological variable is neither unitary nor distinct, Blumer stated: "When caught in its actual social character, it turns out to be an intricate and inner-moving complex." As an illustration, he discussed the relation between a birth-control program and the birth rate of a given people. To understand the meaning of the birth-control program, "we need to know it in terms of *how it enters into the lives of the people*." Nor is the birth rate (a Durkheimian "social fact") simple or unitary, but only seems so. Blumer called for a scheme of sociological analysis very different from that of variable analysis, one based on the the premise that human group life proceeds and is formed by definition. What is needed is to "approach the study of group activity through the eyes and experience of the people who have developed the activity."[22]

Leafing through the sociology journals, one finds that Blumer's words have not been heeded. Though there are rumbles of discontent from many quarters, the old variables turn up again and again, like the bad pennies they are. In an editorial in *Science*, Amitai Etzioni discusses the implications of the forecast of the Organization for Economic Cooperation and Development that not long after 1984, "six or seven times the present volume of new information will be produced." At the same time, the OECD predicted that "the degree of automation of information will approach a hundred times that of today." Mini- and microcomputers allow for centralization, Etzioni acknowledges; they will render the processing of information cheaper and more accessible. "And in a world rich in routine and rut, small computers will be able to take on many of the menial tasks scientists, or their apprentices, now must do." However, there is a price that is exacted for reaping the benefits of the spread of the miniaturized computer. "The very rapid turnabout time compact computers allow between obtaining readings on instruments as well as between data processing runs," Etzioni writes, "practically eliminates the time once allotted to examining the findings, reflecting on their implications, and evolving hypotheses." People will be very sorely tempted, he says, to "keep shooting in the dark," on the assumption that an intriguing correlation or reading will eventually be found. The result may well be that scientists will come to replace a focused effort with trial-and-error search, yielding findings that do not confirm any theorem, but are, rather, no more than an assemblage of data. This would only be a repeat performance of the impact that the use of prepackaged computer programs has made on some areas of the social sciences, where

> the ability to use a prepackaged program to "analyze" a data set, say of the opinions of a random national sample of adults, often results in interpretations that have all the convenience but also the bite of a precooked, frozen TV dinner. This is because existing categories are used even if they do not capture well the variables under study. Thus, opinions are analyzed in terms of sex, age, income, and size of city, even if these correlate poorly with the issues at hand. Much to-do then is made over a difference of a few percentage points between subgroupings (say young versus old), while much greater differences would be found if more suitable but less commonly tapped variables (or combinations thereof) were teased out. Finding such variables, however, requires considerable intellectual, not mechanical, effort . . . .[23]

Rural and urban, black and white, male and female, young and old, middle class and working class—these bloodless and fleshless death masks of the human spirit continue to haunt social scientific analysis. The imagination is caught fast in their moorings. Again and again, one finds examples in research endeavors of how variable analysis leads one astray. In a review of Matilda Riley's *Aging and Society*, George Maddox makes the observation that much research on social processes

> has badly confounded behavior which might be attributable to age (as a proxy for maturation), to cohort (as a proxy for specific historic experiences), and to the interaction between age and cohort at particular points in time within particular environments . . . . If behavioral and social scientists intend to present more than static, quickly outdated, and inadequate characterizations of social and biosocial phenomena, they will have to utilize cohort analysis.[24]

Indiscriminate use of the term "youth" is at least as rife as that of "the aged." In a review of *Youth: Transition to Adulthood*, a report of the President's Science Advisory Committee Panel on Youth, John Clausen enumerates the fundamental features of a "youth culture," as "psychic attachment to peers . . . , a press toward autonomy, concern for the underdog, and an interest in change rather than in the stability of the social order. These features tend to wall youth off from the larger society."[25] In the same vein, sociologists write of the unique features of the culture of blacks or Chicanos or women or the working-class or the aged, as distinct from and alienated from "the larger society" or the (by now hopelessly hackneyed) "mainstream" of American society. This "larger society" is presented as a mosaic which seems to lend itself to disassembling and reassembling, like the parts of an Erector set, depending upon the analyst's point of view. In countless sociological "studies," it is stated that the young or the old, the poor or the working class, the blacks or women or homosexuals are alienated from this "larger society." If even half these studies were to be believed, it would appear that the periphery of the "larger society" is far more populous than its center. But, of course, the sociological investigation may be a ruse for advocating a certain position about economic and political matters; an ideological bias masquerades as sociological analysis. In this way the issues are confounded, and divisiveness is encouraged between the ages, the sexes, the ethnic groups, between the social classes, the categories, the personae—the variables trotted out from the shelves and dusted off for multivariate manipulation, or concocted for the occasion of the research. Edwin Newman writes of how uncomfortable it makes him to "hear the breakdown of voting results according to religion and race and national origin." Though this is an efficacious way to determine the direction that an election is taking, he observes, "it helps to perpetuate divisions that we might be better off without, because it leads people to go on thinking of themselves in a particular way, as members of a particular group, which may have little connection with the issues the election is about."[26]

At least as vexing as the threadbare old variables are those that are taken from the vernacular and incorporated into sociological studies, as well as those that are coined during the course of a research project. In a well-known, though now quite dated, study of the sexual behavior patterns of college students, for example, "nonvirginal women" were classified into six groups—the Loving, the Experimenters, the Sowers of Wild Oats, the Homosexually Inclined, the Remorseful, and the Married. "Nonvirginal men" were classified into Hot Bloods, Pragmatists, Discriminating, Romantics, and Homosexual Variants.[27] The nomenclature in this work, like that which designates varying patterns of adjustment to retirement in another, much more recent study—the "mature," the "rocking-chair men" and the "armored" among the well-adjusted, and the "angry men" and "self-haters" among the poorly adjusted[28]—is at least graphic. But objections to classificatory terms are made on much more serious grounds than that they are often inelegantly phrased. The truth is that we are all a bit of each of the sociological designations at one time or another. Even though one may bend, fold, or spindle a person into one category or another, there is no reason to suppose that this person will remain there forevermore.

This taxonomic mania of some social scientists, this sifting and sorting of human beings into categories old or new, can work much mischief, whether intended or not. In his review of Ladd and Lipset's *The Divided Academy*, a collection of articles based upon a survey of faculty, student, and administrative opinion conducted in 1969 and a smaller follow-up survey conducted three years later, Walter Metzger raises very important questions about the purposes, procedures, and implications of some works of political sociology. The sin in this case was mortal rather than venial; given its sample, its uncommonly long questionnaires, and its operating budget, this survey of opinion on a broad range of academic as well as national issues by the Carnegie Commission on Higher Education presents, Metzger remarks, "an almost vulgar display of technical capacity and empiric riches." In Metzger's review, which ought to be read in its entirety for a full appreciation of its significance, he refers to the benefits to be derived from data yielded by large-scale survey research projects such as the Carnegie project. In this particular survey, he notes, the benefits are not limited solely to descriptive findings: "Thanks to its breadth of interrogation, the Carnegie survey shows up disparities between faculty responses to remote and to impinging issues, and thus reveals at what points an alarmed self-interest comes into play to shape opinion." Because of the extraordinary size of its sample (60,000 full-time faculty members), the respondents can be subdivided extensively, and a number of variables can be subjected to analysis. Both Ladd and Lipset, he says, "are seasoned practitioners of statistical reportage and multivariate manipulation," and the texts and tables they present, derived from the data gathered in the Carnegie survey and in the follow-up survey conducted three years afterward, are "admirably informative and trim."

Ladd and Lipset, however, are after more than the presentation of the data, Metzger writes. They assume "that basic ideological predispositions can be derived from clusters of answers to current political questions, that these predispositions can be located on a continuum running from 'left' to 'right,' and that the relative strength of one factor—'intellectuality' or 'intellectual bent' can account for group differences along that scale." Though the quest for configurations of attitudes is scarcely new, Metzger remarks, what is at issue here is whether the evidence available from the survey can support those that are proposed. Can ideologies be identified by the responses to four questions about specific issues, in addition to responses in which people categorize themselves politically?

If it is held that one thinks ideologically when one answers queries on current questions with some consistency, then these questions may have diagnostic power. On the other hand, if it is presumed that one thinks ideologically when one responds to immediate issues by considering them in the light of one's moral and intellectual commitments, then these questions . . . cannot be regarded as effective probes.[29]

Consistency in responses may mean no more than that the subject is sophisticated in the taking of tests, Metzger reminds us. Therefore, it is advisable to ask questions about ideology if one wants to obtain information about ideology. This was not done in the survey. Nor was an ideological census taken. But what can take the place of asking such questions, if the social scientist wishes to understand what is going on in the respondent's mind? If, Metzger says, one asked William Graham Sumner his opinions about such matters as high tariffs or literary freedom, the responses he would give would reveal a consistent strain of liberalism. If one did not ask him about such matters as the moral value of hard work, one would not learn that he was an arch-conservative.

The rubrics for political positions under which the professors were asked to locate themselves—"strongly conservative," "moderately conservative," "middle-of-the-road," "liberal," and "left"—are, Metzger remarks, more than mere summaries of political positions. Though the social scientist can show a statistical relationship between political opinion and position choice on the basis of responses to these questions, he has no way of knowing whether a professor who places himself in one of these five categories "is responding to convictions in his mind or to the popularity of the labels." Furthermore, the meanings of the labels change in time; and, though respondents were asked to categorize the political views they had when they were college students, it is not clear whether the changes have taken place inside people's heads, or outside, that is, in the labels. Nor is Metzger convinced that the differences between positions are quantitative. The interpretative process, as Blumer would have remarked, is circumvented in surveys such as this one. As a consequence, one is not able to ascertain confidently what people's positions actually are on fundamental issues of social and political life.[30]

The sociological wizardry that "resolves" differences between viewpoints by the expedient of hyphenation ("liberal" and "left" are merged into one "variable" in this study), or that adopts a term, as this one does the term "intellectuality" to "explain" leanings, as in this case toward the "liberal-left," works a good deal of mischief. Metzger calls our attention to the fact that, in this work, the strategem lends itself to the service of documenting anti-academic folklore. The addiction to categorizing and labeling interferes with our understanding of what people are actually doing, and why they are doing it. Blumer, of course, would have predicted that this would happen in any research project that treats "variables" as though their empirical referents were distinct and unitary. The results of such research, no matter how sophisticated the methodology might be, could only be a concealment or a misrepresentation of what is really going on. Ladd and Lipset jestingly suggest, Metzger recalls, that it might be more meaningful to ask an American intellectual whether he reads *Commentary* or *The New York Review of Books* than to ask him to classify himself as a liberal or a conservative. It is Metzger's opinion that Ladd and Lipset ought to have taken their own jest seriously. To ask professors to classify themselves in one of five categories on a predetermined scale is to elicit forced testimony. But "To ask people of learning what they read, and in which authors they find their guides, might well be to increase the chance of gaining entry into that screened interior of thought and feeling where political identities are cast."[31]

"Literary experience," Robert Wilson observes, "is seldom considered to be an important factor in the individual's life history. We correctly search first for the interpersonal events . . . ." But, he goes on to say, we live in a world made up of words: "In emphasizing face-to-face encounters, the more subtle relation between writer and reader via the printed page is often overlooked."[32] To understand a person, it is not enough—and, indeed, it may often be deceptive—to know where he may be placed in the sociological categories, who his personae are. One must know how he thinks, and how his thoughts are shaped. Since I teach in a Continuing Education program, my students are much more heterogeneous than those in the typical undergraduate sophomore or junior class. I have made it a practice to ask my students to tell me what, if any, their reading habits are; and I find this far more revelatory than knowing their age or sex or ethnic affiliation.

If a social scientist insists upon putting everyone in boxes, he will not see human beings, but only his own ghosts. The truth of what it is to be human will elude him. And, before he embarks upon a research project, he will know what his "findings" will be. Time and again in the classroom, I have seen how little the masks, the personae, tell one. In the changing expressions, the gestures, the words of others, there are irruptions of inner life. I remember a Latin American student, perhaps thirty years old, in my Social Problems class one semester. He was preoccupied not with poverty, or with discrimination, or with any of the matters one might assume to be paramount in his life. It was religion that intrigued him. He was deeply offended by what he took to be an excessively secular attitude in Durkheim's *Suicide,* and he talked at length about the meaning of what it is to be a Christian. A zealous Catholic, one might have supposed; but, no, he was a devout member of a Protestant sect. The more he talked, the more attentively I read the essays he had written on examinations, the more he revealed a person who eluded—or is it defied?—the sociological categories. Another student, who played the role of Archie Bunker rather convincingly in class, presenting himself as a prejudiced conformist, a man preoccupied with such matters as "welfare cheating," was nothing of the kind. Art, I discovered, was the ruling passion of his life. The man he presented himself to be—before his wife, before his adolescent children, his co-workers, his fellow classmates—was someone whose part it amused him to play. He had achieved a measure of what Goffman calls "role distance" from this fellow. Yet, only a measure. Listening to him talk in class, watching his reactions to others, I saw how he sometimes fell into the role he had created for himself, and how he had to struggle at times to work his way back out. He was troubled by some of the unhappy things the sociologist is forever talking about, but not at all by others. He said he had no patience with people who would commit suicide; on the other hand, he was bedeviled when we discussed poverty and capital punishment. All people are like this, I thought, listening to his comments—sometimes insightful, sometimes ridiculous; and this is what questionnaires, and even many skillfully conducted interviews miss. I thought of the wisdom of La Rochefoucauld's remark that "We get so much in the habit of wearing disguises before others that we finally appear disguised before ourselves." The "minority" woman in my class who was deeply troubled by alcoholism, the young girl who was coping with a serious illness, the young man whose mother had committed suicide—social issues, social problems, outer reality came through by way of what had happened to them in their lives, and what they were trying to make of it. Over and over again, in the classroom, and more often in office hours, listening to students talk, it has come to me that there must be a special place in hell for teachers who have the Answer for everyone.

One belittles others, and impairs one's own understanding of things, by thinking so rigidly, only in terms of the personae. In an interview with a steelworker that was eventually incorporated into his book *Working*, Studs Terkel recorded the man's, Mike Fitzgerald's, story about what happened when a college boy saw a book in Mike's back pocket:

He walked up to me and he said, "You read?" I said, "What do you mean, I read?" He said, "everybody else reads the sports pages around here. What are you doing with a book?" I looked at him. I said, "I don't know what you're talking about." He said, "All those dummies." I got pissed off at the kid right away. I said, "What do you mean, all these dummies? Don't knock a man who's paying somebody else's way through college."[33]

Mike confides that he would like to run a combination tavern and bookstore, a gathering place for steelworkers and college students, a place "Where a workingman would not be ashamed to quote Walt Whitman and where a college professor would not be ashamed that he painted his house over the weekend." He would like to see the walls between intellectuals and laborers taken down, Mike says, and this is why he would like to have "a book store, a tavern, and a boxing ring in the back."[34]

That social scientists serve as "advisers to the prince" is entirely in keeping with Comte's prevision of the new social order. The application of social scientific thinking to the formulation of social policy has been made, more often than not, in the spirit of the highest ideals espoused by the *philosophes* of the Enlightenment. The development of "scientific selection" of jurors is in the service of justice and human brotherhood, as is the application of the principle of equal opportunity to hiring policies. Yet a Pandora's box has been opened thereby, and it will require more than pure intentions to repair the damages now being done to many. In his review of Nathan Glazer's *Affirmative Discrimination: Ethnic Inequality and Public Policy*, Kenneth Pierce says that the "strange fruit" of the civil rights struggle of the sixties is the sort of nation that has for so long been resisted, one "where a person's race, sex, or national origin carries with it official, governmentally inspired privileges and penalties, where rights have been transferred from individuals to groups, where the clear and direct language of our civil rights laws is circumvented by the agencies that enforce them."[35] Glazer's theme, the subversion of the civil rights legislation of the sixties, the abuses of "affirmative action" in equal employment policy, in busing, and, potentially, in attacking residential segregation, is hardly popular, as Pierce says; but for that very reason, he feels it deserves careful attention. Pierce is satisfied that Glazer has demonstrated in this work that there is reverse discrimination in the marketplace, that there *are* quotas. Furthermore, he finds Glazer's argument that the idolism of statistical ratios can be as un-American, as stupid as the old discrimination, a convincing one. One consequence of this idolism, Pierce remarks, is that "yet another impersonal system has been put between men and women and their work," that anatomy has once again become destiny. We ought to have learned, he writes, the folly of serving goals by sacrificing them. And we ought to learn, both as individuals and as a society, "how to see through the dead symbols that stifle us in every part of life." We did not make sense, Pierce writes, when we classified Asian hamlets as "pacified," "nonpacified" and "mixed." Nor did we make sense when we forced ourselves into categories which are continually revised ("mid-thirties," "type A," and "countercultural" are the examples he provides.) The reason, he says, why we ought to pay attention to Glazer's book and to the new discrimination that is committed in the name of equal opportunity is this: "that we have got to stay alive to the threat our can-do habits of labeling, policymaking, and self-interested engineering pose to the human condition—all the more so when the policies and the slogans are created for the best of reasons." Glazer's approach is not in the scientific, but in the humanistic tradition, Pierce reminds us. What we can learn from it is an appreciation of the *particular* pattern of ethnic freedoms that have developed in the United States, and of the *particular* impact of our present policies.[36]

The sociologist who works in the tradition of the *verstehende* approach looks through and beyond the categories, the symbols, the slogans, the personae, the variables, to see, as Blumer put it, "human beings in their particular world," to grasp a pattern of behavior, a policy, in terms of how it enters into the lives of the people whose actions one is trying to understand. But how rarely this is done! Writing of Lyndon Johnson's Executive Order 11246, as implemented in affirmative action programs in institutions of higher learning, Sheila Johnson found it a significant precedent that the order was amended to include women. She says she finds no reason why there may not be further amendments, "to include gays, spastics, paraplegics, . . . persons over 50," or those in many other categories who might feel justified in claiming that they have experienced discrimination in the job market. The categories that might be incorporated into the province of the Executive Order are all but inexhaustible.[37] More than this, one of the consequences of insistence upon recognition and rights for every conceivable social category is a neutralization of profound and serious grievances, and the cultivation of a carnival atmosphere, in which fundamental issues of human rights are neglected or even deliberately ignored. Affirmative action may become, for many, another instrument by which very old games are played. There are department chairmen at Berkeley, Sheila Johnson reports, who do not care to fill out ethnic identity forms for job applicants or for their departmental faculty. One chairman listed his entire staff as black, because, he said, "they all looked rather tanned to me." Another says he throws a die to determine under which of six columns—the "four minorities," "Caucasian," and "other non-white"—he enters each member of his staff. Professor John Polt is quoted by Johnson as having made the apt observation that Adolf Hitler "did all this much better," and the chilling reminder that the Nuremberg laws computed precisely what fraction of an individual was Jewish.[38] In all this fevered clamor for equal opportunity, it is too easily forgotten that information gathered in innocence today, even in the name of the noblest ideals of humanity, may be used tomorrow for the most nefarious purposes.

Some of the manipulation, the game-playing, may be done out of exasperation with a program that seems all but impossible to implement fairly. And some of it may be due to scofflaw, which has a strong tradition in America. But some of it is shrewdly calculated, bent to the user's best advantage. Any charter, of course, any constitution, any principle or statute or mandate, may be written so as to embody the loftiest human ideals. The measure of people should always be taken in the way they live by a rule, not in the way they phrase it. Above all others, social scientists ought to know that wherever a norm is instituted, there will always be those who will give it the closest scrutiny in order to find in it what might be worked to their personal advantage. As a consequence, a rule that was originally intended to serve as a corrective for an injustice may be so (mis-)applied that other injustices are committed in its very name. Sheila Johnson writes of "a documented case at Berkeley of a student who applied under his father's name and was refused admittance, but who then reapplied under his mother's (Spanish) surname, and was admitted with a large grant." She predicts that, as people see the advantages to be enjoyed by those of a "scheduled caste," ever more individuals "will discover a Cherokee ancestor in their background or will change their names to Ramírez."[39]

The poet, if he attends the work of the social scientists at all, might well ask, Who is under the mask, under the persona? Who is hiding behind the slogan, inside the category, under the rubric? What are the actions cloaked by and compressed within the variable? But the poets themselves have not remained immune from the craze for classifying. For there are poets and poets. On January 31, 1977, The *New York Times* reported that the *American Poetry Review* "has been accused of being antifeminist, racist and antiyouth by a group of 50 well-known poets led by June Jordan and Adrienne Rich. The accusation is denied by the editor, Stephen Berg, poet and translator, who founded the publication in 1971." Some poets seem to be well on their way to committing a social science in poetry:

> The censuring poets say that of 648 contributions in 23 issues, the in-house editors published only 116 by women and that the proportion of contributions by black, minority and third-world writers to white poets was even lower. The figures are disputed by the editor . . . .
> A manifesto has been issued calling for changes in the Review's policies. Among its demands are that "an equal number of highest quality male and female poets" be published; that a different editor be assigned for each issue who is representative of the "female and/or minority" poets, with such poets to be given "one-third of the total space," and that more new writers be published. The manifesto notes the fact that the publication has Federal funding.
> David Ignatow, winner of the 1977 Bollingen Prize for Poetry, has resigned as editor at large of the Review. He went along with part of the dissenting group's statement but issued an independent statement to define his position. In an interview, he said that he was against the censuring group's notion that poetry "quotas" for any sex or race should be mandatory.[40]

So the personae of the magic theater of social scientific classification appear in literature. Indeed, how could it be otherwise? Lucien Goldmann has written of the futility of trying to understand cultural activity "outside the totality of life in the society in which it is developed." One can neither understand a statement that is separated from the individual who has formulated it, he said, nor separate this individual from his social and historical world. "Thus," he maintained, "any radical . . . dualism or pluralism in one's approach to the different areas of human behaviour strikes me as questionable, and condemned in advance as leading to a partial and discordant image of the reality of human behaviour."[41] If much ado is made about representation of female, black, minority or third-world personae in society, it is inevitable that the issues of affirmative action and quota systems will work their way into the literary world. It is no accident that, for every subdivision of the body social, for every "public" that springs from the brow of sociological taxonomy, there is a literary market. Writers who care about having their works published find they must address themselves to one or another of these endlessly subdividing collectivities—the feminist, the third-world, the radical lesbian, for example, which can be (and often are) combined. Thus there are magazines and presses for lesbians, for the older woman, for third-world women, and so forth.

Literature cannot be understood if it is divorced from the social and historical world in which it is created. At the same time, it cannot be merged with these worlds without surrendering a very vital part of itself. In an essay on "Literature as an Institution," Harry Levin puts it this way:

> . . . literature has always been an institution. Like other institutions, the church or the law, it cherishes a unique phase of human experience and controls a special body of precedents and devices; it tends to incorporate a self-perpetuating discipline, while responding to the main currents of each succeeding period; it is continually accessible to all the impulses of life at large, but it must translate them into its own terms and adapt them to its peculiar forms. Once we have grasped this fact, we begin to perceive how art may belong to society and yet be autonomous within its own limits, and are no longer puzzled by the apparent polarity of social and formal criticism. These . . . are complementary frames of reference whereby we may discriminate the complexities of a work of art.[42]

This mixing of celebrated causes with the poetic endeavor evoked protests by some poets against the method of selection of contributions to the *American Poetry Review*. Of course, the issue of the relationship of the arts to politics is a burning one in every age and every society. Two years before this controversy, Joel Oppenheimer wrote of how depressed he felt about "the latest politicizing in the world of poetry." Adrienne Rich, Oppenheimer said, had made some good points about the current state of poetry in a letter responding to a review on this subject by M. L. Rosenthal. But, Oppenheimer comments, somewhere in her letter "the cause takes over." Rosenthal had quoted lines from one of Charles Olson's poems about how women carry themselves, and Adrienne Rich had asked, "Who is Charles Olson to say how women are to move?" To this, Oppenheimer responds,

> damn it, you can lay onto resenthal [sic] all you want, and hang charles for what he's guilty of, but you really can't mean that one.
> —first of all there's the question of what a poet looks at and how, of course, but beyond that is it really a question of olson or any of us telling anyone how to move? we try to see, we try to make sense of what we see, and then we try

to write it down. but the cause is building up steam, and it will run over everything until finally the coming together happens, slowly, and quietly, but as it must.[43]

The late Anaïs Nin said once in an interview that she did not care for classifications, and that therefore she refrained from making what she took to be the necessary intellectual commitments of the feminist. Each of us must make choices between commitments, between selves. Which of the personae is to be superordinate? Who is the First Persona for these, who may be both—the homosexual or the parent, the black or the Puerto Rican, the Southerner or the Catholic, the feminist or the poet? It may well be that no one can do justice to the complexity of his or her own life in any form of literature. How much less can one do justice to the complexity of another's. Perhaps what one thinks one understands about the actions and thoughts, the feelings and motivations of others cannot but miss the mark. One might envy, or pity, the seamless mask, the whole cloth of the costume of the persona, of one who claims to be only and always a militant, believing woman, or black, or homosexual. Few could live long in such a small cloister. Too much would have to be surrendered for the sake of such coherence, too much mutilated. "Unless we prefer to be made fools of by our illusions," Jung wrote, "we shall, by carefully analysing every fascination, extract from it a portion of our own personality, like a quintessence, and slowly come to recognize that we meet ourselves time and again in a thousand disguises on the path of life."[44] We have learned, for Jung is as much a living part of our intellectual heritage as Marx, that we are many beings, that there are many animals inside ourselves. It is not possible to follow *one* leader, to serve *one* cause, without taking some veil of illusion. To declare one of our many selves to be the ascendant self is to declare what it is that we choose to believe in above all other faiths. It is to make a statement about the hierarchy of our values.

Tracing the connections between a person's predilections and his work or family life or place in the community, the social scientist must make decisions about where to place emphases. In a paper on "The Other Self," Martin Price recalls Hampshire's statement in his *Thought and Action* to the effect that we have before us, in ourselves as well as in others, a whole person, always. When we distinguish between features of a person's life, we are making discriminations on the basis of our values. When we emphasize some features and neglect others, we are pointing to that which we think is essential in human life.[45] So it is that when a social scientist looks within a "variable," within a designation even as simple as that based upon sex or age or ethnic affiliation, he finds a little cosmos, one that changes even as it moves. He finds that little worlds are made up of still smaller worlds, that there are ghettos within the ghetto, that his "variable" undergoes a process of mitosis, even as the self does, according to one's beliefs and feelings. In the house of social science itself, there are many mansions: champions of one segment or another of The People and opponents of sexism, racism or ageism are very far from sitting down at a round table together. Thus one writer distinguishes carefully between the "aged," the "minority aged," and the "black aged," since, she notes, the black aged often suffer from poverty as well as from racism and ageism; and black women suffer from sexism, as well. This writer believes that the black aged ought to be studied as a distinctive social category, and not merged with all blacks, or with all elderly people.[46] Another writer, in an impassioned paper reprinted from *Female Liberation* in a book of readings for sociology students, subdivides the category "women" into three major groups: working women, women students, and middle class married women, each with its own interests and objectives. According to her, the exploitation of poor people, and not sex *per se*, is the central issue of the struggle for liberation: women are united by sex, but divided (or at least divisible) by social class and race.[47]

Committing a social science may be just this: surveying, questioning, interviewing, inquiring into the distribution of "variables" without looking inside them to see what they mean to those who are the subjects (or is it the objects?) of research. Committing a social science may mean explaining before understanding, denying inner life, and taking the individual as no more than a repertoire of personae. For it is not by the sum of the parts we play in social life that we truly describe ourselves, but by the way we play each of them, and the choices we make between them, when we must so choose. Perhaps we can be reminded, Martin Price suggests, "of the substantive nature of the self, and of character, by the very conflict between roles, or between the full individual and a particular role he assumes." Writing of George Herbert Mead's concept of the "generalized other," Price remarks, "It is precisely against this submission to an impersonal other that existentialism protests—this surrender of the self as an initiating and free agent to the impersonal anonymity of merely social existence, the loss of authenticity in becoming an object for others to act through or upon."[48]

*You must change your life*, Rilke counseled. Yet, even if one believed that it were within one's power to do this, we do not know whether the transformation must begin from within, or by altering the visible signs of affiliation with social categories. The quest for Identity, the Holy Grail of our time, the search for the quintessential self, is, for some, an inward-facing journey. The Way is through shadowed passages lighted with prayer and drugs, with incantations and meditations. But for others, the Way is eminently social. For them, it is gospel that Society bestows Identity, and that the Way to change one's condition is through change of the outward signs of inner commitment. One begins by changing one's costume, one's name, one's title, one's physical appearance. There is a celebration of the separateness of a social category, and the assertion of its power—Black Power, Woman Power, Student Power, Gay Power, Red Power, Senior Power. This, of course, has been met with counterassertions of, for example, White Power and People Power. "From the effort to admit more and more Americans to the fellowship of full citizenship and equal opportunity," historian Daniel Boorstin reflects, we appear to have begun to think of the barriers which separate people as insurmountable, "and even somehow we begin to celebrate them as desirable."[49] In a chapter on Self-Liquidating Ideals in his *Democracy and Its Discontents*, Boorstin asks how the American ideal of pluralism can be fulfilled without liquidating it.

Given the identification and celebration of differences, and the exploitation of them for ideological purposes as well as for profit, North American society appears to be a crazy-quilt of groups and collectivities, statuses and categories—a grid that may shift its contours overnight. Fads, fashions of dress and hair-style, of speech and mannerism came and went during the sixties, as did the celebrities of that decade. What consonance has this Balkanized outer world, with its myriad personae, with the quintessential self? We are divided and subdivided within ourselves, as Hermann Hesse reveals in *Steppenwolf*. The will to power, the desire for recognition, the demand for reparations paid for past injuries, the cultivation of differences—all these are waged in the arena of the human spirit, as well as in the outer world. Yet each one of these sociological variables acts, as genes act, in concert with the others. Just as genes are not always expressed in material form, so, too, the silent workings of feeling and thought are often hidden from the world of appearances. From the outside looking on, an observer might see a "common" condition: a son is killed in Vietnam, a daughter's mind is destroyed by LSD, a woman is widowed, a man becomes subject to mandatory retirement, there is a divorce.... Yet, in interior life, what happens to one is unique. Life histories, like snowflakes, are never of the same design. The social terrain surveyed by the sociologist is crisscrossed with pathways, each with its crusaders beckoning, its pied pipers and sirens making their invitational music. But it is not given to the social scientist to say which path is to be followed. Nor is it given to anyone to say what another shall make of the journey. In inner life, each of us is a solitary.

Our greatest writers have not always remembered this. They have not always had the gift or the inclination to find the way to the inner life of another. In her essay on "Bloomsbury and Virginia Woolf," Elizabeth Hardwick says that Henry James's story "In the Cage" is one that was written "entirely out of a drastic condescension" on his part. "When characters are seen from the outside," she says, "viewed solely in the glinting suspicions of a sensibility utterly foreign to their own, style tells us the author's prejudices and impatience, his hatreds, his limitations of feeling."[50] Then there is the other risk, no less grave, taken by those who are reaching for an understanding of others. This is the risk that one may become possessed by another person or perspective, that one may seal one's consciousness within another's inner life. Wherever one begins, the task is always the same: to follow the labyrinthine corridors between inner and outer reality, without losing one's integrity, one's selfhood, in either.

In an account of her observations of Esalen, Annette Duffy narrates an argument between participants in a group attending a session on "Healing Your Being." Leo argues with Shirley, who insists we are all living in the Aquarian Age, the time to "go with one's process," the time to "be oneself." But there *is* an objective reality, Leo insists, "there is a right and wrong, and it would be much to the benefit of all the individual beautiful selves if we could all see that and try to do something about it."[51] Leo might have been speaking at that moment for the social scientist who, above all others, is least likely to understate the reality of this world in which we live. It is in an effort to comprehend and explain it that the social scientist devises instruments of description and analysis. But all too easily, and all too often, these instruments are reified: a decade marked off for demographic analysis is infused with a personality (the twenties were Gay, the fifties were Silent, the sixties were so many things). The phrase "older people," or the word "youth," the social category of homosexuals or "the working class" or "the poor"—each is a *deus ex machina* that, though created to reveal certain truths, only serves to darken our understanding. On the other side are those who remain wrapped in the folds and mists of inner life, who dismiss social and cultural realities as chimeras. One strives for a balance of perspective between the two extremes of what Iris Murdoch referred to as "neurosis" and "convention,"

> the first a turning in upon the self and a neglect of the reality of others, the second a passive reduction of the self to the roles that are assigned it by its culture; the first gives us self-enclosed works of high internal coherence, the second journalistic accounts of a life without true persons.[52]

Persons are true so long as the meaning that circumstances and events have *for them* are central to the social scientific task. Perhaps the sin is not in committing a social science, but in presuming to explain with finality that which is always imperfectly understood. There is (and we can be grateful for this) no formula for determining the precise relationship of inner life to outer reality. This must be done afresh with every research undertaking.

Those who believe that only inner life is real are easy prey for the forces of the natural world and of history and social circumstance. They are a danger to themselves and to others, and they condemn themselves to a life that can be only half-examined. At the same time, those who take the masks to be human faces are no less deluded and no less dangerous. The Jungian analytical psychologist Edward C.

Whitmont writes of the consequences of confusion of individuality with the social role one is playing:

the result may . . . often be a state of inflation. Its victim feels great and powerful because he is a fine public figure, but he fails to be a human being or even to make the first steps toward becoming human. Such an inflated over-reliance upon the persona, or identity with it, results in rigidity and lack of genuine responsiveness. Such a person is nothing but the role, be it doctor, lawyer, administrator, mother, daughter or whatever part is so compulsively played. The example of Eichmann has shown how such a role-identified nonpersonality fails to develop a personal, moral responsibility; he has no ethical principles or personal feelings and values of his own but hides behind collective morality and prescribed manners. He has no conflicts of conscience because everything is settled beforehand in a stereotyped fashion.[53]

Whitmont goes on to discuss the consequences of inadequate formation of the persona, and show how personality development is impeded by either one of these difficulties. There is a polarity between collectivity and individuality, he says, and hence

an oppositional and compensatory relationship between persona and *shadow*. The brighter the persona, the darker the shadow. The more one is identified with one's glorified, wonderful social role, the less it is played and recognized as merely a role, the darker and more negative will be one's genuine individuality as a consequence of its being thus neglected. But on the other hand too much concern with the shadow, with one's "bad" side . . . can make for a rather negative, defensive and miserable persona. This . . . will then express itself in stiffness, uncertainty or compulsive, primitive behavior.[54]

No matter how technically sophisticated the gathering and presentation of "social facts" may be—the rises and falls in rates of illegitimate births or divorces, suicides or crime,—they remain manifestations of collective life that have no meaning in and of themselves. Meaning can be conferred upon them only by those whose actions draw them into the statistics, and by the art of social scientific interpretation. Social facts, like any others, do not speak for themselves, but through those who made them come about, and those who read from them the sense of the ways in which our lives are lived.

There are moments in our lives when our age is decisive—perhaps in considering whether or not to make a career change, or to have another child. There are other moments when our sex is central, and still others when neither our age nor our sex matters much, when our ethnic or racial persona determines our destiny—even whether or not we shall live. These beings within ourselves, called forth and expressed through the forms given by history and social circumstance, coexist at certain moments in harmony and peace. But often they are locked in what can become mortal combat. The gods are at war with one another, Max Weber so often said. To live is to strive for balance between the manifold selves, on the edge between inner and outer reality. To live is to choose, and choose again. Of the social scientist who denies this engagement, who confines "reality" to outer life and thinks of feelings and images as epiphenomena of sociological place, it might be said, as Kierkegaard remarked of Hegel, that "his work is full of syntheses, but life is full of choices."

The personae, the variables, the social categories are apparitions of our many selves, frozen, static in the charts and graphs and tables of social science as they can never be in the living of our lives. In *The Book of Imaginary Beings*, Jorge Luis Borges writes of the Simurgh. Firdausi, he says, makes the Simurgh the foster father of Zal, who is father of the hero of the poem in the *Book of Kings*, in which ancient Iranian legends are compiled and set to verse. And in the thirteenth century, Farid al-Din Attar makes the Simurgh a symbol of the godhead. In this allegory,

The distant king of birds, the Simurgh, drops one of his splendid feathers somewhere in the middle of China; on learning of this, the other birds, tired of their present anarchy, decide to seek him. They know that the king's name means "thirty birds"; they know that his castle lies in the Kaf, the mountain or range of mountains that ring the earth. At the outset, some of the birds lose heart; the nightingale pleads his love for the rose; the parrot pleads his beauty, for which he lives caged; the partridge cannot do without his home in the hills, nor the heron without his marsh, nor the owl without his ruins. But finally, certain of them set out on the perilous venture . . . . Many of the pilgrims desert; the journey takes its toll among the rest. Thirty, made pure by their sufferings, reach the great peak of the Simurgh. At last they behold him; they realize that they are the Simurgh, and that the Simurgh is each of them and all of them.[55]

# TWO

## On the Search for Reality

*The reason so few good books are written is that so few people who can write, know anything.*
—Walter Bagehot,
"Shakespeare," *Literary Studies*

    Works that do not resonate with the reality of inner life are dead. And the future of the social sciences is bleak, indeed, if its lore is to be divided between the hollow men, the radical empiricists on the one hand, and those who, to borrow Raymond Aron's apt phrase, are drunk with ideology, on the other. A way must be found to restore the humanistic tradition of the social sciences without forfeiture of all that is distinctive about them. This may be achieved not by social scientists turning themselves into storytellers, but by their recognizing more fully the consonances between social science and literature. It may be that the differences between endeavors are most clearly understood by coming to understand the ways in which they resemble one another. Where the social scientist with humanistic inclinations and the fiction writer who combines romance with social realism meet is on this common ground, in the search for social and cultural realities.
    In the opening lines of his study of the "new journalism" and of what Truman Capote named the "nonfiction novel," John Hollowell writes of the apocalyptic mood of the sixties. "Increasingly," he com-

ments, "everyday 'reality' became more fantastic than the fictional visions of even our best novelists."[1] Throughout that decade, "public events were bewildering, chaotic, almost random, and without meaning." There were changes in the lifestyles and in the attitudes and values of Americans; and American novelists were as confused as many of the rest of us. "Many of the popular books of the last decade," Hollowell says, "reflect an increased concern for social issues and an awareness of the individual's relationship to an explosive social history."[2] Some novelists came to wonder about the possibility of writing fiction at all, and turned to writing documentaries, social commentaries, journalistic reports and confessions in which they were personally involved, and in which they served as their own protagonists. The argument that the novel had died was revived during this period, Hollowell writes; it became increasingly difficult to define "social reality"; and the society was so protean that "the creation of social realism seemed continually to be upstaged by current events." Hollowell quotes Philip Roth, who stated in an article appearing in *Commentary* in 1961 that the actual world was constantly outstripping the talents of the writer whose "meager imagination" was embarrassed by the American reality.[3]

The sense that contemporary life has a quality of unreality about it, creating special problems for the novelist, is not new in American literature, Hollowell reminds us: "Even our earliest novelists—Cooper, Hawthorne, and to an extent, Melville—complained that American society did not offer the depth and stability of cultural materials to sustain a national literature."[4] Even though modern critics may have found the claim that the novel is dead to be exaggerated, they "have nonetheless agreed that certain possibilities for fictional realism and certain possibilities of language are reaching exhaustion." Hollowell refers to Leslie Fiedler's discussion of this question in his collection of essays, *Waiting for the End*, in which Fiedler suggests that the novel will die if the artistic faith sustaining its writers dies, and if the audience need that the novel was created to gratify finds its gratification elsewhere. Here Fiedler is saying, Hollowell writes, "that movies and television have supplanted the novel's cognitive function as 'news' or 'the portrait of provincial life.' "[5]

Nonfiction is preferred to fiction by many readers, as a study of bestseller lists or of the changing proportion of fiction to nonfiction in magazines will demonstrate. It well may be that this is due at least as much to manipulations of what is loosely referred to as the public taste, as to changes in that taste itself. Whatever the causes may be, there has been, with the growing ferment in American society since the end of World War II, a creation of hybrid forms in literature, of fictional techniques combined with the detailed observation of journalism—the "nonfiction novel" and the "new journalism" which Hollowell's book is all about. And in his discussion of the growing popularity of nonfictional forms, Hollowell reminds us that when Lionel Trilling reviewed *The Lonely Crowd*, he "praised the books's literary quality and suggested that the novel's traditional function of examining morals and manners was being better served by the social sciences."[6] Further, in giving examples of works which, like Truman Capote's *In Cold Blood* and Norman Mailer's *The Armies of the Night* confound the customary distinctions between fiction and nonfiction, fact and reality, Hollowell mentions the works of Oscar Lewis, whose *The Children of Sanchez* and *La Vida*, he claims, "*read* more like novels than like works of social science." Works like Lewis', Hollowell says, "demonstrate Trilling's obervation that fiction must now compete with sensitively written social science."[7]

Yet, whether social scientists write with grace and sensitivity or not, they are not engaged in direct competition with fiction writers for the attention of the public. Articles written by social scientists appear most often in journals of social science; only a very few have cultivated a style and a circle of readers reaching beyond the boundaries of their areas of specialization. Nor are social scientists particularly prominent among the authors of the nonfiction "best sellers," which are, more often than not, "how-to" books or autobiographies, memoirs or confessions. Occasionally, a "study" or "report" becomes a best seller for a time; but this is the exception, not the rule, and these works are not representative of what is going on in the field. Indeed, social scientists and fiction writers both compete with television more than with one another. Both have been preempted by the enormous apparatus of the mass media that concocts, in "eyewitness reports" or "special reports," and in filmed narrative, Instant Social Science as well as Instant Romances. Filmed "studies," combining the most superficial elements of social fact and social realism and romance, offer neither fiction nor nonfiction, while pretending to offer both. The mercurial television camera, darting over the surfaces of the social world, peering promiscuously into the corners of our lives, invites any and all to star in the film of the ongoing fiction that a human life is. And, for those for whom the medium has become the message, there is an extended invitation to become an authority overnight on issues that have engaged the intellectual labors of psychologists and sociologists, anthropologists, economists and political scientists during the entire course of their professional lives. Given the exhibitionism of so many in American society, the voracious appetite for quick and comfortable solutions to problems, and the unceasing bombardment of the senses and the mind with counterfeit stories and counterfeit social facts, it is something of a miracle that books are read at all, whether they are works of science or of art.

What is inescapable is that there is no social fact without a social scientific imagination working in its selection and its incorporation into a wider pattern, finding the ways that it radiates outward, toward the past and future. Without interpretation, without the exercise of the imagination, any "social fact," any statistic, any item of testimony is utterly meaningless. Nor can there be a story, when there is no storyteller. Any event, any character, any moral dilemma sleeps until awakened by the exercise of the literary imagination. And a fiction writer, a social scientist cannot be made in one day. It is a lifelong quest, this search for social and cultural realities. Nor is imagination of much use if there is not an accompanying intellectual patience, a self-imposed discipline, to give it form. The crafting of good social science and of good fiction requires a sharp and steady eye and ear, an insatiable curiosity, a passion for the truth of things, an alacrity of mind and spirit—all this as much as, if not infinitely more than, a mastery of techniques. Social and cultural realities do not reveal themselves so easily; there are many snares that might entangle reason and imagination.

But for some twist of fate, there are writers who might have become social scientists, and social scientists who might have become writers. Recalling his student days at the University of Illinois, Nelson Algren said that he had learned a great deal from Bruce Weirich, who taught a course in Shakespeare that Algren took one summer. "I remember," Algren went on to say, "I was also moved by a course given by a sociologist named Taft. It made me decide to be a sociologist."[8] Asked when he decided that he was not going to become a sociologist, Algren replied that this was decided *for* him. "It became a very impractical time to become a sociologist," he said, "inasmuch as there weren't any openings for sociologists. In order to become a sociologist, I guess I would have had to take a master's degree." This was on the eve of the Depression. Though Algren said that he did not even know there was a Depression when he got out of school in 1931, it was difficult for him to stay in school—"a survival thing and I had to borrow money for tuition and so forth, so there was no question of going further . . . ."[9]

For William Foote Whyte, it was the other way around. He had "two strong interests" when he was a student at Swarthmore, he wrote, and these were "economics (mixed with social reform) and writing." Whyte wrote short stories and one act plays in college, and attempted to write a novel one summer. There was value in these attempts at writing, in that they taught him something about himself. Some of his stories were published in the college literary magazine; one was accepted, though never published, by *Story* magazine; and three of his one act plays were produced at Swarthmore in their annual playwriting contest. He had hopes, then, for a writing career. Yet,

> I felt uneasy and dissatisfied. The plays and stories were all fictionalized accounts of events and situations I had experienced or observed myself. When I attempted to go beyond my experience and tackle a novel on a political theme, the result was a complete bust. Even as I wrote the concluding chapters, I realized that the manuscript was worthless. I finished it . . . just so that I could say to myself that I had written a novel.[10]

Whyte wrote that he had come to think of himself as "a pretty dull fellow" who knew nothing about the slums, or about life in mines or factories or fields. He came to feel that, if he would write anything of worth, he would have to go beyond the narrow social borders that, up to that time, had bounded his life; and *Street Corner Society* is the expression of that outward-facing journey, as well as of his interests in economics and social reform.[11]

The rich traditions of social science have accommodated people of very different gifts and temperaments. The reach for understanding of the social and cultural realities ever exceeds its grasp. In writing of the adventure, Godfrey Lienhardt says:

> For the most part men live in society as in the physical world, without reflecting on its nature. But as physical scientists have gone beyond common experience in understanding the physical universe, so social scientists have hoped for a deeper and more systematic knowledge of societies than their members themselves have or usually need in the day-to-day conduct of affairs.[12]

In this quest for the reality of society and culture, social scientists continually try to take the pulse of the beast, following trends for signs of more profound changes, and analyzing the relationship between beliefs and all the forms of human action, between location in sociocultural space and life-chances, fate. The sociologist, who is a sort of anthropologist in home territory, is buffeted about by the variable winds of fad and fashion in the United States. Given the rush with which the news is cast abroad, and the crazed path the automated messengers run from one social and cultural world to another, the social scientist may undertake a study—of guru-worshiping, or of a rise or fall in the divorce rate, or of an apparent shift in attitudes about a political issue—only to find that his subject fades as he pursues it, that the "trend" has already happened, and didn't amount to much; or that other issues have come to preoccupy people.

The evanescence of social and cultural realities affects the social scientist in the classroom just as much as it affects those "in the field." Students in social science classes often have the illusion that the issues burning on their campus and the college community, and the "lifestyle" (one can almost hear Max Weber's groans from the other world at the corruption of this phrase) they say they pursue, are the dominant preoccupations of people throughout the country, if not the world. Often they imagine that they, and what they are doing and thinking at the moment, are of the utmost fascination to those who would understand social and cultural realities; so many of them have come to think of themselves as the vanguard of the Future. There is a provincialism in institutions of higher learning that is very difficult to overcome. When I taught anthropology in Iowa, many students insisted that the course material be filtered through their consensus about How Things Are in society and in the world. It was no different in Baton Rouge, where I taught sociology; there, many students took their college, their community, their state as the measure of all human events and purposes. And many a student in my sociology classes in New Paltz seems to be under the impression that the pulse of the nation beats with the immediate preoccupations of people on this campus, and in the city and state of New York. One finds oneself repeatedly suggesting that there probably *is* no national pulse, but that, even if there were, only two things could safely be said about it: that it is very erratic, and that it is *not* in New Paltz.

The social scientific curiosity may lead anywhere; as Peter Berger says, the parish of the sociologist is the world,[13] and the realities the sociologist studies are far more complex and far less familiar than is commonly supposed. Those, he writes,

Who like to avoid shocking discoveries, who prefer to believe that society is just what they were taught in Sunday School, who like the safety of the rules and the maxims of what Alfred Schuetz has called the "world-taken-for-granted," should stay away from sociology. People who feel no temptation before closed doors, who have no curiosity about human beings, who are content to admire scenery without wondering about the people who live in those houses on the other side of that river, should probably also stay away from sociology. They will find it unpleasant or . . . unrewarding. People who are interested in human beings only if they can change, convert or reform them should also be warned, for they will find sociology much less useful than they hoped. And people whose interest is mainly in their own conceptual constructions will do just as well to turn to the study of little white mice.[14]

Consciousness is transformed when the ordinary, taken-for-granted world, all that seems familiar and real and "given" is seen through the sociological perspective, since seeing is seeing through and seeing beyond. Such are the pleasures of all social scientific discovery, open to those who have, by natural inclination or by conscious cultivation, the gift of a certain kind of curiosity. In every age, there will be those who will cast a cold eye upon social scientists for this very reason, for there is, Lienhardt remarks,

a type of mind which cultivates the virtues of ethnocentricity, represents a distaste for foreigners as realistic and unsentimental common sense, and attributes to itself all the virtues of the civilization to which it belongs. It is a type of mind which will not open itself to the foreign experience which it yet judges with assured disdain, and which humane thinkers, many anthropologists among them, have for long had to contend with.[15]

Social scientists have an openness to the outer world, a quality of self-forgetfulness so distinctive as to be a tribal mark, that would serve a novelist of social realism well. The experience of discovery, the excitement and uncertainty of their adventure, is conveyed by those who write frankly of their field work, who open their field notes to the reader. And it is this discovering that enlivens all scientific as well as all artistic activity. One comes upon the truth that has always been there; it is the task of the social scientist, the writer, to uncover the reality, to reveal, to release it. Writing of Ohnainewk, an Eskimo hunter, Edmund Carpenter expresses this perfectly:

[When Ohnainewk] started to carve ivory, he would hold the unworked tooth lightly in his hand, turning it this way and that, and whisper, "Who are you? Who hides there?" And then: "Ah, Seal!" He rarely set out, at least consciously, to carve, say, a seal, but picked up the ivory, examined it to find its hidden form, and, if that wasn't immediately apparent, carved aimlessly until he saw it, humming or chanting as he worked. Then he brought it out: Seal, hidden, emerged. It was always there: he didn't create it; he released it.[16]

Like many a writer, who has a rather misty idea of what his short story or novel will turn out to be, the social scientist begins research guided by a hypothesis or, more grandly, a theory. But one begins always tentatively, with particular people in a particular place, hoping to be accepted well enough to try to find connections between the life that is going on and the research problem that has engaged one. During his first months in Cornerville, Whyte wrote,

I went through the process that sociologist Robert Johnson has described in his own field work. I began as a nonparticipating observer. As I became accepted into the community, I found myself becoming almost a nonobserving participant. I got the feel of life in Cornerville, but that meant that I got to take for granted the same things that my Cornerville friends took for granted. I was immersed in it, but I could as yet make little sense out of it. I had a feeling that I was doing something important, but I had yet to explain to myself what it was.[17]

Listening, Whyte said, he "learned the answers to questions that I would not even have had the sense to ask if I had been getting my information solely on an interviewing basis." He did ask questions; but he "learned to judge the sensitiveness of the question and my relationship to the people so that I only asked a question in a sensitive area when I was sure that my relationship to the people involved was very solid."[18]

A writer, too, may have this experience, of beginning the composition tentatively, of feeling out the way to meanings, guided by a kind of intuition. When he was interviewed by Ralph Ellison and Eugene Walter for the *Paris Review* series of interviews with writers, Robert Penn Warren spoke of these things. Once he makes a judgment about which character is going to tell the story; once he makes certain objective decisions, Warren said, he *feels* his way toward meanings, rather than following a planned structure. The objective work ought to be done before the fiction is written, he maintained; when he is composing, he tries to "forget the abstractions."[19] Of *Night Rider* and his next novel, *At Heaven's Gate*, Warren said, "I was fumbling rather than working according to plan and convictions already arrived at. When you start any book you don't know what, ultimately, your issues are. You try to write to find them. You're fiddling with the stuff, hoping to make sense, whatever kind of sense you can make."[20]

The temptation is particularly strong, Lienhardt believes, in the social sciences "to give a seemingly scientific basis to attitudes and opinions not derived only, if at all, from dispassionate consideration of fact."[21] Whether wittingly or not, the social scientist may have decided beforehand what his findings will be, and he has to contend with this if his intentions toward portraying reality are honorable. There is always the possibility that he may be creating his own data, so that what he presents as his discovery is his own vision of the way things are, "documented" by "social facts" or testimony that he has contrived, or by statistics which, being neutral, always lend themselves to manipulation for any purpose. Auden's admonition about answering questionnaires and questions on quizzes and "objective" tests, as well as about consorting with statisticians, may have been prompted in part by an awareness of how very easy it is to have people say what one wants to hear. The writer, of course, makes capital of this, but it is anathema in social science. In a review of Wattenberg's *The Real America: A Surprising Examination of the State of the Union*, Sheldon S. Wolin shows how opinion may be systematically organized to promote the structure of control that is in existence:

> One method is to reinforce desired beliefs by disguising assertions as questions. For example, the following statement is described as a "question": "Nader gives a one-sided picture of what America does, leaving out many good things industry does." . . . The insinuated identification of "industry" with America is too obvious to require comment. . . .
>
> Or consider the racism implicit in the following question and the implications of treating it as a precise finding: "Do you feel that blacks in this country have tried to move too fast, too slow, or at about the right pace?" . . . Or recall the "finding" of a Harris poll of 1970 that revealed that 31 percent of the public "would like never to deal with clergymen who keep telling me I have to be for the poor." . . .[22]

The technique, Wolin says, is to pose questions or assertions that are vague or meaningless or even stupid, and then to present the responses to them in precise quantitative form. And he continues:

> The quantitative perfection of meaninglessness, however, is not itself meaningless. Its purpose is to produce a collective force, a manufactured part whose opinion is then identified with the whole. Then the way is open to instill useful beliefs so that the artificial collective will be maintained, along with the dominant position of those who have constructed it. "Questions" are then put whose purpose is to promote the required beliefs.[23]

The tasks of taking surveys, Robert Reinhold notes, have become more difficult and more expensive over recent decades; the public has become more resistant, perhaps because Americans have been oversurveyed, and, as a consequence, the response rate has declined. Those who take surveys and those who depend upon the findings of surveys for making policy decisions are deeply concerned, Reinhold says, and he considers two theories about why the American public no longer responds to surveys as they once did. According to one theory, which is supported by census data, this is because of changing demographic patterns, leisure habits, and trends in family life. Reinhold quotes John C. Scott, field director at the Survey Research Center of the University of Michigan, who maintains that, in addition to higher rates of urbanization and mobility, and increased leisure and vacation time, "The whole home-centered nature of life has changed quite a lot—and even when they are at home it is hard to interfere with television viewing." As a result, interviewers knock at the doors in vain. More often than not, there are not even people around to tell them to come back later. An interviewer now has to come back four or five times before he can obtain a one-hour household interview. Once it took about five hours to obtain the interview, Reinhold reports, but now it takes about seven. According to another theory, the response rate of surveys has declined because the public has become more irritated with them. This, combined with the fear of crime, and thus of strangers, has made people more resistant. Reinhold cites the comment made by Lester Frankel of Audits and Surveys, Inc., that people may be aware that they are *required* to respond to the census-takers, but, "When we go out they think we want to sell magazines when we are really doing a survey on readership."[24]

Whatever the causes may be, the "findings" of surveys cited so pontifically by some social scientists, so magisterially by some newscasters, are suspect indeed. In interpreting them, one must consider not only the methods by which they were conducted, but the purposes for which they were taken, and the motivations that people might have for cooperating or for refusing to cooperate with the researchers. Close scrutiny of studies may reveal that what is reported as fact is fiction, that what is presented as social and cultural reality may often be as fanciful a creation as many short stories or novels. It is not sufficiently appreciated how much reality there may be in fiction. It is still less appreciated how much fiction there may be in many social facts.

Qualitative social science, too, presents temptations and opportunities to the researcher. Here precision in eliciting and reporting what, as Wolin well demonstrates, are distortions of "reality" is sacrificed for the sake of a deeper understanding. Yet liberties are often taken, sometimes with the best of intentions, sometimes with the worst. Of the former, Kai T. Erikson remarks in his book on the Buffalo Creek flood, some authors of recent sociological monographs have used the voices of informants rather casually, admitting "to the truly stunning generosity of 'giving' words to the individuals they quote, either because the informants seemed to be having a hard time expressing what they 'really' meant or because the authors decided to clean up their grammatical idiosyncrasies as a token of personal regard."[25] With this in mind, Erikson takes care to describe the details of his research methods and to explain the manner in which he presents what the people of Buffalo Creek have said to him.

Finding reality was, for Erikson, much more than a matter of knowing when and how to ask questions, and of deciding what to make of the responses to them. Indeed, for all the care that was taken with it, verbal testimony had its limitations. Though he uses quotations freely, Erikson cautions, the reader "must . . . listen . . . carefully for the feelings behind the words"; perhaps this applies especially regarding his chapter on "Collective Trauma: Loss of Communality."[26] The researcher must cope with two interrelated problems. One has to do with the repetitiveness of people's comments, and the other "is that the words people are accustomed to using in everyday speech seem pale and insubstantial when assigned the job of conveying so immense a subject." This difficulty is experienced not only by the survivors who attempt to express their sense of loss, but also by the researchers who are trying to find ways to phrase their questions. At one point in his study, Erikson says, knowing that he could not interview everyone in the group of plaintiffs in the suit filed on behalf of the survivors, he sent out a questionnaire to five hundred people, "asking for a few brief answers to a few crisp questions." And he found that many of these answers "reached so far beyond the questions that I did not really know what to do with them. It was as if I had asked people to compress a world of grief in the space reserved for a sentence or two. 'What do you miss most about the the old community?'"[27]

In his review of *Everything in Its Path*, Michael Harrington suggests that one of the reasons why this book "towers above most of academic social science" is that Erikson studied the facts first, and then worked from them toward generalizations about disaster. Erikson does not pretend to be uninvolved, Harrington observes; he does not present his study as one that is "value-free." "To be sure," Harrington says, "most of the sophisticated sociologists have backed way [sic] from the 1950's pretense of natural-scientific objectivity, but none of them has ever given such a moving and effective demonstration of how subjectivity can sensitize us to substantial truths." Erikson offers us far more than abstract definitions, he remarks, and for this reason, his ideas "resonate in our minds like poems." Harrington expresses the hope that social scientists "will . . . take note of the vitality and creativity of which their discipline is capable."[28] A sensitive and perceptive observer, Erikson assesses the impact of the flood upon the lives of the survivors. An imaginative social scientist, he concludes his work with a meditation upon how all of us may be living in a protracted disaster, how all of us may be, in a way, survivors—of dislocations that destroyed organic community.

In looking for reality, Erikson worked in two directions—from the outward appearances of things toward the inner life of people who shared a common experience, and from the nature of the experience itself and its impact upon their lives outward, toward an understanding of our common condition. He explored the pathways to inner life, in studying children's drawings of the flood (as Robert Coles did in his *Children of Crisis* studies), and in listening to the survivors tell of their dreams. He was attentive to the feelings under and around the words survivors spoke. But he also worked from the particular to the general, from the concrete to the abstract. Future historians, he suggests, may find in the "classic symptoms of trauma" manifest in this disaster—the relativism (an absence of fixed moral landmarks and of established orthodoxies), the sense of impotence, the sensory overload, the diffuse apprehensiveness—the "true clinical signature" of our age.[29]

One can easily imagine how a short story writer or novelist would be attracted to Buffalo Creek; the allegorical possibilities of the disaster are quite apparent. An event such as this flood is studied, Erikson says, as unique, as a story to be told just as it actually happened. This is usually undertaken by dramatists or historians, who "focus on the particularities of the locale, the history of the persons involved, and the contours of the event itself." They arrange its details in such an order that it can be followed as a narrative. But it is also studied because it offers insights into disasters as a *class* of events. This task is undertaken by the social scientists, who "focus on those details that seem to be found in other events of a similar kind occurring elsewhere in the world and pay less attention to those details that are local . . . and to the particular persons involved."[30] In this work, he says, he has approached the disaster in both ways. As a social scientist, Erikson could not but write of this disaster as an instance of disasters, as a case.

However, owing to the nature of his assignment, which was "to sift through the store of available sociological knowledge to see what light it might shed on a single human event," he worked in an order in reverse to that of conventional sociological research. Had he followed conventional procedures, Erikson says,

> I suspect that I would have had difficulty pursuing this study in the cool and measured way most sociological research is done even if the circumstances had been less pressing, partly because the event I was trying to understand seemed so much larger than the professional lens through which I was looking, and partly because the traditional methods of sociology do not really equip one to study discrete moments in the flow of human experience.[31]

Sociologists usually select the scenes that they study with the thought that these will illuminate some more general proposition which has engaged their attention; they select a case because of its value for testing a generalization. Perhaps, Erikson suggests, sociologists ought to work the other way around more often. "The search for generalization has become so intense in our professional ranks," he writes, "that most of the important events of our day have passed without comment in the sociological literature." Even though a science works from the particular to the general, it is his belief that "there are times when the need for generalizations must yield to the urgency of passing events, times when the event must tell its own story."[32] The more one knows and respects a community of people, he says, the more difficult it becomes to think of them as instances of a proposition in sociology—"all the more so," he adds, "if they are suffering in some sharp and private way." His book, then, may be difficult to classify, for it is clinical, historical, and sociological. "I would be content," he comments, "to think of these pages as an example of what C. Wright Mills called 'social studies' and let librarians worry about the shelf on which they should be placed."[33]

*Everything in Its Path* is the work of a humanist, of a sociologist who interweaves passages from Santayana's *The Last Puritan* and Dostoevski's *Notes from the Underground* with his own evocative writing, who invites readers to *see* as well as to hear the people he writes about:

Wilbur was born in Kentucky in 1922. He has a strong mountain face, streaked here and there with thin scars and a little out of line. "I was caught under a slate fall," he says matter-of-factly, "and it busted my face up." His breathing is measured, labored, not as if he is gasping for air, but as if he is carefully rationing his intake, making every lungful count. He is one of five brothers, all of whom worked underground, all of whom have black lung in one degree or another, and all of whom had retired on a disability pension by their early fifties.[34]

The chapter entitled "Individual Trauma: State of Shock" contains a number of ideas one may find in Terrence des Pres's *The Survivor* and in the last chapters of Alvarez' *The Savage God*. The section on "The Furniture of Self" was written with a Jamesian sensitivity to and appreciation of the meaning of things, of possessions: "To lose a home or the sum of one's belongings," Erikson writes, "is to lose evidence as to who one is and where one belongs in the world."[35] Erikson knew his subject so well that he recognized immediately that the remark of a coal company official, to the effect that the disaster was "an act of God," and that the dam was "incapable of holding the water God poured into it" was, for the people of the hollow, tantamount to blasphemy.[36]

Erikson's methods were, in some ways, those of classic social science. Like James West in Plainville and Whyte in Cornerville, he wanted to get the feel of things first, and was drawn to a street corner—or "the nearest thing" to it on Buffalo Creek, "Charlie Cowan's gas station."[37] He acquainted himself with what had been written about disasters as a class of events, and he studied the transcript material that had been compiled for the legal action that was to be taken on behalf of the survivors. He asked people questions; he listened to them talk; he observed them as they went about the business of their daily lives, or what, after the disaster, was left of them. In his analysis, he moved from the particular to the general, from observed fact to concepts and theories. But because of his awareness of the larger meanings of the Buffalo Creek flood, and his sympathy for those who had endured it, the abstractions never get the better of him, never obstruct his vision.

In his "Notes on Appalachia," Erikson takes many exceptions to the conventional portrait of "the mountaineer." It is a portrait, for the most part, of adult men, he says. And it includes many features that are not peculiar to Appalachia. It is artificial, because the people it is supposed to represent are changing even as the portrait is being drawn.

Therefore, no matter how recent it is, it will always reflect the past, and not the present living reality. Any such portrait, he reminds us, can only understate the contrasts to be found in whatever is real. The depiction of types, of patterns, which is the social scientific task, is at once a guide and an impediment to understanding reality. Since things both change and remain the same, as people do, the social scientist is continuously engaged in the effort to balance these dual aspects of reality, that which happens only once, and that which happens over and over again. It is not appreciated enough how difficult it is to distinguish between the two. Either way, one runs the risk of losing the sense of reality. It is possible to construct an "ideal type," to abstract a general pattern by taking away all that is particular about a general phenomenon, and, by that very act, to miss its essential meaning. On the other hand, it is possible to become so intrigued with the concrete, the unique, the particular, as to miss seeing how often appearances are *re*appearances. What is real, what is true is that both are present in every human being, in every relationship, in every situation and event.

When the anthropologist constructs a "still life" of a community, he has this double vision, of the living reality and of the design or pattern of which it appears to be an individuation. The social scientist sees the world he studies through the eyes of those who inhabit it. But at the same time, he sees it through the lens of the social scientific tradition. Somewhere in the spaces between these two perspectives the truth of social and cultural reality moves. In his study of the ghetto, Ulf Hannerz finds that the people of Winston Street think in terms of a dichotomy of ways of life. On the one side are the "respectable" people, or the "good" people, or, less commonly, and perhaps with a shade of self-mockery, they speak of the "model citizens" or of the "middle class." On the other side are the "undesirables," the "no goods," the "rowdies" or "bums" or "trash." These labels are used most often by those who see themselves as counted among the "respectables," of course. But, looking more closely at the ghetto community, Hannerz finds that the reality is far more complex than this depiction of two internally homogeneous groups standing in opposition to one another implies. "This folk model of social cleavage is not a particularly accurate description of what real lives are like," he writes, "or of how they are intertwined. Above all, . . . these two categories are only the opposite poles of a rather complex continuum."[38] Though the native's understanding of the social and cultural reality must be known by the social scientist, it can only be a part, though a very vital part, of his own. Hannerz conceives of the social and moral vocabularies of those who live in the ghetto as forming an image bank; one draws from it to fit one's position and the immediate situation. This ought to be emphasized, he says, because simple dichotomous labels appear all too often in social scientific writing about poor black people or about the lower classes. The reason for this may be that "the observers have simply accepted the moral taxonomy of the natives as an acceptable way of ordering descriptions of the community, or because a similar dichotomy fits the outsider's moral precepts, or his concern for 'social problems.'"[39]

Hannerz adopts the terms "ghetto-specific" and "mainstream-oriented" modes of action, although he does not make this dichotomy the only basis for classifying lifestyles and people. Beginning with this, he describes four lifestyles that, he thinks, more accurately reflect the realities of Winston Street than the dichotomy of the ghetto view. These four, the mainstreamers, the swingers, the street families, and the street-corner men are, he says, "ideal types" that can only approximate the reality that is ghetto life.[40] The reality he finds is a world made up of smaller worlds, both in flux, between and within which people live their lives.

Seeing these worlds steadily and seeing them whole is the task of the social scientist. Hannerz is in search of the deeper meanings of what people do and what they say. He considers why Ghetto Man is so often made the topic of street-corner sociability, why men become so personally involved and find such gratification in their story-telling sessions about this Ghetto Man. He is each of them and all of them, this image of natural masculinity,

a bit of a hero, a bit of a villain, and a bit of a fool, yet none of them all the way. He is in fact a kind of a trickster—uncertainty personified.... He applies his mother wit or is plainly lucky some times, as Big Bill in front of the judge, and this helps him come out victorious or at least unscathed. But not all the time, for native wit and luck have their limits, for instance when David left his bottle behind and the police were watching, or when Brenda came home and prevented Charlie from sneaking out with the gorgeous chicks from North Carolina. Anyway, when Ghetto Man succeeds, he is a hero . . . ; if he fails, it is natural because he was up to no good.[41]

The significance of Ghetto Man is fully understood by understanding that men living the ghetto-specific lifestyle "are constantly morally and intellectually besieged." All of them must cope with the same problems of role ambivalence. They need one another for support of the sort of masculinity that they have achieved. Listening to the tales these men tell, connecting them with the way their lives are lived, Hannerz unearths a "type conflict" they endure about their masculinity. Reminiscences, he finds, "may be like myths, sociability a kind of mythmaking." Street-corner mythmaking, with its reminiscences and tales, cannot resolve this conflict, but it can at least alleviate the burden of it somewhat. "This is why," Hannerz writes, "the men 'running their mouths' under the street lamp, in the barber shop, or on the front staircase are doing something important."[42]

Social and cultural realities are as elusive as the psychological. We are forever becoming another of who we are; and social and cultural worlds, too, are forever coming into being. The world-view shared by those who live in the ghetto community, Hannerz writes, "is a complex phenomenon with a changing structure and composition. Attempting to analyze it we are constantly faced with the danger that we depict it too statically and in terms too intellectually clearcut to represent well the vague moods of an entire community."[43] Throughout this work, Hannerz tries to see the ghetto culture as something always in process. The task of the social scientist is to arrest what will not hold still in order to describe and to analyze it. Reality, ever moving, ever changing, does not easily yield up its truths.

In his chapter on "Mainstream and Ghetto in Culture," Hannerz considers some of the most profound questions that beset social scientists. These are: in what ways a culture may be said to exist, what its components may be said to be, what an understanding of social and cultural reality suggests about the nature and extent of human freedom, and what a study of poor people may have to contribute to the formulation of just social policy. Following a painstaking review of the meaning of the concept of the "culture of poverty," Hannerz finds it "obvious . . . that man is not a mindless cultural automaton; some of the doubts raised against the notion of a culture of poverty may be reactions against tendencies to view culture as an oppressive tradition which people can only slavishly follow."[44] The culture of the ghetto community, he finds, is not all-of-a-piece; in some ways, those who live there

> form one group, while in other ways they are divided into several. They may all share the understanding of what it means to be black in a white society; somewhat fewer are directly involved in the problems of being both black and poor; and unemployed male alcoholics are a yet smaller number who face some of their common problems in cultural processes of streetcorner mythmaking. This heterogeneity must be taken into account as we try to arrive at an outline of the distribution of shared culture in the ghetto community.[45]

Nor does Hannerz confine his discussion to the meaning that poverty has in the ghetto. Recognizing that "black people are not just any poor people but an ethnic community existing under very special circumstances in American society," the last pages of this chapter are concerned with "Prospects for black culture."[46]

Writing of his field experiences, Hannerz comments that, when he was introduced to people, the fact that he is Swedish was emphasized, and he thinks that this may have created a special position for him: he was clearly distinguished from other white people. Being Swedish gave him an advantage in doing his research. Because of it, he says, "I was not quite so readily assimilated into the perspective of black-white conflict."[47] The anthropologist, both stranger and friend, as Hortense Powdermaker would have it, may, by virtue of his training, be able to give a more insightful picture of the human side of ghetto living than other social scientists—or, at least, Hannerz thinks as much. Perhaps by describing life as it is lived from day to day, he suggests, the anthropologist can offer something other and more than the social-problems studies of life in the black ghetto. Black nationalists and intellectuals, he comments, have often said that much of the attention that social scientists have given to the ghetto is both degrading and dehumanizing. He quotes Ralph Ellison, who wrote in "A Very Stern Discipline" (in *Harper's Magazine* in 1967) that the sociological formulas are drawn from life, and yet the complexity of Harlem escapes sociologists. They abstract Harlem, and reduce it to proportions they can manage, Ellison wrote, and he was unable to recognize Harlem or the people of Harlem in their work. While he felt that the sociologists capture the struggle in Harlem, the poverty and the sordidness, he wrote that there is another quality, the source of the strength and the promise of the people of Harlem, that sociologists ignore at their peril. It is this quality that Ellison identified as the proper subject for the Negro American writer.

In reflecting on Ellison's thoughts, Hannerz writes that we have tended to read the novels and autobiographies of black writers, rather than social scientific writing, in our search for the reality of the ghetto. "Of course," he continues, "there are things these writers can do which no social scientist can get away with. In a way, Ellison is criticizing sociologists for being sociologists" since it is their task to make abstractions. Perhaps, however, Hannerz goes on to say, the reality of the ghetto eludes sociologists because those who live in the ghetto have been viewed by them as "cases" of social problems. Thus, even though sociologists clearly believe that those who live in the ghetto are victimized, the image that comes through in sociological studies is one of "failure and impotence." One who writes in the anthropological tradition, Hannerz suggests, might illuminate this more human side of the ghetto reality more clearly than other social scientists, this endurance and strength and promise of the people of Harlem of which Ellison wrote. For it may be, Hannerz says, that "soul" can be grasped only in a grassroots context, "and anthropology as a form of consciousness may be better able to inquire into these personal terms of life while at the same time remaining more systematic than the literary view of the black experience."[48]

Every tradition, in science as well as in art, is at once a confinement and a means of liberation of consciousness. Nor will any two observers working within the same tradition see and report the same things. This Hannerz appreciates, and writes about in his introduction to *Soulside*. The social scientist and the fiction writer, working at the same moment in time and in the same place even, will perceive and re-create different "realities."

It is sometimes assumed that, by the very nature of the differences between the social scientific and the literary perspective, the social scientist cannot but miss the mark. To this way of thinking, the realities in his studies are not realities at all, but fictions of social scientific invention, whereas the realities in the short story or novel are seen to approximate fact. However, simply because many social scientific works compare unfavorably with some works of fiction—because they are not evocative, or are not memorable, or do not contribute particularly to any understanding of their subject—does not mean that this is inevitable. Perhaps those social scientists responsible for stiff, dead writing have ruined the reputation of their humanistically inclined compeers. Perhaps the voices of those who are scientists with a vengeance, joined with those who believe they have found an answer for everything, have created such a din that they have driven many who care for the life of the mind to a despairing silence. Some have suggested that a moratorium ought to be declared on publishing any works in social science for a year, so that one might gather one's wits and sweet reason together. But there are social scientists who write very well, indeed. Books like *Everything in Its Path* and *Soulside* open a social and cultural world of people to us, and deepen our understanding of that world and, through this, of ourselves. A gifted social scientist can see very far into things, and through them. If his work is lifeless and without meaning, this is because of a failure within him, a failure of his powers of imagination or observation or analysis, and not because of a fatal flaw in social science.

Much the same may be said of literary works. It is impossible to generalize about "the writer" or "fiction," as Aldous Huxley remarked in an interview conducted by George Wickes and Ray Frazer for the *Paris Review*. Writers are a diverse group, he said,

and fiction is a genus of which there are many species. I think that certain species of fiction quite clearly call for a certain locale. It's impossible that Trollope could have written except where he did write. He couldn't have gone off to Italy like Byron or Shelley. He required the English middle-class life. But then look at Lawrence. At the beginning you would have said that he had to stay in the Midlands of England, near the coal mines. But he could write anywhere.[49]

If two Negro American writers wrote novels about Ulf Hannerz's Winston Street, they would create two different works. Their ways of seeing would be different, and two different "realities" would be perceived, each with its truths and its fictions. For no two sensibilities are alike. Nor is any place the same for a writer when he is middle-aged as it was for him when he was young. And, as social scientists well know, being *of* a place or a people as well as *in* them, or a part of them, does not always grant the gift of sight. Quite the reverse for some writers: it may blind them to much that is there. Certain discoveries may be made more easily by the stranger. This is apparent in *Soulside*, and also in that celebrated work by another Swedish social scientist, Myrdal's *An American Dilemma*. We shall always see through a glass darkly, social scientists and writers alike. Each of us has his own angle of vision, his own point of view, his own ear, so that it cannot be said (though it often is) of any writer that the Truth lies in his or her own sensibility. Truth is not one, but many. And it moves about; it does not stay still.

How do writers work, and what does this suggest about the ways in which they resemble, as well as differ from, the social scientist's approach? The *Paris Review* interviews are a rich source of information on this question. When Algren was asked how he arrived at *The Man with the Golden Arm*—"thematically," as interviewers Alston Anderson and Terry Southern put the question, "rather than a war novel?" he replied,

... if you're going to write a war novel, you have to do it while you're *in* the war. If you don't do the thing while you're there—at least the way I operate—you can't do it. It slips away. Two months after the war it was gone; but I was living in a *living* situation, and ... I find it pretty hard to write on anything in the past ... and this thing just got more real; I mean, the neighborhood I was living in, and these people, were a lot more *real* than the Army was.[50]

*The Man with the Golden Arm*, Algren said, did not "write itself." At the same time, it was not a contrived work. He said that the situation was there and it struck him, and he responded to this. He had worked for almost two years on the book before he ever ran into a drug addict. He did not know much about drug addiction; he was writing the book about a card dealer. It came to him that the "dope angle" could have great dramatic force, but, he said, he did not know anything about drugs. "I thought it would be better to lay off if you don't *know*," he recalled, "and I didn't see how you'd go about finding out about something like that deliberately, so I dropped it. Somehow

I didn't fit it in." The book needed a "peg" to hang everything on, he told the interviewers, and just when he was preoccupied with that problem, he was hanging with drug users. But still, it took him a very long time to make any connection between drug addiction and the book. When he asked his agent for her advice, she insisted that he use it. "I hung it on there," he said, "without really knowing a great deal about it. It was an afterthought. I got the mood of the thing, but I didn't have much time to, you know, do it thoroughly." He learned more about it *after* the book was published.[51]

Algren and his interviewers discussed some of the same issues the participant-observer confronts in going about his research. The interviewers asked him if he felt he ought to try to use heroin, since he was writing a book on the subject, and Algren replied, "No, I think you can do a thing like that best from a detached position." When he was asked if the people he was writing about might have put him down as an eavesdropper, he said that, for the most part, they were amused by his work. They thought it was an odd way to make a living. However, after the book was published, Algren recalled, one junkie who liked it very much was trying to persuade another junkie to read it. Finally, the latter said that he *had* read the book, and that he objected to a passage in it where someone takes a shot and then talks "for about four pages." "It ain't like that," the junkie said, "a guy takes a fix and he goes on the nod." The junkie who had liked the book a great deal pointed out that, if Algren *really* had known what he was writing about, he could never have written the book, because he'd be in jail. And Algren said of the writer, "you have to compromise. But the book was somehow incidental to my relationship with them, inasmuch as they always had some hassle going on, and--well, this needle thing wasn't always up front, you know."[52]

Algren made a distinction between working as a social scientist and working as a writer. Remarking of another writer that he is "too journalistic for my taste" and that "I don't get anything besides a social study" from reading his work, Algren said, "It isn't enough to do just a case study, something stenographic."[53]

A social scientist is, of course, much more than a stenographer; he, like the creative writer, must edit, must make some sense and order out of the chaos that is reality. Artists and scientists alike must come to terms with their traditions, must be aware of the continuity of things, if their work is to live. What Katherine Anne Porter said of the writer in her interview for the *Paris Review* may be said just as well of the social scientist:

> nothing is pointless, and nothing is meaningless if the artist will face it. And it's his business to face it. He hasn't got the right to sidestep it . . . . Human life itself may be almost pure chaos, but the work of the artist—the only thing he's good for—is to take these handfuls of confusion and disparate things, things that seem to be irreconcilable, and put them together in a frame to give them some kind of shape and meaning. Even if it's only his view of a meaning. That's what he's for--to give his view of life. Surely, we understand very little of what is happening to us at any given moment. But by remembering, comparing, waiting to know the consequences, we can sometimes see what an event really meant, what it was trying to teach us.[54]

When Erikson talked with the survivors of the Buffalo Creek flood, when he listened to them tell of their dreams, he was in search of the way the meaning of the immediate tragedy could lead to an understanding of the meaning of their lives, and from that, of all our lives. Meditating on the "Loss of Connection" with community that people experienced after the flood, a loss beyond restoring, Erikson writes of how human relationships began to crumble. Neighborhood customs, family traditions, community ways had been torn away by the disaster. Marriages began to fall apart. "Marriage, too," he reflects, "is something of a community affair. It is validated by the community, witnessed by the community, commemorated by the community, and every married couple in the world knows something about the pressures exerted on that union by interests outside of it." Once the community that provided the context for the marriage had been destroyed, husbands and wives who had formerly been devoted to one another found "that they did not know how to care for each other or to work together as a team or even to carry on satisfactory conversations . . . ."[55] In *Soulside*, Ulf Hannerz listens to the jokes and tales the men tell, the wonderful adventures of Ghetto Man, and searches for their larger meaning. He finds how sociability works as a sort of myth-making, and reminiscences as myths, remembering that "leisure is the time for taking care of moral and intellectual business."[56] In and of themselves, a flood is just another part of the news, the Winston Street neighborhood just another ghetto. The universals there do not speak for themselves. Without the explorations of the social scientist, they would remain hidden to us, as they so often are to the people who experience a disaster, or are part of a cultural world.

The search for the universal may explain, in part, why the Lynds wrote about "Middletown" and Lloyd Warner of "Yankee City," why Whyte wrote of a place called "Cornerville," and West of "Plainville," and Hannerz of "Winston Street." The social scientist adopts a pseudonym for the community he studies (West went further; he adopted one for himself as well) if he feels this is necessary to protect the anonymity of people who entrust him with their secrets. Indeed, it is standard practice to begin research studies by promising not to reveal actual names or places. It has become a matter of professional ethics to report facts about fictional places and people—though it is easy enough, most of the time, to find the actual names. (In this as in other respects, Erikson's work is the exception rather than the rule: there was no point in his disguising the locality of his research, since he was asked to serve as one of a group of consultants to a law firm that was preparing a suit on behalf of the survivors of the Buffalo Creek flood.) Invented names for places and people may do more than simply serve as a device for protecting their anonymity. It may be that the social scientist writes of Springdale or of Jonesville, of Cornerville or of the New Deal Carry-out shop on Tally's Corner to draw our attention to the universals, to keep us from stumbling over particularities and losing our way in them, to prevent us from staring at one detail of a canvas. The task of the social scientist is to connect social and cultural realities to the larger realities of all human association.

Many a writer, too, consciously pursues the universals, though coming around toward them by way of a very different path than that taken by the social scientist. In his *Paris Review* interview, Frank O'Connor said that a theme is something that matters to everyone. In his view, a writer must have a theme, a story to tell:

The moment you grab somebody by the lapels and you've got something to tell, that's a real story. It means you want to tell him and think the story is interesting in itself. If you start describing your own personal experiences, something that's only of interest to yourself, then you can't express yourself, you cannot say, ultimately, what you think about human beings. The moment you say this, you're committed.[57]

There are echoes of Katherine Anne Porter's statement in O'Connor's: a story, to be a story, must have a point. And the writer is one who has a point of view, and must write in a way that will draw the reader in, making him, as O'Connor sees it, a part of the story. Interpretation is everything; stories do not speak for themselves any more than the social facts do.

The writer "needs three things," Faulkner maintained, "experience, observation, and imagination." Faulkner went on to say that any two of these, and at times any one of them, can be put to work in the absence of the others.[58] It is difficult, however, to see how a writer could work without imagination and still write effectively. Perhaps Faulkner did not intend this remark to be taken in full seriousness, since he followed it by saying that the writer tries to create people in whom we can believe, in situations that are moving and at the same time believable, and that he tries to do this in a way that is moving. He was speaking about his feeling that the amount of a writer's work that is based upon personal experience is not an important issue; obviously, he said, a writer must use the environment he knows as one of his instruments. Gradually, the full significance of what he was doing came to Faulkner: after he had written *Soldier's Pay*, he said, he discovered

> that not only each book had to have a design but the whole output or sum of an artist's work had to have a design. With *Soldier's Pay* and *Mosquitoes* I wrote for the sake of writing because it was fun. Beginning with *Sartoris* I discovered that my own little postage stamp of native soil was worth writing about and that I would never live long enough to exhaust it, and that by sublimating the actual into the apocryphal I would have complete liberty to use whatever talent I might have to its absolute top. It opened up a gold mine of other people, so I created a cosmos of my own. I can move these people around like God, not only in space but in time too.[59]

The social scientist, too, needs experience, observation, and imagination; and the best of social science, the works that will endure, are those in which all three are interwoven. Yet, while the risk for the social scientist is that he may miss seeing the detail—the trees, the risk of the writer is that he may miss seeing the forest. It would seem that the social scientist and the writer work from different directions toward the same achievement, the discovery of the universal. Still, they are sometimes very close to one another. Algren, who once thought he might become a sociologist, but who also said that he believed it is not enough to do a case study, was asked by the interviewers for the *Paris Review* if he was trying to dramatize a social problem in *The Man with the Golden Arm*. He replied:

> Well, there's always something wrong in any society. I think it would be a mistake to aim at any solution, you know; I mean, the most you can do is—well, if any writer can catch the *routine lives* of people just *living* in that kind of ring of fire to show how you can't go out of a certain neighborhood if you're addicted, or for other reasons, that you can't be legitimate, but that within the limitation you can succeed in making a life that is routine—with human values that seem to be a little more real, a little more intense, and human, than with people who are freer to come and go—if somebody could write a book about the routine of these circumscribed people, just their everyday life, without any big scenes, without any violence, or cops breaking in, and so on, just day-to-day life—like maybe the woman is hustling and makes a few bucks, and they get a little H just to keep from getting sick, and go to bed, and get up—just an absolutely prosaic life without any particular drama to it in their eyes—if you could just do that straight, without anybody getting arrested—there's always a little danger of that, of course—but to have it just the way these thousands of people live, very quiet, commonplace routine . . . well, you'd have an awfully good book.[60]

Reality, to paraphrase a revolutionary, lies in the streets; it only remains for the writer, the social scientist, to discover how to pick it up. Some writers do not believe that literature can or ought to lend itself to social reforms or the making of revolutions; others believe this passionately. Sometimes a writer's work reflects his beliefs about these matters, and at other times, not. Social scientists are divided on this issue, also. Some believe that social scientific knowledge has no value or point other than its political utility, and others violently disagree. Unlike writers, social scientists are very explicit about this issue in their work.

In the quest for realities, the writer invents, makes up, narrates. He appeals to our senses, our emotions, as well as to our reason. And there are writers who eschew any appeal to reason at all. Joyce Cary said that philosophers are "always bores," and that "A novel should be an experience and convey an emotional truth rather than arguments."[61] In contrast, it may be said that the social scientist is always arguing in his work. It is the *ideas* that guide and inform his work to which the social scientist is most closely attentive. Perhaps the difference between writer and social scientist has its roots in temperament. Speaking of his own preference for biography, history, and fiction, Aldous Huxley said, "I think one can say much more about general abstract ideas in terms of concrete characters and situations, whether fictional or real, than one can in abstract terms."[62] *Grey Eminence*, he said, *The Devils of Loudun*, and other works convey general ideas through specific lives and incidents; and he continued:

I think that probably *all* philosophy ought to be written in this form; it would be much more profound and much more edifying. It's awfully easy to write abstractly, without attaching much meaning to the big words. But the moment you have to express ideas in the light of a particular context, in a particular set of circumstances, although it's a limitation in some ways, it's also an invitation to go much further and much deeper. I think that fiction and, as I say, history and biography are *immensely* important, not only for their own sake, because they provide a picture of life now and of life in the past, but also as vehicles for the expression of general philosophic ideas, religious ideas, social ideas. My goodness, Dostoevski is six times as profound as Kierkegaard, because he writes *fiction*. In Kierkegaard you have this Abstract Man going on and on—like Coleridge—why, it's *nothing* compared with the really profound Fictional Man, who has always to keep these tremendous ideas *alive* in a concrete form. In fiction you have the reconciliation of the absolute and the relative, so to speak, the expression of the general in the particular. And this, it seems to me, is the exciting thing—both in life and in art.[63]

Huxley was, of course, speaking of fiction, and not of poetry. Robert Lowell suggested that "on the whole prose is less cut off from life than poetry is."[64] For all his gifts, Lowell remarked, Browning's people seem *made up* to the reader, whereas in Frost's poems the reader feels that the people are *real*. Frost's poetry, Lowell suggested, "has the virtue of a photograph but all the finish of art," and he found this an extraordinary achievement for a poet. Prose writers seemed to Lowell to have a "kind of sympathy and observation of people" far more than poets do.[65] Many more fiction writers than poets, one might say, are able participant-observers. Therefore, they are drawn into the same field of vision as social scientists are.

How much observing is enough? This depends upon the writer's needs and abilities. It is probably true that many writers are not wholly conscious of how much listening and looking they actually do when they are away from their typewriters. Some writers are even disdainful of the suggestion that they do "research" before they write. Robert Penn Warren said that one writer might need to do quite a bit of research, whereas for another, researching might be "poison." However, Warren maintained that one doesn't "work up" literature; rather, one *is* "worked up" about something. "You see the world as best you can—with or without the help of somebody's research," he continued. It was his contention that one ought to be interested in events and books simply because one is a human being, not because one can use them as a writer. Researching for a book, he said, struck him as obscene—that is, researching in order to find a book one might write: "Once you are engaged by a subject, are in your book, have your idea, you may or may not want to do some investigating. But you ought to do it in the same spirit in which you'd take a walk in the evening air to think things over."[66]

Even so, and even if one is writing a fable or a work of science fiction, the writer draws from social and cultural realities. No matter how proficient a writer may be in telling a tale, once he moves away from the familiar circle of personal experience, he has to do some hanging about on street corners, some eavesdropping; he has to scout the social terrain, if his work is to be taken seriously, if it is to be believed. In *Fact and Fiction*, John Hollowell discusses the approach that Truman Capote (who coined the term "nonfiction novel") used in researching the material for *In Cold Blood*. He "began his research with stacks of documents, public records, and interviews with Holcomb residents close to the case." Capote, however, "wanted it both ways," Hollowell reminds us; he wanted "the impeccable accuracy of fact *and* the emotional impact found only in fiction. In order to reconstruct conversations by the deceased family, he elicited and tirelessly double-checked the recollections of neighbors who were present." And, once he gained the confidence of the killers, he was granted access to their diaries, letters, confessions, and to the accounts they had written especially for him to use. Through all these resources, Capote achieved a reconstruction of what was going on before the murders, though he had not yet even arrived in Holcomb.[67] Capote did research as a social scientist would. Yet he presented his "findings" as a novelist does. In the "new journalism" and the "nonfiction novel" the reader finds a *celebration* of the social and cultural realities, researched by the writer and then cast in literary form. Some critics, and some writers, too, are very critical of this blending of fact and fiction. It is Hollowell's judgment that *In Cold Blood* is, on what might be called a symbolic level, closer to fiction than it is to journalism: "Capote's treatment of the 'facts' creates a context of meaning beyond these particular killers, this particular crime. He weaves the facts of the case into a pattern that resonates with the violence of an entire decade of American life."[68] Just as Erikson did in *Everything in Its Path*, Capote, in *In Cold Blood*, connected a particular series of events to a wider reality, bringing the crafting of a novel as close as it may ever be brought, perhaps, to the crafting of social science.

In composing a literary work, Robert Penn Warren maintained, even a work of objective fiction, one writes "from the inside not the outside"—the inside of oneself. "You have to find what's there," he said. "You can't predict it . . . . of course you have to have common sense enough and structural sense enough to know what is relevant." All the same, he believes that the writer does not choose a story; the story chooses the writer.[69] The protagonist of the novel *In Cold Blood*, the chief character of the report *In Cold Blood* may have "chosen" Capote, whose fascination with him, Hollowell suggests, "casts suspicion upon his claims of objectivity." Capote said that after he had been working on the project for several months, things suddenly came together. Hollowell quotes Capote's statement to an interviewer to the effect that there was something in the material that appealed to something within himself. Perry, Capote said, made him decide to write *In Cold Blood*. For Perry was a character that was also in Capote's imagination.[70]

It may be that events, situations, a certain people, preexist in the social scientist's imagination, and that the research projects are chosen because they flow from this. It may be that there was something more than "mere" chance, something more compelling than an intellectual problem and a combination of circumstances that brought Whyte to Cornerville, Erikson to Buffalo Creek, Ulf Hannerz to Winston Street. Perhaps "coincidence" is a word we use when we speak of a mystery that we cannot penetrate—at least, not yet. If the writer works from the inside outward, there is a world in there that is brought to life, not so much *by* him as *through* him. In some way, even without his always being aware of it, he absorbs the outer world, and tries to shape it in his writing so that, when he offers it to us, we can recognize the truth of it, and the truth of ourselves. If a writer can take in very little, if eye and ear are poorly developed, his imagination flickers. The writing becomes contrived, forced; we cannot believe it because it has no depth and no scope. Writing is discovering, and the richer and deeper the imagination—the more of the outer world one has taken in for transformation—the more there will be to discover. Indeed, like Keats, the writer's pen may never glean his teeming brain, for the outer world is inexhaustible.

Usually the social scientist works the other way around, from the outside inward. Whether he has chosen the problem and the site of research or it has chosen him, he, too, must find what is there. Like the writer, he is an explorer who cannot predict what he will find. The richer his imagination, the keener his eye and ear, the more gifted he is in what Cooley called "sympathetic introspection," the more he will discover to bring back to us. If the social scientist has read very little, thought very little about the matters he has undertaken to study, he will not sound the meanings of what he sees and hears. What is in the outer world that may be mined as truth will elude him. Lacking an inner life, wanting in imagination, a social scientist may master the most sophisticated techniques, yet never find social and cultural realities.

In Britain and America, Tom and Elizabeth Burns write, sociologists who have turned to literature "have treated it as a kind of quarry for fossil specimens of classes of events and stereotyped actions, performances, or social roles." But in Europe, there has been "far less of the anxiety about demarcation rules which afflicts the English speaking academic world." And there, the sociology of literature "flourishes under its own colours, particularly in France."[71] Long ago, Ferdinand Tönnies spoke of "genitive sociology,"[72] a proclivity sociologists have toward planting a flag marked "of sociological significance" on every event and issue, toward ferreting out "sociological insights" in works of fiction, indeed, toward expressing approval of something by the simple device of claiming that it is ultimately sociological. Of all the social scientists, sociologists may be the most inclined to this genitive tendency. This legacy from the Encylopedists has led to conflicts in colleges of liberal arts, and to something approaching fratricidal warfare in combined departments of the social sciences. It seems to scholars in the humanities to operate as a sort of territorial imperative. "The Sociology of Death," an unfriendly colleague in English remarked in the halls of a university not long ago, "now, what might *really* be opportune would be a course in the Death of Sociology." Scholars in other disciplines are not in the position to cast the first stone, of course. Still, the mechanical application of what is loosely and superficially called "Marxist thinking" to works of fiction and drama, and the combing of literary works for documentation of what the sociologist already "knows," is intellectually barbaric. Sometimes it is mindless, but at other times it has a sinister cast. Northrop Frye has clearly delineated the limitations of documentary approaches to literature:

In the first place, they do not account for the literary form of what they are discussing. Identifying Edward King and documenting Milton's attitude to the Church of England will throw no light on *Lycidas* as a pastoral elegy with specific Classical and Italian lines of ancestry. Secondly, they do not account for the poetic and metaphorical language of the literary work. Documentary criticism in general is based on the assumption that the literal or real meaning of a poem is not what it says as a poem, but is something to be expressed by a prose paraphrase derived from the poem. Thirdly, they do not account for the fact that the unique quality of a poet is often in quite a negative relation to the chosen context. To understand fully Blake's *Milton* and *Jerusalem* one needs to know something of his quarrel with Hayley and his sedition trial, but one also needs to be aware of the vast disproportion between these very minor events in a very quiet life and their apocalyptic transformation in the poems. Similarly, one may write a whole shelf of books about the life of Milton studied in connexion with the history of his time, and still fail to notice that Milton's greatness as a poet has a good deal to do with his profound and perverse misunderstanding of the history of his time.[73]

Turning the topic around, there are also severe limitations to what a writer can achieve, if he seeks to create a world of characters, scenes, and events beyond those he has known and experienced, without any knowledge of them. There is much a fiction writer could learn from ethnographies by sensitive field workers. Just as every writer whose works have the ring of truth in them has absorbed some understanding of human psychology, so, too, he has in some way absorbed social and cultural realities. One must know the "given" before one can rebel against it. While the psychological and social facts ought to be understood, for nothing can take their place, the writer needs to cultivate eye and ear in order to apprehend them; he must become a kind of field worker. Those creative writers who have worked as journalists have learned much of great value; and work as a social researcher would be of value to those who write in every genre. Nor does a knowledge of the lore of social science necessarily interfere with the creative process. Quite the reverse is true in certain cases. For Saul Bellow, an impressive command of anthropology and sociology enriches an extraordinary literary imagination.

Some writers have maintained that working as literary critics threatens their creative force. But any kind of criticism, Robert Penn Warren maintained, is good, if it "gives a deeper insight into the nature of the thing—a Marxist analysis, a Freudian study, the relation to a literary or social tradition . . . ." What ought to be kept in mind, he emphasized, is that there is no one correct *kind* of criticism, there is no *complete* criticism. Rather, what we have are different perspectives, each offering different kinds of insights.[74] Writers and critics have much to teach social scientists, and much to learn from them as well. In an informative essay on this very subject, George Steiner writes, "The Marxist sensibility has contributed a sociological awareness to the best of modern criticism. It is the kind of awareness realized, for example, in Lionel Trilling's observation that Dostoyevskyan plots originate in crises in monetary or class relationships."[75]

In their search for reality, writers and social scientists alike need those faculties that Matthew Arnold thought necessary if culture is to be saved at all—curiosity and disinterestedness. Reality, the truth and sense of our lives, ever eludes us—writers and social scientists both. Of course, this does not matter so much; it is the hunt that matters, not the kill. Neither the "informant" in the field report nor the character in the novel, neither the social world in the ethnography nor that in the short story, can ever be more than an approximation of the living reality. "Real people are too complex and too disorganized for books," Joyce Cary said. "They aren't simple enough." All the great heroes and heroines "are essentially characters from fable, and so they must be to take their place in a formal construction which is to have a meaning."[76]

Aldous Huxley said this, too: that "fictional characters are oversimplified; they're much less complex than the people one knows."[77] We cannot know characters in fiction as we know persons in life, Martin Price writes. If we say that fictional persons are more "real" than actual persons, this

> conceals more problems than it clarifies. Actual persons are curiously open; they have lives yet to live, they impinge upon us in direct ways. We confront them; we can affect them. We see them as coming closer to us or receding, and if they recede we may miss them. In all these respects, and countless others, real persons have an urgency that the persons of fiction cannot have.[78]

If a fictional character spills over a work of fiction, demanding a work of his own, he does not spill over into our lives, Price goes on to say. Rather, he goes only into another fictional work. For the social scientist, the actual persons remain, "curiously open," with some part of their lives before them, after he folds up his tent, packs away his camera or his tape recorder, and takes leave of "the field." They, too, are much too disorganized and complicated to be contained in any social scientific report. And if that report is sensitively written, and the research done by a social scientist who was both curious and disinterested enough to keep some moral and intellectual distance between himself and his "subjects," they, like fictional characters, can be unforgettable. Good writing and good social science evoke and convey some portion of that reality, that living reality, that is slways larger than all science and all art.

The measure of a civilization, Tocqueville thought, could be taken by the conditions of its prisons. For Simone de Beauvoir, it is, rather, the way the old people are treated. For Brendan Behan, it is the age of the whores, and for Henry Miller, the quality of the home-baked bread. Many writers and social observers have their own keys, no doubt, to the kingdom of the quality of social life. Yet, although cleverness does not appear to be a gift lavishly bestowed upon the human race, it is far simpler to make a keen observation, a pithy remark, than to labor patiently for a fuller understanding of the meaning of one's own time.

Where does one look, and how does one look for reality? An artist is "a man who has antennae," Henry Miller said, one "who knows how to hook up to the currents which are in the atmosphere, in the cosmos." All that we think, already exists; we are only intermediaries. The elements that make up a scientific truth or a great work of art "are already in the air, they have not been given voice, that's all. They need *the* man, *the* interpreter, to bring them forth."[79] Through this strange alchemy we know as creativity, the truths of an age are given form and voice; they become known to us.

To know one's own time, which is what writers and social scientists are after, is a task fraught with difficulties. It demands sensitivity, and at the same time a kind of ruthlessness, since looking everywhere and listening to everything at once, one sees nothing, hears nothing. It requires that rarest of gifts, the talent for grasping how another experiences his life. At the same time, it requires that one keep a certain moral and intellectual distance. Those of us who wish to understand others, and the essential meaning of our time, whether as social scientists, creative writers, or silent philosophers, must achieve a dwelling-apart of the spirit. Part of our selves must remain outside, but not too far outside—and not so much of ourselves that what we make of our vision is no more than an exercise in taxonomy or a release of bile. On the other hand, without empathy, a work of social science or of literature cannot come to much. And one who does not know himself can never know another, or ever make much sense of his world or of history. Yet there is the risk for those gifted in understanding how others experience their lives, the risk that one may become possessed by a person or a perspective, that once one finds one's way inside another's head and body, one will not be able to find one's way out again. Those who have empathy are the very people for whom this risk is gravest; these are the most easily overwhelmed by the forces inherent in people and events and situations. Jung has said that every man has his story. But not every man has the gift or the desire to tell it. Those elected to this task, of telling the stories of the lives of others, must follow the intricate and fragile connections between inner life and outer reality without drowning in the one, without surrendering integrity, selfhood, to the other.

What will come of one's work, what future generations will make of it, if it endures, can never be known. In a fascinating inquiry into oral and printed literatue, Robert Escarpit remarks that Defoe's *Robinson Crusoe* and Swift's *Gulliver's Travels* both belong today to juvenile literature, and that, very probably, Defoe would have been surprised, and Swift infuriated, to know this. Though the writer is betrayed in a way by what Escarpit calls "creative treason," his work is given "a new lease of life" by this very betrayal. For "creative treason," Escarpit says, "is simply a shifting of values, a rearrangement of the poetic pattern." It is not always so drastic as in the cases of Defoe or Swift: "Instead of being a spectacular piece of carving, it is almost always content with being an infinity of subtle warpings and minute shiftings which add up to a complete metamorphosis of the original work but still preserve its individuality."[80]

When the learned historians, the archaeologists of far future time, scavengers of the ruins of our own, search for the reality of our lives, how much will they learn from our social scientific studies and our literature? By what signs shall the truth of our time be read? How ought writers and social scientists to leave their signature, that we may communicate with them? What will they make of our works? Through reading them, will they come to know us better than we know ourselves?

We trust that they will be more merciful than we have been when we look backward. And it is easy to imagine that they may be amused by our histrionics, our hysteria, our gloom. Surely they may wonder why we could not behave ourselves better, why our private lives are in such disarray, and why we want for a genuine public life. Perhaps they shall come to pity us for having laid waste so many of our powers. Whatever their final judgment of us, they cannot but wonder what it is we are now trying to tell one another, and why. We leave them embarrassed with riches—with our floodtide of printed materials, our records and files and documents and memoirs, our confessions, our oral histories, our catenae of tapes and filmstrips that might encircle the whole tormented planet ten times over. Each of us, whether with graffiti or diary, with portfolios of drawings and paintings, or with albums of photographs or a repertory of films and recordings . . . each of us, with our scribblings and squeaks and squawks, seems to be in need of the services of an untiring amanuensis. It may happen that even the most stout of heart among tomorrow's archivists will come to curse our inventiveness, the proliferation of technological toys that makes it possible for us to stir up so great a commotion. Indeed, if life *were* fair, we ought to be doomed to reincarnation, doomed to return to earth to sift through the noise and clutter of our lives until we put it all together more coherently.

It is very likely, still, that much will be lost—much of value. As always, many feel called upon to speak for their age, but few are chosen. And that choice, of what will survive and what will perish, turns on chance and the judgment of one's contemporaries, neither of which has ever been remarkable for generosity. From time to time, there is an effort made to rescue unpublished works from oblivion; a "home for unpublished books" is opened, or an unpublished library of copyrighted manuscripts. Recently it was recommended that an American Diary Repository be created, "a central clearinghouse for the preservation and use of the diaries written by its people."[81] These and other gathering-places for works that might otherwise be lost forever are sites for excavation by the scholarly gravediggers of the future. Such sites, out-of-the-way, castaway, far from the places where the time capsules with their calculated treasures are buried, attract the archaeologist, whose profile was finely drawn by Loren Eiseley:

No one, I suppose, would believe that an archeologist is a man who knows where last year's lace valentines have gone, or that from the surface of rubbish heaps the thin and ghostly essence of things human keeps rising through the centuries until the plaintive murmur of dead men and women may take precedence at times over the living voice. A man who has once looked with the archaeological eye will never see quite normally. He will be wounded by what other men call trifles. It is possible to refine the sense of time until an old shoe in the bunch grass or a pile of nineteenth-century beer bottles in an abandoned mining town tolls in one's head like a hall clock. This is the price one pays for learning to read time from surfaces other than an illuminated dial. It is the melancholy secret of the artifact, the humanly touched thing.[82]

It is the archaeologist who has the gift of making the artifacts, the *things*, speak, of giving utterance to the seemingly inert, of reading messages in stones, history in potsherds. But tomorrow's archaeologist, unlike his predecessors, is doomed to comb a vast and cluttered beach. Just as we are covering the earth with our depredations, we are filling the air with our talk, our cries. Our appetite for "social facts" has become—or been made—insatiable. What fine screen shall the social historian of the future use, to sift what has value and meaning from the dust?

So many of us seem to be going to confession to one another, moving toward a future where pop artist Andy Warhol said each of us will be given fifteen minutes to be famous. Social scientists and fiction writers alike, by the very nature of their calling, listen in on these private confessions (though they cannot grant absolution). And the height of ambition seems to be to make one's public confession in an Astrodome. The television cameras are, of course, at the ready to receive them. Discoveries of the Way, the Truth, the Life, follow upon one another as the night the day—Vitamin E, soybeans, Pyramid, now Pendulum, Power. Debut follows upon debut; the "coming out," the declarations, the manifestoes . . . each claims its quarter of an hour. A woman discovers the lesbian in herself, and, from this, the lesbian in Everywoman. And she goes to tell it on the mountain, rewriting history as well as prehistory, reshaping it so that it leads to the moment of her discovery. A man has a vasectomy, and creates an entire political science from the experience. Someone has a trans-sexual operation, and makes a book—and a fortune—from a transition that, Jung taught, each of us must inevitably make, if we live long enough. A retirement, an abortion, a move from one occupation or region to another . . . each is analyzed, dissected, reconstructed, formed into a book or film. We are behaving like Martial's poet, caught up in the fever of wanting to give a public reading at every possible opportunity, to whom Martial made the amusing rebuke, "*currenti legis et legis cacanti* (you read to me when I am running and you read to me when I am defecating)."[83]

We behave as though every turn we make on the road must be not only noticed, but endorsed, and preferably applauded, by all others. We behave as though each of us has the assignment of refashioning history and society. Wanting shared meanings, wanting rites of passage, each of us makes up our own, waiting impatiently in the wings for our moment on the stage, our dramatic presentation of the Self coming of age, the Self in midlife crisis, the Self experiencing a divorce or unemployment or alcoholism, the Self contemplating dying. There is this craving for performance on the stage because the search for authenticity is, for so many, an odyssey in the outer world.

It is the task of the writer, the social scientist, to explore the deeper meanings of these things. People "running at the mouth" are doing something important, as Hannerz discerned. Their talk reveals something about our common condition. But one must see *through*, one must listen for the meanings *under* the words. Instead of parroting their words, or putting them on tape, or taking photographs of their unmade beds because they make an interesting composition, or seem to confirm a hypothesis, one must work for true understanding. What people say, what they do, what they look like—all these matter, and an account of human affairs that is silent about these things is without life. But in and of themselves, they do not constitute reality; they do not make their own meanings. In *Everything in Its Path*, Kai Erikson saw how an event forced people to inquire into what it was that their lives were made of; for many people from Buffalo Creek, the flood was the moment of truth. Erikson searched for the meaning the disaster had for them. Reaching back into the history of Appalachia, he gave that meaning depth. And finding in the flood an allegory of a condition we all share, as survivors of a disaster that destroyed the sense of community, he gave it universality. In social science, as in literature, reality lies under the surface of things. Those who find it are those who balance the keen observer's eye and ear with a sense of history and a lively imagination.

# PART TWO

*I have often said and oftener think, that this world is a comedy to those that think; a tragedy to those that feel.*

—Horace Walpole, Letter to
Sir Horace Mann, 31 December 1769

# THREE

## Satirist and Sociologist: Some Likenesses

> *In proportion as men know more and think more, they look less at individuals and more at classes. They therefore make better theories and worse poems.*
> —Thomas Babington Macaulay, "Milton," *Essays and Biographies*

Satirist and sociologist ... an unlikely pair. Yet the eighteenth century provided a hospitable climate for the renaissance of satire and the birth of the social scientific temperament. Social criticism, Morroe Berger writes in his work on the novel and social science, "has probably always been an aspect of art but seems to have grown in importance in the eighteenth century, especially on the eve of the French Revolution."[1] The same could be said of sociological analysis. There are other parallels. Both satirists and sociologists, however else they may differ, have worked with categories, classes, types, rather than with individuals. Furthermore, there have been times when both professions have had a very busy traffic in evangelists. Perhaps one could never guess from outward appearances (their stock in trade) that they share a common lineage. Perhaps, too, if one looks through appearances, one might find some intriguing resemblances between the two.

"Like Wesley," Peter Berger remarks in his *Invitation to Sociology*, "the sociologist will have to confess that his parish is the world."[2] So, too, is the parish of the satirist, whose eye is trained on the "outside of things," as Leonard Feinberg puts it, "the surface, the behavior."[3] Both satirist and sociologist look at things from a certain distance. The satiric perspective is always one of detachment. The sociological perspective, too, except for that of the symbolic interactionists, who would put themselves out of business if they looked only at the outside of things, is always at a remove. From the beginning, sociology has been concerned with the external, with the world of appearances, with the surfaces of human affairs, with all that seems more sharply and clearly visible to the dispassionate observer. Moral distance seems to be both price and prize of the satiric vision, and of the sociological understanding.

Waugh did not appreciate the judgemnt of those who saw his characters as types, Feinberg observes. Indeed, Waugh declared that the "novelist has no business with types," that types are the property of economists, politicians, advertisers, and "other professional bores." The artist, Waugh insisted, is concerned with individuals.[4] Nonetheless, it is the satirist more than any other creative writer who fashions types, types representative of the follies and hypocrisies, the venial and mortal sins of their contemporaries—perhaps of all humanity. The satirist uses types, Feinberg suggests, "because he is usually concerned with Man rather than men, institutions rather than personalities, repeated behavior patterns rather than uncommon acts. The type is an aesthetic compromise between an abstraction (which is dull) and an individual (who is unique)."[5]

Sociologists would, one supposes, have to be numbered among Waugh's "other professional bores," since it is the very nature of their task to classify, to reach for an understanding of what is general and recurrent. Early in the sociological enterprise, one searches for the character, the essence of a society, among the tables of the census-takers; one follows the rises and falls of the social facts—birth rates, divorce rates, unemployment rates—and the ebb and flow of migration patterns, the changing forms and fortunes of the family, of sect and church, city and suburb, of social classes, for signs of the meaning of what is happening around us. Like the satirist, the sociologist thinks in terms of Man, not men, of institutions, not personalities. Alas for sociology, however: there is no "aesthetic compromise." Sociologists work with the (dull) abstractions. Not driven by aesthetic considerations, the sociologist constructs "Ideal Types" and social categories—the "Protestant ethic" or "rational-legal authority," the "middle class" or the "aged." These could never captivate the reader's imagination as a Pangloss could, or any one of the brothers in *A Tale of a Tub*. Though there are moments when the satirist's pen seems about to yield up a human character, the pen of the sociologist never seems to be in a like danger.

"The chief effect of satire is pleasure," Feinberg maintains. It "may also provide a fresh perspective, detachment, or balance." But in essence what satire offers is aesthetic pleasure.[6] What, in contrast, is the chief effect of sociology? What purposes are served by compressing the desire for or dread of having children, or the crime of passion, or the bitter divorce into a statistic? The better to see the social fact, the societal terrain; perhaps even the better to see it whole and see it steadily. Both the satirist and the sociologist are preoccupied with the social arrangements; both are inclined to take the panoramic view. Both would be more likely than other writers and social scientists to appreciate fully the wisdom of George Eliot's remark that "There is no creature whose inward being is so strong that it is not greatly determined by what lies outside it." Both, too, attend the masquerade of their own historical time and place in part, at least, as visitors. Both look at the whole affair—the masks and costumes, the rituals and games and intrigues—as foreign observers might. Both, ultimately, write about what they have seen as foreign correspondents might. Both grind away at a fine lens which, when lifted to the eye, grants the viewer the ability to find what lies under the appearances. But the sociologist tends to see patterns within and under patterns. And the satirist tends to see things as if he were gazing into a trick mirror.

Perhaps the sociologist would be a satirist if he had kept the child's gift for playfulness. Perhaps both are social reformers, or even utopian thinkers in disguise. Feinberg does not think that this is true in the case of satirists. "While idealists from Plato to modern social planners have dreamed of perfect societies," he writes, "satirists from Aristophanes to modern skeptics have ridiculed utopias."[7] The satirist of Utopia, he suggests, uses the device of the *reductio ad absurdum*. Still, the reader of satire is not wholly convinced that there is not a disenchanted utopian thinker within many a satirist. While the purpose of Plato's *Republic* or of More's *Utopia* or of Bellamy's *Looking Backward* was hardly to amuse, the purpose of *Candide* or *Gulliver's Travels* was far more than that. If a satirist truly despaired of people's ever coming to their senses or feeling genuine remorse for their own evil-doing or genuine compassion for the suffering of others, he might never take up his pen at all.

Scratch the soul of a sociologist, Samuel Stouffer is said to have remarked, and you will find a Methodist minister. A priest still lurks within the breast of many a sociologist: Alvin Gouldner reports that he and Timothy Sprehe polled 6,762 members of the American Sociological Association on a variety of questions, and found that, of the 3,441 who responded to the mailed questionnaire, more than a fourth of the sociologists said that they had thought of becoming clergymen at one time or another.[8] It was Auguste Comte who invented the "dreadful word" sociology, as Raymond Aron calls it; and it was Auguste Comte who envisioned a new social order with a priesthood of sociologists. There was undoubtedly something of the preacher-reformer in many of the fathers of the discipline. Indeed, one who is claimed by sociologists as the founder of modern demography, Thomas Malthus, *was* a divine. In France, Gouldner reminds us, it was the ambition of the early founders of sociology to establish a religion of humanity.[9]

In his book on *The Satirist*, Feinberg observes that, while the satirist resembles the Outsider much more than he does the True Believer, he differs from him "in always being aware that his detachment is a pose, and that he really *is* involved in his society to the extent that most people are . . . ."[10] This may be true of the sociologist as well. One suspects that, beneath the "objective" surface of the presentation of his judgments, and within many a "concept" or "working definition," there are strong feelings and opinions about the way things are and the way things ought to be. Why should not the sociologist be driven by the same desires, troubled by the same prejudices, predilections, and passions as any other thinker? A social category can become the personification of some force a sociologist feels elected to combat or defend with the only weapons available to him—questionnaires and interviews, charts and graphs and statistical tables. There are many ways to labor in the vineyard. The appeal to reasonableness in one's readers is just as legitimate (though probably even more foredoomed to fall on deaf ears) as the appeal to the sense of the ridiculous.

It often happens, of course, that the sociologist loses his way in the maze of abstractions and statistics he constructs. Perhaps, having taken the veil of social science, he dooms himself to a lifetime of labor in a cold and austere cell, spinning phantoms from "conceptual frameworks" and paradigms and formulae, shadows of the very real, very human dilemmas and griefs that may have brought him to the doors of social science in the first place. Perhaps, in the end, he drifts further and further away from a true understanding of human action. Though Robert Coles does not address himself directly to the demon of the social scientist in his essay on "Understanding White Racists," he *does* direct attention to what happens to some intellectuals (he calls them "well-to-do" ones, at that) "who write about subjects like 'the authoritarian personality' and 'white racism' (for the government, foundations, or editors)": one has a right, he says, to expect that they will write with "a measure of concreteness and common sense, not to mention some evidence that what is handed down as virtual law has somehow been tried out in the world 'out there'. . . ." The pronouncements of the social scientists, Coles maintains, ought to be tested against the economic and political, the social and psychological realities, which most people "live out rather than try to fit into theories or prophesies."[11]

Whether with concepts and theories, or with the "raw data" accessible to the ear and eye of the participant observer with his relaxed pace and many-faceted curiosity, the sociologist may harbor a stubborn utopian vision in the thickets of his reports. As in the case of the satirist, his attention wanders back again and again to the hiatus between received opinion and reality, between the ideal and the actual. What Bergson said of humorists may be true of at least *some* of them, that they are moralists disguised as scientists. Surely the same applies to many sociologists. The ability to see through appearances, which is the mark of the opportunist, is a necessity for those who have a strong conviction about how things ought to be. But what happens so often is that moral and ideological conviction cloud the observing eye. Probably the moralist is fated to wrestle time and again with his demon, so that his vision alternates between sharpness and dimness, so that he sees now with radiant clarity, and then again through a glass darkly. It is apparent to those who read works in social science that the authors waver from page to page, first discussing things as they are and then things as they ought or ought not to be. It is as though the social scientist cannot make up his mind as to whether he is writing as a scientist or as a moralist.

No doubt this can all be traced to Positivism and thence to its fervid founder, this moralistc bent in sociology. Certainly it is the mark of one of the most outstanding of the sociologists, Emile Durkheim. His preoccupation with the nature of the bonds between the individual and the collectivity, and his concern about the social genesis and consequences of *anomie* brought him to the study of a subject seemingly quite remote from sociological interest, the subject of suicide. In this work, which was first published in France at the turn of the century but not translated into English for another fifty years, Durkheim had to construct his own charts and maps and statistical tables. His was an unrelenting effort to demonstrate that suicide is a sociological and not a purely psychological "phenomenon." An advocate of social realism, he insisted on the significance of the suicide rate. He took pains to show how the suicide rate of a collectivity fluctuates in accordance with varying social conditions. He arrived at types of suicide, the "egoistic," the "altruistic," and the "anomic," not by working from the individual instance of suicide to a general category of cases, but by classifying sets of social conditions which account for varying rates of incidence. "Disregarding the individual as such," he wrote, "his motives and his ideas, we shall seek directly the states of the various social environments (religious confessions, family, political society, occupational groups, etc.), in terms of which the variations of suicide occur. Only then returning to the individual" could the ways in which these general causes "become individualized" be studied.[12] What could be more withering to the romantic imagination, more inhospitable to the tragic sense of life, than this dogged, chilling rationalism? To analyze the "fluctuations" of the suicide rate, to refer to suicide as a "sociological phenomenon," to discourse on sociological types of suicide—if one did not know better, one would suspect Durkheim of writing satirically.

It is instructive that suicide was not a topic of which satirists were particularly enamored. Perhaps they had other more pressing things on their minds. Perhaps, again, there is more to it than that. In *The Savage God*, Alvarez observes that suicide was no longer imaginatively possible, so far as literature was concerned, in the Augustan age. He reminds us that the eighth edition of *The Anatomy of Melancholy* was published in 1676, and that the second edition of *Biathanatos* appeared in 1700, and he goes on to remark that "by that time the spiritual temper of the time had cooled considerably": melancholy had metamorphosed into spleen.[13] In Hume's attack on the moral prejudice against suicide, Alvarez suggests, we find the exasperation of this great philosopher with the old superstitions. "For the great rationalists," Alvarez writes, "a sense of absurdity—the absurdity of superstition, self-importance and unreason—was as natural and illuminating as sunlight."[14]

The rationalists also believed, it may be recalled, that the institutions of society can and ought to be subjected to the same critical appraisal as that to which the things of the natural world had been subjected. Such was the thinking of the *philosophes*, recognized by many to have been the true founders of the social sciences. What was the attitude in the air at that time toward suicide? Alvarez tells us that Walpole had made the fretful remark in a letter to Hannah More that "It is very provoking that people must always be hanging or drowning themselves or going mad." It would be difficult to say which attitude— this vexed and rather bored approach, or that which advocates a ponderous analysis of fluctuations in suicide rates—is in sharper contrast to the emotions that led to the Werther epidemic, or to the literary excesses of the Romantics. For the Romantics, woe to any who did not die young by the hand of Fate or by their own. Rimbaud referred to himself as a *littératuricide*, Alvarez recalls; and Coleridge chose a death by opium. He "deliberately poisoned his creative gifts by an overdose of Kant and Fichte," Alvarez remarks, "because to survive as a poet demanded an effort, sensitivity and continual exposure to feeling which were too painful for him." What metaphysics had begun, opium finished. So far as writing poetry is concerned, "the last thirty-odd years of his life were a posthumous existence."[15]

One could just as effectively poison the creative spirit enmeshed in the Romantic agony by an overdose of Durkheim. His analysis of suicide would be just as lethal for the literary imagination as any text by Kant or Fichte. The reader must turn page after page of this learned treatise on the consideration of the relationship between "psychological states" or "cosmic factors," and the types of suicide, before he will come upon an individual form of any of them. (Durkheim provides as an example of the "ideal type" of "egoistic suicide" a passage from Lamartine's *Raphael*.) In a rare expression of private sentiment, Durkheim wrote, "Sadness does not inhere in things; it does not reach us from the world and through mere contemplation of the world. It is a product of our own thought."[16] But less than a dozen pages after this, another table is presented, this one on the "Distribution of the Different Kinds of Death Among 1,000 Suicides (Both Sexes Combined)."

The rationalists vindicated suicide, Alvarez says; the arguments of the *philosophes* led to a revision of the punitive laws that decreed that the bodies of suicides were to be mutilated and that their properties were to revert to the Crown. But the ransom paid for this liberation may have been a fully human understanding of an action (the scientifically minded prefer the word "behavior"). Attention was drawn away from the individual and toward the societal; suicide was thought of as a "social problem." Granted that the attitude of the Church toward one who committed suicide was brutal, Alvarez writes; at least it was rooted in a concern for his immortal soul. But the scientist's tolerance, he suggests, may be rooted in indifference. Suicide had become "an interesting but purely intellectual problem, beyond obloquy but also beyond tragedy and morality." Alvarez may be addressing all Durkheim's intellectual heirs when he remarks, "All that anguish, the slow tensing of the self to that final, irreversible act, and for what? In order to become a statistic."[17] This is the poet's consummate reproach to sociologists. Perhaps Walpole's irritable witticism is, at least, a salute in the suicide's direction, which is more than one can say for the sociologists's elaborate computations.

Whenever human suffering or joy is compressed into a statistic, there seems to the humanist to be a defiance of understanding in the very name of it. The meaning of the act or state seems to have been hollowed out; the passion, the motive seem to have been forced into something alien to their true nature—a quantity that is arranged on a "table" or a map. In "Under Which Lyre," Auden forbade the classification of human beings and of their actions; he forbade thinking in Types.[18] However, the satirist's approach to suicide—or, indeed, to any social problem—could not be innocent of the sin of sociology. Like the sociologist, the satirist is interested in deviations from some norm or other;[19] though, in contrast to the sociologist, the artist is ascendant over the moralist in his writing. In his *Introduction to Satire*, Feinberg maintains that the satirist is not so much motivated by the desire for reform as by an aesthetic desire for self-expression.[20] This proclivity to a playful and critical distortion is apparent in satirists "while they are still youngsters—long before they have any genuine concern with morality."[21] The sources of satiric material, Feinberg writes, are hypocrisy, folly, and vanity (and none but the most incurable idealist would deny that these are inexhaustible sources in *any* age), and the special talent of the satirist is his gift for distortion of the familiar. It is his *technique* that sets him apart from other writers, a technique that encompasses "controlled vehemence," a vehemence not always necessarily that of the moralist. "He is more interested in inadequacy than achievement," Feinberg contends, "injustice than justice, illusion than truth."[22]

Still, the satirist, like the sociologist, begins with people as much as with ideas. There are human beings at the starting point; in his essay on "Gulliver," Irvin Ehrenpreis says that "Swift's imagination worked in terms of people." Swift, he observes, "did not invent a set of values to defend, or objects to attack; he started from human embodiments of those values or vices, and he addressed himself to people whom he wished to encourage, refute, or annihilate."[23] What is interesting is that the people with whom both satirists and sociologists begin their enterprise are soon overshadowed by the circumstances of their own time, or by the moral infirmities of human beings in any time, as well as by being thought of in the mass. Man rather than men, as Feinberg put it; institutions rather than personalities.

The satirist did not take suicide as a central topic. If he had, the result would provide an interesting basis for comparison with the work of Durkheim. There is a social problem, however, to which both the satirist and the sociologist have addressed themselves. This is the problem of overpopulation. The differences between the way it was handled in the classic treatise and satire on the subject reveal something about the differences between the sociological and satiric temperaments. In meditating upon the madness of mindless reproduction, the father of modern demography, Thomas Malthus, devised the formula that unchecked population growth increases geometrically, but that the means of subsistence increase only arithmetically. He went on to compute, without benefit of a calculator, the ratio of population to the means of subsistence. This he reckoned as 256 to 9 by our own time, and as 4,096 to 13 by the twenty-first century. The "positive" checks, including war, pestilence, famine, and the effects of unwholesome occupations and environments, serve to increase the death rate. The "preventive" checks, which include "moral restraint" and late marriage, serve to reduce the birth rate. As a divine and a humanitarian, Malthus could not but favor the preventive checks, though he was not sanguine, especially in the first edition of the *Essay*, about the likelihood that the operation of the preventive checks would be as impressive as that of the positive checks upon population growth.[24]

Malthus' *Essay* was, among other things, a sharp rebuke to the optimism of Condorcet and Godwin, who thought humanity to be on an ascendant pathway. Indeed, in his reply to Malthus' work, Godwin wrote of a day he thought to be near at hand when everyone in the world would be fed from a single flowerpot. It is fascinating to reflect that the child of Godwin's union with Mary Wollstonecraft brought forth the vision of Frankenstein from the scientific laboratories which, her father believed, seemed destined to deliver us from privation. But that is another story. The moral temper of Malthus' *Essay* haunts his intellectual descendants, the "neo-Malthusians," who appeal to the social engineers of "developed" as well as "underdeveloped" nations to keep their wits about them, to use reason in implementing programs based on the preventive checks. The much-discussed policy of triage, applied to the choice of which nations ought to be given foreign aid by their well-endowed neighbors, is a curious blend of rational calculation and humanitarian sentiment which clearly stands in the Malthusian tradition.

Swift, too, considered this complex and weighty matter. Indeed, he wrote about it nearly three-quarters of a century before Malthus' famous work was published. Rather than addressing himself to the question of overpopulation in the world, Swift chose to narrow his focus to Ireland. In *A Modest Proposal*, he remarked the "melancholy object" for any traveler in Dublin or in the country, "when they see the streets, the roads, and cabin doors, crowded with beggars of the female sex, followed by three, four, or six children, all in rags and importuning every passenger for an alms . . . ." Swift, however, had no preventive check to propose. It might be said that he put his faith in the exercise of another way of reasoning. "A young healthy child," he contended, "is at a year old a most delicious, nourishing and wholesome food, whether stewed, roasted, baked or boiled; and I make no doubt that it will equally serve in a fricassee or a ragout." He estimated that a child could be depended upon to "make four dishes of excellent nutritive meat" when one is dining with the family or with a particular friend, two dishes for entertaining friends, and, if the family is dining alone, "the fore or hind quarter will make a reasonable dish, and seasoned with a little pepper or salt will be very good boiled on the fourth day, especially in winter." Surely, Swift wrote, "no gentleman would repine to give ten shillings for the carcass of a good fat child."[25]

The contrast between how the computations are phrased in Malthus' essay and Swift's satire is striking. Malthus wrote of the ratio of the population, increasing in geometrical progression, to the means of subsistence, increasing in arithmetical progression: 256 to 9, 4096 to 13, and, a few thousand years hence, in figures that are all but unimaginable. Swift, on the other hand, suggested a price of ten shillings for a good fat child's carcass, which ought to make up to four dishes of excellent meat for the more parsimonious of "persons of quality and fortune throughout the kingdom." Indeed, Swift even went to the trouble of computing the number of children responsible for the "melancholy object" of the tourist's eyes at 120,000. He opined that only one-sixth of them need be reserved for breed, one male for every four females ("which is more than we allow to sheep, black cattle or swine") sufficing for this purpose. If Swift were writing of this matter today, his satire might be written as a tale of science fiction: There is a mutation. A Lilliputian is born, a perfectly formed miniature human baby who is easily nourished by a nibble of alfalfa and a thimbleful of dew. Eventually, there is a nation, and then a whole world populated by Lilliputians, who find that they must engage in warfare against the cockroaches. The victors will inherit the dubious estate of the earth.

"The tragedy of the population problem," the poet Dom Moraes wrote, "is that though every single individual born is desirable, people in the mass can be lethal without their wanting to be."[26] Even if it were granted that the first part of this statement may be true, neither social scientists nor satirists could get on with their work if they dwelled overlong on the tragic sense of things, whether their subject were suicide or overpopulation. For the social scientist, the profound compassion, the pity and love for one's fellows—"all your fellows and brothers in this world of appearances," as Unamuno writes, "these unhappy shadows who pass from nothingness to nothingness, these sparks of consciousness which shine for a moment in the infinite and eternal darkness"[27]—can lead only to despair of ever finding a solution to a social problem. The satirist, too, must be master of his compassion. If the wit and the imagination are to be sustained in this form of literary creation, the satirist must keep a steady eye fixed on the general, the societal condition. In this respect, at least, Malthus and Swift were much alike.

Yet the satire *A Modest Proposal* seems closer to despair than Malthus' essay. The moral instruction in it stings; it is informed by a darker imagination. Malthus, of course, was a divine. He appealed to the use of reason, to prudence. His thought was that, once they realized the folly of their ways, his readers would educate others and practice themselves the measures he advocated for control of the birth rate. But Swift was a divine, too, one with a genius for marrying playfulness to moral outrage. A pamphleteer all clothed in wit, he expected far less of the human race than Malthus. Nearly three-quarters of that fateful century divided the publication of the two works, the one addressed to the situation in a particular country, the other to a seeming law of nature. One might think that Malthus, given his premise, would be the gloomier prophet of the two. Yet it is he, not Swift, who offers men of reason and good will a way out of the dreadful dilemma. Indeed, as is so often the case with a prophet who is a social scientist at heart (or the other way around), the chance for redemption, the conditions for solution, are implicit in the presentation of the problem.

"Human life," Sartre has a character say in one of his plays, "begins at the far side of despair." Perhaps much satire begins there, too. Indeed, a renaissance of satire is not unlikely. It may be that the doomsday prophet-scientists—ecologists, demographers, economists, sociologists, the whole somber lot—are hastening this, with all their lurid portraits of the world-to-come. In Russia, satire appears to be doing well enough.[28] The need for it is just as urgent in Lilliput as in Brobdingnag. Apocalyptic visions abound; the comprehensive statements of the condition of the contemporary world in *The Limits to Growth*[29] and *An Inquiry into the Human Prospect*[30] overwhelm the reader with a sense of futility, with terror and perplexity and disillusionment. The horizon is dark with portent, and the little solutions (if that is what they are) offered by such true believers as the behavior modifiers are hardly cheering to the humanistically inclined. In the face of all this doomfulness, there seem to be few alternatives to silence for those with the gift for writing or for appreciating literature. Of course, there is always poetry; there will always be poetry so long as humanity endures. There is satire, too. The temptation to write it ought to be very strong for the sociologist. A recent prediction made by demographers is that, within two hundred years, the population of the earth may number 250 billion souls, and, in about 1,750 years, the sheer physical weight of people then on the earth may exceed the weight of the earth itself. According to these calculations, if people do not learn to control their breeding habits, our descendants may pull the planet out of orbit. This sort of thing is irresistible to the satiric mind: as with the Tarot cards, the technological toys are consulted by those whose curiosity about the future is matched by their dread of it. Sociologists, who work with these materials so closely, are brought to the very brink of poking fun at the apocalypse.

In an essay on the state of contemporary fiction, Eric Larsen suggests that satire may become hysteria, and that the extent to which it does "serves as an index of the degree to which . . . there is a dissociation of some essential kind between the individual perceiver and the external world in which he exists."[31] It is in satire, perhaps more than in any other form of writing, Larsen contends, that the question that troubles the contemporary writer becomes most acute, the question of "how to connect, how to belong, how to make a work tell." The world of the satirist is being reduced, according to Larsen, and therefore the satirist must direct his aim at a target that grows ever more vast. "As the real connection between himself and that vast target diminishes," Larsen writes, "the risk increases . . . that his work will become manic rather than intelligent."[32] There is a double meaning in Larsen's observations that every sociologist ought to explore. One, of interest for the sociology of literature, is the effect that the growing distance between the writer and the outer world may have upon literature. The other, of a very personal significance, is the effect that the growing distance between external reality and the *social scientist* (as far as the writer from the center of power and the forces of social change) may have upon his work. The social scientist, too, must resolve the problem of "how to connect, how to belong, how to make a work tell."

The ideas that sociologists work with are rich with possibilities for satiric formulation: bigotry, urban devastation, class conflict, the abuses of power are only a few that come immediately to mind. In his *Invitation to Sociology*, Peter Berger remarks that the very "presence in an intellectual discipline of ironical skepticism" about its own enterprises "is a mark of its humanistic character," and that sociological study could "profit greatly from those insights that one can obtain only while laughing."[33] Now, it would be uncharitable to make the general comment that the masters of sociology lacked wit. It would even be untrue to say that *all* of them *utterly* lacked it: Max Weber is said to have remarked that, in matters of religion, he was "absolutely unmusical." It must be granted that this was a witty way of putting it. Still, though they had many illustrious qualities, one is hard put to imagine Weber or Durkheim, Simmel or Marx in a fit of laughter, or writing with the intention of consigning others to that condition. The reader of their tomes has the impression that they were *grim* about it all, about charismatic authority and anomic suicide, about dyads and the proletariat. One is not amused when reading the classics in sociology. Intrigued and instructed, yes, often; but not amused. Where is their imagination? one wonders—not what C. Wright Mills called "the sociological imagination" necessarily, but imagination of *any* sort? Peter Berger warns sociologists well against giving ontological status to the masquerade. Yet is this not what so many of the intellectual heirs of the masters seem to be doing?—making boxes in which to put everything, counting and measuring and stuffing the things people do and say into concepts and social categories, tidying them up until they fit into these grim little boxes? One searches in vain to find the raging, thieving, envying, lusting, bewildered, anxious, and often silly and pathetic being who, with all the others, makes and unmakes the social arrangements every day. And finding him, keeping him in mind, one is no longer engaged in an intellectual exercise; one is engaged in a moral workout.

The path from sociology to satire must necessarily circumvent the vital concerns of symbolic interactionism. If one wants to write satire, one cannot afford to detain oneself too long with the view-from-within. There are works which include both the objective and the subjective perspectives on a social issue or social problem. For example, in Simone de Beauvoir's *The Coming of Age*,[34] Part One presents "Old Age Seen From Without," whereas, in Part Two, "The Being-in-the-World," Beauvoir quotes from diaries and essays and autobiographical notes written by artists and philosophers about the experience of growing older. Such a work, with passages written by Chateaubriand, Gide, Montaigne, Yeats, Schopenhauer, Tolstoy, Michelangelo, and others on old age, has a strong appeal for the humanistically inclined sociologist. For the humanistic sociologist, there is at least as much value, if not more, in the remark of an eighty-two-year-old woman that "*Age puzzles me.* I thought it was a quiet time. My seventies were interesting, and fairly serene, but my eighties are passionate"[35] as in statistics about the number of people in the population aged sixty five or over, or in projections of life expectancy. But neither the sociologist nor the satirist can remain with the view from within. Swift put the matter wryly in *A Tale of a Tub*, remarking that "in most Corporeal Beings, which have fallen under my cognizance, the *Outside* hath been infinitely preferable to the *In*." Swift writes that he has been persuaded of this opinion by many observations he had made, among them this, that "Last Week, I saw a Woman *flay'd,* and you will hardly believe, how much it altered her Person for the worse."[36]

To suggest a likeness of inclination and of moral temper between satirists and sociologists is not to deny the differences *within* the ranks of those of either calling. Pope was Pope and not Voltaire, after all; Thurber was someone else than Mark Twain. On the other side, the sociology of Durkheim is quite distinctive from that of Pareto, and Max Weber was far more and other than the shadow of Karl Marx. To complicate matters still more, Pope was not even always himself. The selves of any person are never fully realized.

"Those satirists who circumvent the limitations of satire most successfully," Feinberg maintains, "are writers who combine satire with other literary appeals."[37] This might be said of sociologists as well. Those who become stuffy, who lose the gift for playfulness, who allow themselves to become mired in certain theories or ideologies fall prey to the limitations of their endeavors. In the utopia Marx and Engels envisioned in *The German Ideology*, the social arrangements will make it possible for one "to hunt in the morning, fish in the afternoon, rear cattle in the evening, criticize after dinner." For many people today, this utopia has just about arrived. Though they may suffer from guilt because of it more than did the aristocrats of the past, many people of moderate means in the Western European countries and the United States are free to move from one post to another in society. Conversions from one religious or sexual or ideological affiliation to another are so commonplace today that shifts in the occupational and professional spheres are hardly newsworthy. There is always a risk involved, of course; a priest who had permitted himself to be defrocked remarked that he was more free without his collar, yet missed the platform that collar had granted him. There is little to prevent many a person from "doing" sociology in the morning, thundering from a pulpit in the afternoon, singing in a choir in the evening, and writing (perhaps satire) after dinner.[38]

It is not altogether impossible that sociologists who have literary ambitions may turn to writing satire. The literary achievements of psychoanalysts and psychiatrists are well known: Erik Erikson, June Singer, and Robert Coles have distinguished themselves as writers, as did Freud, Jung, and Otto Rank, among others, in an earlier day. Other social scientists have tried their hand at creative writing. Among the sociologists who have done so are Peter Berger and Everett

Hughes, and among the anthropologists, Laura Bohannan, Robert Redfield, and Claude Lévi-Strauss, who includes an original play in his *Tristes Tropiques*. Saul Bellow had done graduate work in anthropology before devoting all his energies to creative writing; and Alfred Kroeber studied literature before he chose to become an anthropologist. In *Blackberry Winter*, Margaret Mead says that she and her friends exchanged poetry as naturally as they exchanged letters. In this book, as well as in Margaret Mead's *An Anthropologist at Work: The Writings of Ruth Benedict*, the reader's attention is drawn to the poetry of Sapir and Benedict, and the many references in their correspondence to the vocation of the poet.

In *The Coming of Age*, Simone de Beauvoir contends that the writer creates out of his own substance. He needs a continually enriching inner world to sustain him, she says, and he must always have access to it. In this way, according to her, the writer is less fortunate than the painter, for whom the "world provides . . . an inexhaustible source of colours, lights, varying subtleties of tone, and shapes."[39] But the *outer* world is inexhaustible in possibilities for the satirist, too. And it is the natural intellectual habitat of the sociologist. Because of the detachment which he struggles to win and to sustain, the sociologist may come to see the outer world as a visitor, a stranger, perhaps even an intruder might see it. The fascination for cultural differences, rooted in a belief in the fundamental brotherhood of humanity, quickens the searches and researches of the great masters of anthropology—Tylor and Morgan, Boas and Malinowski, Mead and Benedict, Kroeber and Murdock. The sociologist is a sort of anthropologist in his own quarters. Having learned how to look beyond a particular situation or place, he seeks to understand *what is* from many points of view. The sociologist's training encourages movement from one perspective to another, seeing through and seeing beyond the perimeters of private experience. The sociologist, like the satirist, should find it difficult to forget that the emperor—*all* emperors—are naked.

There was a time not long ago when there was a sort of literary social science, or social scientific literature, which reached its finest expression in Montesquieu's *Persian Letters*, Cadalso's *Moroccan Letters*, and Oliver Goldsmith's *Citizen of the World*. The tradition is there (one can see it carried forward in *The Silent Traveller*, and in

Saul Bellow's *Henderson the Rain King* and the inveterate scribbler *Herzog*), for describing, as though one were an astonished visitor, what other people take for granted as natural and right. Given his perspective and his detachment, the sociologist with literary inclinations may discover the satirist within himself—once his pen is loosened from the moorings of scientism. He may find a note of irony creeping into his descriptions of manners and morals, of norms and institutions. If he happens to have been an idealist in his youth (one suspects that many sociologists took the veil out of a desire, when very young, to save the world; *this* one did), he may find that it is the loss of faith that grants one the power to see through things—faith in the likelihood that the Good Life can be built on this earth, faith in the perfectibility of mankind, faith that reason and dignity and the rights of mankind will one day prevail.

Very early in the study of sociology, one learns how one's perspective is shaped by where one happens to be standing in historical time and in social circumstance. It is only much later that one comes to appreciate that one's perspective is not only a matter of this, but also of how long and how keenly one has been observing things. The sociologist may be the shadow of the satirist, and the satirist the shadow of the sociologist. In the works of both, there is a realization of a portion of the heritage bequeathed by the *philosophes*. That it was rich we know. And it was in the brow of the *philosophes* that so much of social science and modern society were formed—and from which both, today, must free themselves for further flight.

# FOUR

## *On Compassion*

> *There is much suffering in the world, but there is one kind of suffering which it is a privilege to endure, the suffering of those who suffer because they want to make a world worthy of man—the suffering of those who know that defending the realm of the mind means imparting culture to an ever-growing number—of those who know that the realm of the mind is not for the privileged, that possessing culture is not a question of privilege, and who know that the life of culture throughout the centuries, if it depends first on those who create it, depends less on those who inherit it than on those who desire it. . . . . Let each man choose his own way of alleviating this suffering; relieve it he must. That is our responsibility to man's destiny—and perhaps to our own hearts.*
> —André Malraux, "Forging Man's Fate in Spain," revision of speech delivered at dinner in honor of Malraux and Louis Fischer, in *The Nation*, March 20, 1937

The American, Jules Henry scolded, "makes conflict into a god; and although sociology swells its chest with a thousand 'conflict theories,' it has none on compassion."[1] Com-passion: "feeling with"; "sorrow and pity," as the Webster's Collegiate Dictionary defines it. Moral sympathy. We know very little about this, which may be the very heart of civilization, and upon which the very survival of the human race may come to depend. Nor do we instruct our children in it much; there is no paragraph, indeed not even a sentence about it, between "compass" and "compensation" in *The World Book Encyclopedia*. It is still a mystery, why one person feels compassion so keenly that he takes care not to bring harm to any living creature, and why another—the "sociopath" or the "psychopath"—can be brutal to others and feel no remorse. Another mystery is why the same person may be deeply affected by the suffering of one, and unmoved by that of another. Writing of the plight of the American Negro and the urban poor, Lewis Coser remarks that, "The sociology of social perception, a sociology elucidating why people sometimes look and why they sometimes look away . . . still is to be written."[2]

Some measure of compassion entered into the conception of Swift's *A Modest Proposal* and Malthus's *On Population*. There is a measure of compassion, too, in the field reports of many an anthropologist, and in the vocational choice of many a sociologist (American sociology began, Boorstin writes, as "substantially a Science of Minorities" devoted to giving "respectability and aggressiveness to pluralism")[3] as well as in the thrust of data-gathering and theoretical arguments on the inequities in North American society. Perhaps compassion is nowhere more apparent in sociology than in classes on social problems and in those devoted to specific problems in contemporary society—the plight of minorities; the plight of the elderly; urban devastation; mental illness; drug addiction; alcoholism; poverty; juvenile delinquency. Indeed, in the third edition of Merton and Nisbet's *Contemporary Social Problems*, Nisbet writes that, just as there is a history and a sociology of emotions such as jealousy which, though they are individual sentiments, are expressed in ways prescribed by the norms of society, so, too, there is a history and a sociology of compassion:

Compassion is a timeless and universal human sentiment, but its objects and intensity vary from age to age. In the same way that certain social conditions became, at the beginning of the nineteenth century, objects of rationalist regard, conceived as intellectual problems, they became also objects of moral regard, conceived as moral problems. Sudden reflections of this growing compassion are to be seen in the literature of the age, notably in the English social novel, where such problems were effectively brought to the attention of society.[4]

Defining it as "the gradual widening and institutionalization of compassion," Nisbet names humanitarianism as one of the two historical currents whereby social problems have come to be so widely recognized in modern Western society. The other historical current is secular rationalism. Poverty, crime, ethnic conflict, population growth—these are all believed to be susceptible to effective human intervention. Like society itself, they are seen to be the work of human beings; and what man has wrought can be undone and remade by man. The very concept of social problems would be incomprehensible to the mind imbued with the tragic sense of life, with the belief in implacable Fate, in Necessity, in unknowable, blind, all-powerful force. Nisbet finds it is "no accident that serious awareness of social problems in western Europe first entered the European mind during the Enlightenment," for this was the age when Reason was endowed with the power to bestow understanding, control, and even redemption of the earthly estate, the human portion.[5]

That the social arrangements ought to be changed and could be changed to bring them nearer to the Good Life: this, Nisbet suggests, was the first moral attitude necessary for the recognition of social problems; the second he identifies as humanitarianism. Recalling Tocqueville's discussion of the broadening of compassion in his *Democracy in America*, Nisbet writes that it was not so much a growing humanitarianism of the upper classes as "the tendency toward equalization of social ranks that followed the American and French revolutions" that accounts for the institutionalization of compassion in modern society. Tocqueville had written that one consequence of the extension of political and civil democracy was a widening of the social field of recognition of suffering. When social ranks approximate equality, Tocqueville maintained, people tend to think and feel alike; and those who suffer are no longer seen as enemies or as strangers. When one looks across at others, rather than up or down, one can readily imagine what it is like to be in their place.[6]

The founders of sociology had a radiant vision of its mission, that the central task of the discipline, its gift to the world, would be the shaping of a moral science, a "religion of humanity." The ethical sensibility, the moral bond between people, some believed, was unfolding through time; and it was the task of the high priests of the new order to foster the realization of this in the world-to-come. It was believed, and it is still believed by some, that man's inhumanity to man will diminish as reason is put to use in modifying the social arrangements. According to this view, the more enlightened the members of a society become, the more valiantly will they oppose torture, tyranny, slavery, all forms of oppression and violence and cruelty. We have come far, some say: Theodore Rubin writes that we *are* progressing, that there is less cruelty in the world today, and greater awareness of the need for compassion, than ever before.[7] Historical perspective supports this, at least to some extent: Horace rode unmoved, indeed unseeing, past the crucified slaves. Caesar wrote the calm report in *The Gallic Wars*, translated by this once-upon Latin pupil to read these chilling words, "In this way, our troops, without any risk, were able to go on killing them as long as daylight lasted." In our time, it is the *absence* of social protest against injustice, tyranny, cruelty, exploitation that is seen by many to be the greatest social evil of all. If one were to use enrollment in sociology courses, so many of which are in essence social problems courses, as a gauge of humanitarian concern in contemporary society, one might think we were on the very eve of the millennium. There is, Nisbet observes, "a reciprocal relation between moral consciousness in a society and the perceived existence of social problems."[8] Certainly, there is little in the way of a social ill, an evil of the societal system that has gone unremarked, at least by sociologists!

What is the nature of this moral consciousness? How are choices made between the objects of moral regard, so that one sociologist dedicates both life and work to the cause of women, another to that of the aged, a third to that of a minority? One must know something of the "personal realities" of the sociologist[9] in order to answer this question. We know far too little about this matter, and about what happens to moral concerns when they become intellectual concerns of the individual social scientist. For one cannot love or pity an abstraction, a persona.

Compassion may be the key, perhaps even the master key, to understanding more fully the nature of social science and the demon that drives individual social scientists. One is aware, whether dimly or keenly, of what it was that attracted one to the study of human affairs, of social arrangements; of what people or condition or problem *out there* evoked a response within oneself. One is aware of a fundamental conflict, also—that between the desire to know simply and purely for the sake of knowing, and the desire to know in order to act effectively. There are other conflicts: one cannot know it all, one cannot love and pity it all, at least not as a social scientist. Some problems seem more pressing, some issues more vital than others. One must decide what one will work for, what one believes is most important. This is always a moral as well an an intellectual decision. It is also a fatal decision: one must narrow the field in order to see more clearly. To explore the nature of compassion is to engage in a humanistic, not a scientific endeavor. Perhaps for this very reason, the subject has been neglected. This is a scandal; co-feeling, fellow feeling ought to be a subject of the greatest fascination to social scientists. And surely, without it, society would not be possible, and culture would come to an end.

The Baganda have a saying: He who has not suffered does not know how to pity. This is Unamuno's teaching in his *Tragic Sense of Life*, that the awareness of the resemblance of the self to others is the provenance of compassion. And this awareness can only come through suffering. All consciousness, Unamuno wrote, is consciousness of suffering and of death. Consciousness is co-feeling, according to him; and co-feeling is compassion. To look closely at the universe is at the same time to look inward. Then one contemplates and feels all things in one's own consciousness. Then one apprehends not only the abyss of the *taedium vitae*, but of the tedium of all existence, "the bottomless pit of the vanity of vanities." In this way, one comes to pity all things. In this way, one arrives at universal love.[10]

Unamuno believed that love personalizes all that it pities. One loves and feels pity for all things when one feels all things within oneself. According to his philosophy, we can only pity, we can only love that which is seen to resemble ourselves. The more clearly we grasp the resemblance of anything to ourselves, the more we come to love it. But how can anything be personalized, be seen to resemble ourselves, except by the use of our imagination? To Unamuno, imagination is the life-force of compassion:

On hearing my brother give a cry of pain, my own pain awakes and cries in the depth of my consciousness. And in the same way I feel the pain of animals, and the pain of a tree when one of its branches is being cut off, and I feel it most when my imagination is alive, for the imagination is the faculty of intuition, of inward vision.

Proceeding from ourselves, from our own human consciousness, . . . we attribute some sort of consciousness, more or less dim, to all living things, and even to the stones themselves, for they also live. And the evolution of organic beings is simply a struggle to realize fullness of consciousness through suffering, a continual aspiration to be others without ceasing to be themselves, to break and yet to preserve their proper limits.[11]

In the brief life that each of us is given, we strive for completeness, for the realization of all the possibilities of the self. In the spiritual journey, the odyssey in inner space, we encounter our many selves—the male and female, the young and old, the Jew and Christian, the black and white, the rich and poor, Eskimo and Andaman Islander, Navaho and Iroquois. The more keenly we become aware of our own multiciplicity, the more does our co-feeling, our compassion emcompass. Inward vision grants us awareness of our kinship with the infant being born, and with the mother delivering the infant, with all who are young and with all who are old, and with the dying . . . with all men and all women, with the prince and the pauper, the beautiful and the deformed . . . with all animals, and with insects, and with vegetables and minerals, too—with the stones, "for they also live" . . . with the very earth, and the solar system in which it spins . . . and with all universes. The more deeply we look within, the more conscious we become of the suffering and the death, the being and the nothingness, not only of all fellow creatures, but of hills, trees, stars . . . for we contain all these, and all these contain our selves.

Or so the Spanish philosopher believed. It follows from this that the more limited the imagination, the narrower the compass of one's compassion. If the imagination is alive, one does not need to "become" another in the flesh in order to feel compassion for that other. A man whose imaginative powers are highly developed does not need to change his body into that of a woman in order to apprehend what it must be like to be a woman. If there is imagination, compassion can flower, between black and white, old and young, rich and poor. In her autobiography, Margaret Mead writes of her first—and only—experience of having been discriminated against. She speaks of

> being born a serf or slave, a woman believed to have no mind or no soul, a black man or woman in a white man's world, a Jew among Christians who make a virtue of anti-Semitism, a miner among those who thought it good sport to hire Pinkertons to shoot down miners on strike. Such experiences sear the soul. They make their victims ache with bitterness and rage, with compassion for fellow sufferers or with blind determination to escape even on the backs of fellow sufferers.[12]

Experiences like these, Mead says, can lead one to become a fighter against injustice, the injustices committed whenever the personae are taken for human beings. Yet, she reminds us, the fight for human rights has been valiantly waged by many who never experienced the injustices against which they took up arms. *Both* sorts of fighters are needed, Mead says, those who have been unjustly treated, and those who have witnessed injustice and who have been morally shocked by what they have seen. Mead believes that the point of John Howard Griffin's *Black Like Me* "was precisely that he was not black." Therefore, he could tell people things that no black person had thought to tell them. She finds it no accident "that some of the most impassioned statements about woman's rights have been made by men," and that Europeans have inspired, and even led anti-imperialist movements in colonial countries—"Europeans who were outraged by the consequences of social arrangements through which they, as members of a privileged group, had never suffered."[13]

Imagination, however, is not enough; it must be strengthened by encouragement, by moral instruction. It is all too human to resist the awareness of that which is unpleasant—the awareness, for example, of the silent workings of aging and dying within oneself. In her introduction to *The Coming of Age*, Simone de Beauvoir tells the story of how astonished Buddha was when, as Prince Siddhartha, he first saw "a tottering, wrinkled, toothless, white-haired man, bowed, mumbling and trembling as he propped himself along on his stick." When the charioteer explained what it means to be old, the young prince cried out, "It is the world's pity that weak and ignorant beings, drunk with the vanity of youth, do not behold old age!" And he bade the charioteer to return quickly to the palace, asking, "What is the use of pleasures and delights, since I myself am the future dwelling-place of old age?" Because he was born to save humanity, Beauvoir observes, Buddha took all of the human condition upon himself, and he saw his own fate in the person of an old man. In this, she remarks, he was different from the rest of humanity, who evade what distresses them about the human state.[14]

Under certain social conditions, one is encouraged to see one's own fate in the fate of others: there is moral instruction about what imagination gives everyone to apprehend. Samuel Johnson wisely remarked that "It is not sufficiently considered that men more frequently require to be reminded than informed." Therefore, in a society in which there is separation between sexes or generations or castes, one may become fully conscious of the sharing of a common humanity with another only after many years. In an interview held on January 13, 1974, Louisiana State Senator Edgar Mouton spoke of the time, in 1964, when he first ran for the State Senate from Lafayette Parish. "I was born and raised here," he said, "and I had never shaken hands with a black person before I ran for office." Even though black people had worked for his family, Mouton said, he never shook hands with a black person; and the first time this happened was traumatic for him. "And sure enough," he said, "the first was named Mouton, a black Mouton." As he became more involved with the poverty program, Mouton said that he "learned to greatly respect the feelings of the blacks." After one campaigns among the blacks for a time, one begins to understand all that they have endured.[15] One day, Mouton recalled, he spoke at a meeting where he was the only white person present. At the end of his brief talk, the blacks began to ask questions of him. During this session, which lasted for three hours, a black man promised Mouton that if he could answer a certain question for him, he would give him his vote. A few days before, the man told Mouton, he was driving down the road with his seven-year-old son, and they saw a lineman working on a power line. The boy told his father that he wanted to be a lineman when he grew up. But the power company did not hire black people, the man told Mouton. How, he asked, could he tell his son that he could not be that lineman because he was black? Mouton had no answer to this question. "It opened my eyes," he said, "that this fellow had the same feelings for his son that I have for my daughters."[16]

It is imagination that makes it possible for a man to write a novel with an unforgettable woman character, which makes it possible for a historian to bring another time, or a biographer another human being, vividly to life. One can live in the midst of great suffering and remain unaware of it, unmoved by it. One can also live in a community where there is no sign of suffering, and yet be keenly aware of the brutality and pain, the hunger and want endured throughout the world. Of the first it may be said that the imagination sleeps, and of the second that it never sleeps. What is inescapable is that imagination is expressed through social and historical circumstance. So it is with compassion, of which, Unamuno thought, imagination is the life-force. The objects and the intensity of compassion, as Nisbet reminds us, vary from time to time and from place to place. The handicapped, the poor, slaves and prisoners, victims of torture, aging people, homosexuals—these are but a few of the social classifications of people for whom both creative writers and social scientists have sought to arouse moral sympathy.

To what end is this moral sympathy aroused? In order to elucidate what is distinct about the sociological approach, Nisbet discusses four other approaches to social problems: the religious, the legal, the journalistic and the artistic. The artist's approach, he observes, can be found "in all spheres of art, painting, drama, poetry, but nowhere so compellingly as in the social novel." He calls attention to "the mordant depictions of lower-class misery under the impact of the new industrialism," which can be found in the works of Dickens and Zola among others, and which were, "for many millions of readers, the indispensable means of perceiving what actually lay around them." Later, the works of Shaw, Ibsen, Wells, Galsworthy, and Samuel Butler brought "the cankering social and moral problems that had lain long concealed behind the thick folds of Victorian respectability" to the attention of their readers. In the United States, Nisbet reminds us, social novels "have had enormous impact in their illumination of prostitution, poverty, crime, job and family dislocation, juvenile delinquency, alcoholism, narcotics, ethnic segregation, and other social problems."[17]

The religious, legal, journalistic, and artistic approaches to social problems all have an element in common, according to Nisbet, and this is their moral commitment. In contrast, he describes the sociological approach as one in which the causes of social problems are sought, as well as the ways in which they are related to other areas of social life. Whereas the objective of the artist may be dramatization, and that of the journalist exposure, of the social conditions that breed social problems, Nisbet states that the objective of the social scientist is knowledge: the sociologist is after hypotheses, not action. "The social scientist," Nisbet maintains, "is interested in making the protection of society his first responsibility, in seeing society reach higher levels of moral decency, and, when necessary, in promoting such legal actions as are necessary in the short run for protection or decency." Since he is a scientist, however, his professional responsibility is to treat any social problem in precisely the same way in which he treats any other sphere of human behavior or social activity.[18]

In this passage, Nisbet reminds us that a concern with social problems "has been an integral part of the main tradition of sociology." Sociology as it is known today "was born in the practical interests of its titans quite as much as in their theoretical interests." He mentions Durkheim's *Suicide* and Thomas and Znaniecki's *The Polish Peasant* as two classics that have had great impact upon the development of sociological theory. Through a consideration of specific social problems, the authors of these classics were led from analysis of a social problem and a search for practical solutions to an analysis of society itself, of norms and of social relationships, which illuminated understanding of social organization as well as of social *dis*organization.[19]

In reflecting on the significance of the study of social problems for sociology, Nisbet writes that "The itch of curiosity has generally had more to do with the history of science than has the spur of moral conscience." Nevertheless, he emphasizes the fact that the theoretical concerns of contemporary sociology are rooted in the attention that Le Play, Durkheim, Thomas, and others gave to social problems. Even though sociology is clearly distinct from social work, Nisbet remarks, studies of social problems continue to provide insights into the very nature of society. But "knowledge for what?" the student of social problems ever demands. To this Nisbet responds that it is an error to assume that there is a fatal contradiction between the desire for knowledge and the desire to act upon such knowledge as we have, in the name of our noblest ideals. One is not forced to choose, Nisbet contends, between the quest for knowledge and the action that a concerned citizen is now and again inclined to take. There is a need for both; and science and action are interdependent. All the social sciences are confronted with two major challenges, Nisbet suggests—the challenge of social action, and the challenge of social policy that is or ought to be the context of action.[20]

For the social scientist, there is a natural connection between moral concern for the condition of others, rooted in compassion, and social action. The ethic of humanitarianism upholds what might be called the norm of interference: people are responsible for alleviating one another's suffering, for intervening in one another's lives, for working in one another's best interests by modifying the social arrangements. It was in this spirit that André Malraux wrote that it is a privilege to endure suffering for the sake of making a better world. It is the spirit of the Enlightenment joined to that of Positivism: to free those suffering under the yoke of want and oppression is to act in the name of the religion of humanity; social institutions are the work of human, not divine beings, and are therefore knowable and modifiable; humanity is One; knowledge is power.

There is another path that compassion may lead one to take. One may ask, How deeply can compassion carry one into the experience of another, how much can one truly understand of another's condition? In our society, those who have endured a common suffering, a common loss, are encouraged to seek one another out, to band together. Those who have lost a child, those afflicted with the same mental or physical condition form a circle in order to give strength and consolation to one another. But sorrowing cannot be fully expunged by communal sharing of it; a measure of every grief must be borne alone. Only in its outward form is the suffering of one exactly like that of another. This is the other face of compassion, the sense of separateness that accompanies the sense of pity. It is as much in our consciousness, Unamuno believed, as the awareness of our resemblance to others. Aware of our separateness, he said, we are aware of our limitations: Pity is akin to love, but also to powerlessness. Compassion is born, he thought, out of the *collision* of knowledge with power. In writing of these things, he recalls the words spoken by a Persian who was said by Herodotus to have told a Theban at a banquet, "The bitterest sorrow that man can know is to aspire to do much and to achieve nothing."[21]

In contrast to the norm of intervention is the norm of *non*intervention, and this is related to the awareness of one's separateness. Anthropologist Robert Dentan found that the Semai of Malaya observe the "principle of non-interference," which appears to call forth the "feeling that human relationships are insecure in the sense that one is always essentially alone." Dentan cites a proverb of the east Semai, which literally means that

"thinking thinks by itself." The sense is that the thoughts of the heart only the heart can know. "You cannot know my grief," says a west Semai man. "You feel grief, but not the real grief. For you it *must* always be like a movie." An extension of this feeling is the general opinion that sympathy is "useless." "What good does it do an unhappy person to have another person upset?" people ask.[22]

Recognizing one's essential separateness from all others, the Semai teach that one ought to refrain from active intervention in the lives of others. No matter how benevolent one may feel disposed to be, one should not, because one *can*not, take the suffering of others upon oneself.

Compassion, Unamuno wrote, begins with those close to oneself, and then widens into a universal co-feeling. In itself, in the pity and the sorrowing, there is no necessary thought of how the suffering might be redeemed. Indeed, for Unamuno, compassion leads to contemplation, contemplation of the finitude and mortality of all things. This is why, when he writes of universal love, he writes of the "tragic sense of life." What can be done? Nothing can be done.

This fatalism is in counterpoint to the moral indignation, the anger in literary works that have the theme of some form of human suffering.

Thus, James Agee, in writing of the Alabama sharecroppers, creates passages like this that read as lamentations:

On the day you are married, at about sixteen if you are a girl, at about twenty if you are a man, a key is turned, with a sound not easily audible, and you are locked between the stale earth and the sky; the key turns in the lock behind you, and your full life's work begins, and there is nothing conceivable for which it can afford to stop short of your death, which is a long way off.[23]

Here as elsewhere in this complex work, Agee expresses the tragic sense of life, the sense of the immutability of the laws governing human destiny, the encounter with the implacable face of human fate. "Born otherwise," he says with savage simplicity, "he would break his shell upon other forms of madness."[24]

Jules Henry, too, in his studies of the families of emotionally ill children, brooded on the inevitability of human suffering, and found that the recognition of this is the source of compassionate feeling. Tragedy did not pass out of the world with the passing of the Greeks, he wrote; rather,

The difference between the ancient and the modern "tragic motif," as Søren Kierkegaard pointed out, is in the nature of the determination of action: in the ancient tragedy, destiny was determined by the gods or by fate, while in modern tragedy it is determined by what Kierkegaard calls our "inheritance"— what our parents did to us because the culture had done it to them. The understanding that in both cases the individual is bound, so that he has little choice, is the beginning of compassion; and our ability to suffer with these people because we know they cannot escape is the essence of sorrow.[25]

*The individual is bound, so that he has little choice.* This is the first principle of the tragic sense of life . . . but also the first principle of social and cultural determinism. The anthropologist sees "culture" as the force moving through people's lives. The sociologist might see another force—"society" or "the socioeconomic system" or the "social structure." Or, as an advocate of a certain ideology, a social scientist may name the social stratification system or the Oedipus complex or the "geographical environment" as the prime mover in the unfolding of human destiny. Whatever their intellectual differences, all social scientists are engaged in a common endeavor: the search for the "determinants" of human action and historical and social reality, and the ways in which these determinants are interrelated. Although the sociologist may differ radically from the biological determinist in his understanding of the causes of criminal behavior, both are agreed that the causes are knowable, and that they may be invoked to explain why the criminal does what he does. But to the sociologist, these causes—flaws in the social environment, faults in the social arrangements—can be altered, and even eradicated. There is a rejection, perhaps even a defiance of the principle of Necessity in social science. To the sociologist, much can be done: that which binds the individual can be loosened; circumstances fostering human suffering are corrigible. The very spirit of social science is counter to the tragic sense of life.

The belief in the efficacy of human intervention has all the power and passion of a religious faith for many contemporary thinkers. The demand for justice, George Steiner reminds us, has always animated the spirit of Judaism, which "is vehement in its conviction that the order of the universe and of man's estate is accessible to reason." Marxism, Steiner observes, "is characteristically Jewish in its insistence on justice and reason, and Marx repudiated the entire concept of tragedy. 'Necessity,' he declared, 'is blind only in so far as it is not understood.'"[26] But tragic drama is born of the exact contrary to this, born of the belief that "necessity is blind and man's encounter with it shall rob him of his eyes, whether it be in Thebes or in Gaza."[27] This is the wisdom of the ancient Greeks, and Steiner believes that the tragic sense of life that flows from this is the most outstanding contribution of "the Greek genius" to our heritage. Man can do nothing but endure—or perish—at the hands of his fate. There is no reparation; there are no compensations; there is no justice:

> Tragic drama tells us that the spheres of reason, order, and justice are terribly limited and that no progress in our science or technical resources will enlarge their relevance. Outside and within man is *l'autre*, the "otherness" of the world. Call it what you will: a hidden or malevolent God, blind fate, the solicitations of hell, or the brute fury of our animal blood. It waits for us in ambush at the crossroads. It mocks and destroys us. In certain rare instances, it leads us after destruction to some incomprehensible repose.[28]

We cannot know, we cannot contemplate this "otherness," this force, Nicola Chiaromonte says in his thrilling essay on "Simone Weil's *Iliad*," because, in order to know or contemplate it, we "would have to know where, in this world, the human and intelligible end and where the divine begins"; we would "have to have a sense of sacred limit."[29]

This, the "sense of sacred limit," the social scientist does not write about or speak of in the classroom. Indeed, to do so might be tantamount to heresy. The social scientific understanding of the nature of the world does not lead to withdrawal and contemplation of the tragic nature of life, of the vanity of all things. Rather, it leads to making recommendations and giving advice to those in positions of power, and, for some, to intervention, to action directed toward change, even transformation, of the social arrangements. A consummate social scientist, Jules Henry, despite the fact that he wrote so eloquently of his sense of the ineluctability of the fates of these people to whose tragic lives he came as witness, opened his account of what he has seen with the reformist spirit that enlivens all social science. His book, he declared in the preface, was written for children. It was his hope that "it will help reduce the misery in their lives." And he hoped, too, that "some parents, because they have read it, will be able to save themselves some suffering by avoiding some mistakes with their children." They may come to understand, he wrote, that we usually do not know what we do to children.[30]

To the question, What can be done? the social scientist answers that much can be done, that things can be otherwise. It is not Necessity that is blind, as Marx would have it, but ourselves. Yet the social scientist is caught on the horns of a dilemma. Programs and social movements are often founded upon the desire to alleviate the suffering of people in social categories, of the personae of gender or age, of ethnic or religious or social class affiliation, of statistical "groups" defined in terms of social and economic characteristics, of an objectively defined collectivity. It is not possible, Unamuno taught, to feel compassion for an abstraction; one must personalize in order to experience love and pity. The richer the imagination, the more readily and intensely one feels compassion for *all* others who, beneath their masks, beneath the surfaces of the world of appearances, resemble the manifold self. When the alleviation of the suffering of a collectivity becomes a cause, one becomes a champion of a particular segment of the social universe—a tribe, a religious sect, "the proletariat," "women," or "the aged." In consequence, the savior of one "people" can become the destroyer of another, or even of those in the group elected to be saved who resist the defenders who act in their name.

"There is much suffering in the world," Malraux said. This "advanced" age has been host to death and destruction on a scale unparalleled by that of any earlier time. It seems to some whose lives are dedicated to the alleviation of human suffering that there is no progress, that every small victory is followed by massive defeat. Despair, not hope, seems companion to compassion to those who are deeply sensitive to human suffering. Each of us needs, John Cowper Powys wrote,

> to escape from the thought of the horrors of life somehow; for those who pretend they can face them are either lying to others or to themselves.
> No man—not even the noblest saint—can face the horror of what can happen, has happened, and is happening to human beings in this world.
> For this is the nature of our life upon earth that we can only live by forgetting the intolerable.[31]

Perhaps the only "progress" that has been made is that the torturers and murderers, the oppressors and exploiters of the contemporary world try to conceal or to justify their inhumanity, whereas, in earlier times, they did not feel they had to make an account of their actions. Again and again, Solzhenitsyn has called upon writers to light up the shadows and corners of societies around the world where there is evildoing. Solzhenitsyn believes in the efficacy of exposure because he believes that people in power fear the condemnation of the public.

Power *collides* with knowledge, Unamuno thought; and out of this, compassion is born. Many thinkers have suggested that the lust for power destroys compassion, that these two feelings pull in opposite directions. Decades ago, the American novelist John Dos Passos saw a fundamental opposition between pity and the will to power. He wrote of pity as a "corrosive," and argued that one of the consequences of pity is a "failure of nerve":

> The corrosive of pity, which had attacked the steel girders of our civilization even before the work of building was completed, has brought about what Gilbert Murray, in speaking of Greek thought, calls the failure of nerve. In the seventeenth century, men still had the courage of their egoism. The world was a bad job to be made the best of, all hope lay in driving a good bargain with

the conductors of life everlasting. By the end of the nineteenth century, the life everlasting had grown cobwebby. The French Revolution had filled men up with extravagant hopes of the perfectibility of this world, humanitarianism had instilled an abnormal sensitiveness to pain, to one's own pain, and to the pain of one's neighbors.[32]

How useless compassion seems, when one considers the weapons available to world leaders today. In their power games, they are playing petulantly, arrogantly, most unwisely with the future of the species.

To Comte, the founding father of sociology, it seemed clear enough: in the new social order, warriors would be replaced by industrialists, and priests by scientists. Fatality, Comte insisted, is modifiable; knowledge can be power in the realm of society as it had proven itself to be in the realm of nature. Today we have only begun to attend to the warnings of the ecologists; we have only begun to learn that what was once thought to be a conquest of nature was a ravening pillage of its gifts. The doubts that trouble social scientists today, about the reaches of human understanding and control, about what is possible for humanity, are not all of modern origin. There were the gloomy forebodings of Malthus, sounded at the very time that the *philosophes* were celebrating the wonders of the world-to-come. Later there were Durkheim's somber reflections. Pareto warned that today's redeemers may be led tomorrow to the scaffolds; he argued that an aristocracy which loses its capacity for brutality, which becomes "excessive" in its humanitarianism, is doomed. And, too, there was Max Weber's dark prevision of the iron cage. Scions of the Enlightenment, the social sciences are predicated upon a vision of a better world. Yet, by the very fact-gathering and exercise of reason extolled as the pathways to a better world, social scientists are uncovering a Malthusian nightmare on a "plundered planet." All along the roads to utopia are torture chambers, concentration camps, mass graves. Perhaps the evolution of morality, or the broadening or institutionalization of compassion were impossible dreams. Perhaps the notion of evolution is itself a misapprehension of the way things change in society and culture. Comte did not see, Unamuno shrewdly observed, that the three "ages" or "stages" of theology, metaphysics and Positivism can, and do, coexist. Or, if evolution is indeed a law governing society as well as nature, we may be no more than the "missing link" ourselves, as Konrad Lorenz suggested. We may be no more than the connecting bond between the primates and truly compassionate beings.[33]

If there is a genetics of altruism, as the sociobiologists suspect, it is quite possible that self-sacrificing actions are linked to compassion. However, as social scientists, and particularly sociologists fully appreciate, hereditary predispositions depend upon the grace of the social environment for their realization. There are many factors to be taken into account in an analysis of the sociocultural context of compassion. It can happen that the conditions of life are so extreme for a people that only the uncaring can survive at all. It is also quite likely that people who live in a society in which a strong sense of the past is cultivated are more compassionate than people who live in a society in which there is little concern for ancestry. An impoverished imagination, an inability to apprehend one's connection with all life, an indifference or blindness to the condition of others may be due to an ignorance of human history. Loren Eiseley put this beautifully when he wrote, "There should be a kind of pity that comes with time, when one grows truly conscious and looks behind as well as forward, for nothing is more brutally savage than the man who is not aware he is a shadow."[34] There is also the strong possibility that the willingness to project oneself into the situation of another is dependent upon the manner in which the young child is socialized.

In a passage in his book on kibbutz society, child psychologist Bruno Bettelheim discusses the relationship between empathy and the introject. According to psychoanalytic theory, when the young child fears or actually experiences the loss of those upon whom he is completely dependent, he transfers the psychic energy he invested in the object to the mental image of the object. This is introjection, and through this he defends himself against the terror of abandonment and helplessness. Now, in the kibbutz, Bettelheim writes, there is no profound sense of mutual belonging, of possessing and at the same time of being possessed by significant others. Since the child is neither physically nor emotionally dependent upon particular persons, he feels their loss much less keenly than would his counterpart who is reared in the nuclear family. Bettelheim believes that the fact that the kibbutz child does not introject his parents—and, according to him, introjection probably cannot occur in normal persons much later than at the onset of the latency period—is crucial to understanding his personality.[35] Bettelheim's observations are also applicable to the personality formation of a child reared in a conjugal-natal unit that is embedded within either a composite unilineal or a composite conjugal-natal ("extended") family.

What is significant for our understanding of the nature of compassion is that Bettelheim suggests that introjects "are what later endow the child in our culture with both a deep empathy for others (because he carries some other person within him), and a capacity for living independently (because with introjects to keep him company, independence is never again a being wholly alone)."[36] Thus young people who grow up in the context of a nuclear family can imagine themselves in the place of another person. But youths reared in the kibbutz do not. The only exceptions to this failure to project oneself into the feelings of others are peers. But peers, Bettelheim says, are essentially alter egos who, though they protect one from feeling alone, have not been made introjects out of a dread of abandonment.

It is instructive that Bettelheim noted that the young kibbutzniks found it difficult or impossible "to comprehend (much less respond to) a hypothetical question, when to answer it would have required them to step outside their own frame of reference."[37] Whereas many youngsters growing up in the United States come to imagine what it might be like had they been born of the other sex, or, later on, of another ethnic group or social class, youth reared in the kibbutz do not seem to do this. Of course, they have no difficulty, Bettelheim says, in conceiving of things as being different from what they are. But they could not conceive of *themselves* as being different in their thinking and feelings and actions. This, he believes, is less due to living in a community in which all the answers have already been worked out than to the absence of introjected persons with whom people hold "inner conversations, talks that require them to recognize the introject's viewpoint and their own at the same time."[38] On the kibbutz, then, the freedom to hold a continuous "collective monologue" with age-mates may be won at the price of what George Herbert Mead called the "inner conversation." According to Mead, it is through this interior exchange that the social self continually unfolds.

A grasp of child-rearing practices and the broader culture and personality perspective from which they are studied is vital to an understanding of why compassion, or, indeed, any individual sentiment, is expressed in a particular pattern. One must see things as the people themselves see them; one must work as an anthropologist or sociologist of everyday life if one is to interpret the social arrangements correctly. Still, many questions remain open, and call for further analysis. For example, the capacity for empathy varies greatly among people in a generation that experiences the same child-rearing practices, just as an appreciation of history, a sense of the past, varies among those living in the same social environment. The narrower the focus of the social scientist, the more reluctant he is to make generalizations. But, on the other hand, the narrower the focus of study, the more acute are the insights gained thereby.

At the other extreme are the "macro-sociological" studies, through which the nature of an entire community or society is explored. From this perspective, it might be said that compassion has been institutionalized in the modern state, that personal violence—man's inhumanity to man—has been outlawed, and that the state itself has claimed a monopoly on force. This works in theory, however, far better than in fact: outlawed or not, personal violence goes on in the modern state; indeed, Etzioni writes that it has been on the increase during the 1970s.[39] Every day, in the newspapers and over the radio and on television, one hears of cases of child abuse, wife abuse, murder, assault, rape, violence in jails and prisons, acts of terrorism; indeed, one social observer writes of our prevailing state as one of "social warfare."[40]

One thing seems clear, and that is the relationship between compassion and nonviolence. A discussion of nonviolence from a macro-sociological and macro-anthropological perspective affords many insights for the student of compassion. In a paper entitled "Man Has No 'Killer' Instinct," Geoffrey Gorer identifies "gentle societies" in which people do not find pleasure in dominating or wounding or killing one another. These, he says, are "small, weak, technologically backward, and living in inaccessible country; only so could they survive the power-seeking of their uninhibited neighbors." Among these are the Arapesh of New Guinea, the Lepchas of Sikkim in the Himalayas, and the pygmies of the Ituri rain-forest in the Congo. What they have in common, Gorer writes, is not only a great enjoyment for the "concrete physical pleasures—eating, drinking, sex, laughter—" but also the fact that they do not make a strong distinction between ideal male and ideal female characters, and "particularly that they have no ideal of brave, aggressive masculinity."[41] A child growing up in such a society does not suffer from a confusion of sexual identity, according to Gorer. The model for a boy or a girl "is of concrete performance and frank enjoyment, not of metaphysical symbolic achievements or of ordeals to be surmounted. They do not have heroes or martyrs to emulate or cowards or traitors to despise." The people in these societies value peace, and discourage quarreling and jealousy. Gorer remarks the sharp contrast between these gentle societies and that of the cannibals in the New Guinea highlands, who uphold an aggressive ideal of masculinity. In general, he believes, this ideal is celebrated in all societies whose people extol the martial virtues, and kill whomever they define as their enemies or inferiors. They kill them with self-righteousness, and even with joy. "Mankind is safer," Gorer observes, "when men seek pleasure than when they seek the power and the glory." In this essay, which was first published in the mid-1960s, Gorer expressed the hope that the "youth international" will succeed in redefining the concepts of the "real man" and the "true woman." For it is on this redefinition, as well as on the celebration of shared sensual pleasure, that, he believes, the true brotherhood of humanity ultimately depends.[42]

There is another possibility, and that is that compassion is sex-linked, that the more female, specifically maternal feelings are cultivated in a person, the more compassionate that person—male or female—will be. Unamuno wrote of the maternal quality of compassion. And Anaïs Nin, in writing of a time when she nursed her brother through appendicitis, said that she felt he was more than a brother to her; he was her *child*, as well. She felt herself to be his second mother as well as his nurse. "I love my brother," she wrote, "and there are times when I know this love . . . makes me feel man is a brother; it created a pact which has disarmed my power to do man any harm." She wrote of feeling "life and love and pain in the womb, always, as if in our own body."[43]

Theories of innate differences between the sexes are not very popular at the present time. The controversy between Nature and Nurture is unceasing, and today the environmentalist position is in intellectual fashion. There are those who believe that the causes of man's inhumanity to man are to be found in the nature of social organization; there are others who believe that they lie in the nature of the beast. Cruelty, oppression, slavery, war—these, Rousseau contended, are *social* inventions, societal institutions. The quarrel between Rousseau and Hobbes turns, as all differences of opinion of this sort turn, on a quarrel about the nature of human nature. Without a natural sympathy between humans, a propensity to imagine how another must feel, there can be no compassion. But with it, the human race has scarcely begun to realize all that it is possible to achieve in life on this earth.

Statistics are cold, and sociological analysis ought to be dispassionate. Yet a case can surely be made that both are presented to serve humanitarian interests, to arouse compassion in those who study them. In the camera they have a lively, and some say a deadly, competitor. As with love and with desire, compassion may be aroused through an appeal to the senses, and particularly through an appeal to visual perception. The express purpose of some "photographic essays," forms of photojournalism, is to awaken moral sympathy, if not moral indignation, in the viewer. Photographs can be powerful inciters of social protest. In 1975, *Minamata* was published, a work by W. Eugene Smith, formerly a photographer for *Life* magazine, and his wife, Aileen, who was born in Tokyo. *Minamata* is the work of witnesses to the suffering and death caused by methyl mercury poisoning of people in the fishing and farming community of Minamata, a city on the western coast of Kyushu. For over two decades, the Chisso Corporation, a chemical factory, released toxic wastes into Minamata Bay, committing what Smith has called "industrial genocide" upon the people of the community. The Smiths traveled for three years throughout Japan, gathering facts about the history of the Chisso Corporation; and they united with the people of the community in their struggle for compensation for the ravages of this chemical poisoning. They interviewed the executives of Chisso, and participated at hearings and in demonstrations. Their involvement was intense: Smith was beaten severely by Chisso hirelings, and nearly blinded.

In his review of *Minamata*, which is, he says, "the most passionate instance of pamphleteering since Ralph Nader aimed his lance at Detroit," Paul Theroux writes of the book as "a humane and deeply-felt document" throughout which "the photographs of appalling brilliance tear at the heart." Although, he says, we have known for some time of the violence that industry has done to our planet,

> never have I seen this fact so poignantly recorded as in one of the opening photographs in "Minamata," a tragic history of 20 years of suffering in a small prefecture in southern Japan. It is an eerily-lit Pietà: a mother holds the naked ruined body of her daughter, who has been made deaf and dumb and physically incapable by the progress of methyl-mercury poisoning . . . .[44]

The Minamata Pietà to which Theroux refers was entitled "Tomoko in Her Bath."

How well W. Eugene Smith understands "the visceral power inherent in the photographic image," Hilton Kramer exclaims:

> Every image is a mode of persuasion. It urges us into belief, and brooks no argument. Its aim is the conversion of feeling. It does not engage us in debate, or invite disinterested discussion. Its purpose is to alter our perception of the world we inhabit.
> This is the great advantage that images—especially, in our time, photographic images—enjoy over more discursive forms of expressions: They speed us to the point of perception with a velocity that renders "objective" argument irrelevant.[45]

In this review, Kramer tells us that Smith regards the very notion of objectivity as suspect. His mission, Kramer says, is to convince us that an evil, but a reversible evil, has befallen humanity.

Photographs have this power, that they make witnesses of all who view them. Because of the camera, the people of a small village across the world may be converted into neighbors, even into friends and kin. Through the photographic image, the viewer can enter into the lives of the people taken as subjects. The imagination is quickened; one can find oneself reflected in image after image; through them, one can recognize the common condition of all humanity. When James Agee explained why he cared so deeply for the camera, he compared it with scientific instruments and the phonograph record, all of which, he thought, could not but record pure truth.[46]

Long before the camera was invented, however, Blake wrote that "The eye sees more than the heart knows." In his review of a number of European films about "The Age of Fascism," Alfred Kazin recalls Blake's words. There is more than we know what to do with, Kazin remarks, in all this filmfeast for the eyes. How, he asks, can we distinguish "between the unending news show on film and 'reality'?" Films, Kazin observes, are an *impersonation* of reality. Like newspapers, they give us the surfaces of ongoing life. And World War II, he says, "has become the longest running movie of all time." Indeed, thanks to the camera, for many people World War II has mythic proportions as great as those of the Civil War. Has it become no more than a movie? Kazin asks. Films are, he says, "insidious . . . one of the great drugs of our time, as irresistible as sex and liquor." The danger is that too many of us may come to depend upon them for our understanding of history and of the workings of the human heart. These no film can give us. Films "simply cannot deal with the moral complexity, the moral actuality, of a world dominated by totalitarian terror."[47]

Smith's photographs were intended to "speak for themselves," to arouse compassion in every viewer. They tell of suffering and of death. But they do not tell us how to alleviate the suffering. This can only be suggested by films, just as films can only suggest the causes of suffering. We have learned a precious lesson from the picture magazines, John Szarkowski writes, and that is the lesson that "There is no equivalent of the syllogism in pictures. The photograph may suggest, but cannot define, intellectual or philosophical or political values. It can only describe appearances." The belief that photography should aspire to perform the functions of language, Szarkowski remarks, may be "even farther from the mark than the notion that it should emulate painting."[48] Cause and cure—these are the province of language, of meditation and argument and social scientific analysis, of utopian vision and ideological polemics. For many, this is where compassion leads, and why it dies—to language, to words that, rather than informing feelings, may come to supplant them. Gandhi spoke sadly of the hardness of heart he so often observed in educated people.

Margaret Mead has argued that we have only begun to tap the power the camera has for arousing compassion. We are in need of ways, she contended, "to think about the four billion people on this planet which will not turn them into statistics or vast faceless masses." It is the camera, she believes, that can bring others to us in all their immediacy. She suggests that our "capacity to feel and think and act is deadened and anesthetized" by abstractions and statistics about "the poor" or "the elderly" or the "L.D.C.'s" ("Least-Developed Countries"). Photography makes it possible for us to gaze directly into the eyes of another. Through it, distances can be spanned that, before our time, were formidable if not insurmountable. "As once the people of small villages wept for the death of a single child," she writes, "we can again take the world to our hearts."[49]

Still, not every photographer would maintain that his mission is the awakening of compassion; not every photographer thinks of himself as first an envoy in the cause of human brotherhood. One cannot be certain of the photographer's intentions, always. Nor does one always know what it is about a photograph that compels one to be responsive to it, or leaves one unmoved by it. "It is hard to say," Susan Sontag observes, whether the photographs that Smith took in Minamata "move us more because they are documents of real suffering or because they are superb photographs of 'agony' conforming to surrealist standards of beauty." She suggests that the photograph he took "of a dying youth, writhing on his mother's lap, is a possible image for Artaud's Theater of Cruelty."[50]

Walker Evans, whose celebrated photographs of the Alabama sharecroppers during the Depression are often cited for their propagandistic value, said of his work, "They weren't part of the social protest of the time or intended to be heart-wringing. They were a record of what's what. You can't do anything about poverty that way. That's too naive."[51] Indeed, according to Hilton Kramer, Walker Evans was one of the most widely misunderstood artists of his generation. The cultural ethos of the 1930s contributed heavily to an interpretation of Evans' work as social documentary, Kramer comments, and of Evans as "an artist defined by his empathy for the poor and the dispossessed and for the humble circumstances in which their lives were so accurately observed." But Evans' sensibility was shaped not by the Depression, but by "his fateful immersion in the literary and artistic culture of Paris in the 1920s." And Evans was very open about acknowledging his debts to Baudelaire and to Flaubert. According to Kramer, he "was a man profoundly detached from the common woes of the human spectacle." He was interested not in the social fate of his subjects but in their aesthetic effects. A "chronicler of anonymous architecture and artifacts," Evans "was most at home, spiritually and artistically, where human actors had quit the stage . . . and left the eloquent debris of their past free to be examined and 'taken' . . . as a permanent statement of feeling." If we compare his pictures for the Farm Security Administration with the pictures of other photographers working on that project, Kramer suggests, we will "find that they actually tell us a lot less about the social condition of his subjects than they do about the photographer's own esthetic interests."[52]

Even if it could be established that the explicit purpose of the photojournalist is to capture images of suffering in order to arouse compassion in the viewer, this purpose is not always realized. The moral distance between sufferer and viewer is not always spanned by the photograph. Indeed, it can happen that an image of suffering only serves to alienate the viewer from the subject. For, although nothing could be more real than suffering to those who are enduring it, the apprehension of suffering, as that of beauty, must be achieved through the eye of the beholder. What may arouse pity in one person may arouse resentment in another, resentment for having been reminded of what one prefers to forget, or for having been made aware of one's powerlessness to help others, or for the guilt that is often attendant to feelings of pity. No photographer, no orator, no artist is in absolute control of the consequences of evocation.

There is another possibility. That is that those who suffer may see the artist or photographer as an intruder upon their privacy, their only claim to human dignity. People may consent to be models because of economic need, yet they may remain convinced that artists or photographers or journalists are voyeurs who exploit anguish in order to gratify their curiosity or to tell the "big story." This is an age when the appetite for sensationalism seems as gluttonous as it is depraved. All through the agony of Vietnam, the suffering and death were brought before the eyes of everyone in the world who could see, and who happened to look—in newspapers and magazines, on television and news films. Only the blind failed to witness the nightmare of war come to life in photographic images. The photographs were shown for many different reasons—for their shock value, for their propagandistic value, for the purpose of keeping people abreast of "news as it happens," as well as for arousing compassion. The power of the photographic image is undeniable. Yet, once unleashed, the effects are unpredictable. Just as there were those brought to the very edge of sanity by photographs of suffering, those for whom their visual impact was all but unendurable, so there were those who were angered by them, who claimed that they were contrived or exaggerated. There were those, too, whose prurient or sadistic appetites were whetted by what they saw. It should never be assumed that the meaning of a photographic image is inherent in it. Indeed, it is possible that the work of art or photography can be understood without much knowledge of the artist. But the very act of understanding demands the complicity of the beholder. In photojournalism and in art, as in social science, interpretation is all.

The powers of every art form, like the powers of social scientific analysis, seem, like the Polynesian *mana*, to be morally indifferent; photographs, words, statistics can all be used to serve good or evil ends. One cannot predict confidently what will come of the uses of these powers—compassion on the one hand, brutality on the other. The professor's hope of arriving at some universal truth in discussion following the showing of a film may be a vain hope. What students of social problems learn from a film depends less upon the film than upon the moral sense, the ability to think and to discern that they bring to it. The images brought to us, through painting, through music and photography and dreams, vivid and compelling as they so often are, can be no more, no other than images. Indeed, because they *are* images, what students see on films may even corrupt the very source of sympathy: without flesh, without substance, without the immediacy of physical presence, a rush of pity may all too easily be quelled. What follows after this is all too often a diatribe, or a show of boredom, or distaste.

In the course of their professional work, anthropologists and sociologists are forced to specialize, to become intellectually and (though they may not acknowledge it) morally engaged with a certain people and their problems. For one, it may be the urban poor, for another the migrant workers, for a third those who are in prison. Whatever the choice, the social scientist comes up against the boundary stone: What must be considered first, before all other considerations? And, what must be done first, before any other measures are taken? For, in every theory about the social and cultural realities, and in every technique devised for use in studying them, there is an idea, a vision of what human nature and society are. If one is dominated by moral concern, by feeling, one may be brought to despair, to a sense of impotence. John Cowper Powys wrote:

> The origin of Pity; who can trace it or sound it? From what fountain in the abyss does it spring? It is irrational. Reason can tell us only of Justice, of weighing merits, of rewarding the good, of punishing the evil. This strange feeling, that suddenly wells up in the heart—it is like fresh water from beneath the salt sea of our life; and it breaks all laws; it overbrims all measures; it contradicts all values of weighing and calculating.[53]

If, on the other hand, one is dominated by intellectual concern, by abstractions, one may forget one's humanity. One may even come to preach, if not to practice, *in*humanity. If one chooses one being out of the multiple selfhood as the only authentic one; if one chooses to sacrifice one's uniqueness, one's individuality in the name of service to a collectivity, one surrenders the power to love at all. So much savagery is committed in the name of love and pity. Social scientists should know better than anyone else that consecration of unwavering loyalty to those within any circle defined as kin is achieved at the cost of clearly defining its perimeters. Those beyond the circle come to be seen as faceless, without souls or feelings; they become the Other; they become objects, fair game. Once Unamuno, who wrote the classic work on compassion, spoke of these things to the Hispanic scholar Walter Starkie. He and Unamuno were walking down the Gran Vía in Madrid a little before the Civil War, Starkie recalled, and Unamuno spoke bitterly against Marx's and Lenin's theories as these had been followed by their devotees in Spain. "There is no tyranny in the world more hateful than that of ideas," Unamuno exclaimed. "Ideas bring ideophobia, and the consequence is that people begin to persecute their neighbors in the name of ideas." Unamuno told Starkie that he loathed and detested all labels, and that the only label he could accept for himself would be that of "ideoclast or idea-breaker."[54]

No one can save the whole world. But anyone may live compassionately; anyone can respond to the life-force of compassion, the imagination, in one's daily round. Compassion takes root in inner life; those who remain mysteries to themselves, who have no way to their own inner lives, cannot see themselves in other people, cannot see their fate in the fate of other people. It may be possible to teach the young in a society to be humane without recourse to the imagination. Through a system of positive inducements to humane behavior, an application of learning reinforcement theory, children can be discouraged from behaving inhumanely toward animals as well as people. But, since there is no transformation of feelings, the removal of rewards for humane behavior may prove fatal to the moral enterprise. Furthermore, learning reinforcement, like any method, can serve both God and the devil. It could conceivably be adopted in the service of discouraging as well as of encouraging humane behavior. Society is possible, George Herbert Mead taught long ago, cooperative endeavor is possible, because people are able to take one another's point of view. And this is possible because of the use of the imagination which, according to Mead, is socially grounded. In contrast to Watson and his school of behaviorism, Mead sought understanding of the *sources* of overt, observable actions. Watson and his followers, Mead observed, took the stance of ordering "off with their heads." Their school excluded the covert aspect of behavior—thinking and imagining.

Yet many have commented on the distrust of the imagination in contemporary society. Once James Agee's impassioned paean of praise for the camera as superior to the printed word was very unusual. Today, in retrospect, Agee can be seen as a precursor, for photography is exceedingly popular. This, Hilton Kramer suggests, may have to do with the belief that the photograph can give us "reality." For whatever reasons, he says,

contemporary sensibility has become deeply suspicious of the fictive impulse. It yearns for the verifiable—for images than [sic] can be tested, if only in theory, by the standards of common experience—and is increasingly restive, if not resentful, in the presence of the purely imaginary. For the same reason that novels are now less eagerly read than works of biography and history and personal confession—and even poetry, long considered the very essence of imaginative invention, has been swamped by the confessional mode—photography appears to enjoy a legitimacy denied to the more traditional forms of visual expression. Perhaps because the world of common experience has become a more difficult and problematic place for most of us, we are all the more desperate to have its "reality" triumphantly reaffirmed in our art.[55]

The reality of a photograph, Kramer reminds us, is a contrivance of timing and technique. And the camera alone is equipped to convey—and does convey—an "illusion of absolute veracity." Students often tell their professors in the social sciences and the humanities that they "understand" films much better than they understand the written word. When asked just what it is that they understand, they often say that they cannot express it in words, either. But, except by thought, how are all the images that flood the eye to be comprehended? It may be no accident that violence, brutality, cruelty all seem to grow in direct proportion to the voracious appetite for films, that films are devoured by those who feel a need to fill an inner emptiness. If there is nothing in the head or the heart that responds to the image given to the eye, one does not know what it is one is seeing. The richer the imagination, the more informed the mind, the less need one has for the evidence given by the senses. The more completely we know ourselves, the more fellow feeling we naturally come to have.

If Freud was right, the earliest encounters with the Other are decisive; and therefore, some people will always be more compassionate than others. Even so, by separate paths, people arrive at the same place. Let each choose his own way of alleviating the suffering of the world, Malraux wrote. One responds to the problems of minorities, another to those of the poor, a third to those of the aged. In a book which contains the wisdom of philosophers of the non-Western world, the anthropologist Paul Radin quotes a philosopher of the Oglala Dakota, whose words were recorded by Francis Densmore in a *Bulletin* of the Bureau of American Ethnology: "I have noticed in my life that all men have a liking for some special animal, or plant, or spot of earth," the man told Densmore. "If men would pay more attention to these preferences and seek what is best to do in order to make themselves worthy of that toward which they are so attracted, they might have dreams which would purify their lives."[56]

Martin Luther King once said that undeserved suffering is redemptive. So, too, may be the *apprehension* of undeserved suffering. Some say that civilization, indeed, the very survival of life on this earth, is conditional upon compassion—not upon cleverness or brute strength, not upon creativity or charisma or even luck, so much as upon compassion. People are so very much alike; the differences between one person and another are small. Yet the difference in the measure of compassionate feeling makes it seem as though one had been born only yesterday, whereas the other had been living on this earth for a thousand years.

# PART THREE

*Vision is the art of seeing things invisible.*

—Jonathan Swift, *Thoughts on Various Subjects*

# FIVE

## *Witnessing*

> *There's no art*
> *To find the mind's construction in the face.*
> —Shakespeare,
> *Macbeth*, Act I, Scene IV

"Peering and peeping persons" Yeats found us to be, and for that, "hawkers of stolen goods"—with our ravenous noses, our sharp eyes. Each social scientist in his time plays many parts—the gossip and the interrogator, the translator and interpreter, the spy and the confessor—all in the service of our calling, as witnesses of a particular time, a certain place. Our surveys and statistical analyses, our questionnaires and interviews are all intended to realize the single mission of interpenetrating separate cultural spaces, of making the inhabitants of separate social worlds known and intelligible to others. Our "methodologies" are secular rites through which we celebrate human resemblances and differences and, through that, the bonds between people of every age and persuasion and condition.

But so often we imagine things. We imagine that we do not intrude in any significant way upon that which we describe and analyze. We imagine that we do not stand in the light of those whose words are copied down in notebooks or recorded on tape. We imagine that what we are told is the truth, the whole truth, and nothing but the truth.

We imagine that we understand the circumstances of the lives of other people, the forces they feel are moving through them. Sometimes we even imagine that a moral law is established because a statistical majority say that they subscribe to it. And we imagine that our witnessing is disinterested, that we are innocent of any motive but that of curiosity. As if curiosity were innocent!

Corrupted by a rigid scientism and the ideological commitments that wear its mask, we remain strangers to the nature of imagination itself. We have always understood ourselves to be engaged in a scientific, not an artistic endeavor, and the "language" of social science tells the tale. Social scientists have spun a dense, gray fog of verbiage out of its traditions, a kind of limbo to which it remains condemned, a world that is neither art nor science. Whether intentions have been pure or not, social scientists have aroused suspicions on all sides because of this, the "language" of social science. Over thirty years ago, in his essay on "Politics and the English Language," George Orwell wrote of the use of pretentious words "to dress up simple statement and give an air of scientific impartiality to biased judgments."[1] Orwell made it quite clear that he was not referring to the literary use of language, but only to "language as an instrument for expressing and not for concealing or preventing thought." Political language, he warned, "is designed to make lies sound truthful and murder respectable, and to give an appearance of solidity to pure wind."[2] Very recently, J. M. Cameron stated that "The corruption of language is the worst corruption of culture." In reviewing Paul Robinson's *The Modernization of Sex*, a work in which, he says, the reader is offered "horrific specimens of the dense jargon of modern writers," Cameron suggests that the impenetrable jargon of Masters and Johnson

—Robinson misses this—is an important rhetorical weapon (compare the prose of the literature put out by the Church of Scientology); it softens up the half-educated public who are grown accustomed to the idea that what is important and improving is always framed in obscure incantatory prose, whose passion for "meaningful communication," "new values," "new parameters of significance," is a kind of intellectual masochism, so that when something intelligible does come through it is embraced with sobbing relief.[3]

But do not social scientists report what they actually see and hear, regardless of the church in which they worship? Are they not clearly different in this respect from poets and fiction writers, who create their characters from a broth of personalities who ride the subways, hold forth in saloons, play golf in retirement villages, pick cotton in the summer? Is not the social scientist a dispassionate observer, and the creative writer an inventor, the one a photographer and the other a painter at the side of the road of the moving pageant of history? The social scientist seeks out the prototype, the writer the protagonist; the social scientist takes pains to drive out the very imaginative powers without which the writer cannot find his voice. Indeed, is it not true that the aim of the social scientist would be death to literature--that is, to "do a study" so precisely that anyone could follow in his steps and duplicate his "findings"? In writing a description of his work, the social scientist addresses himself to a public that will presumably judge the worth of his endeavors in terms of how well they could be replicated. There is literary writing, and there is scientific writing. In *The Ascent of Man*, J. Bronowski refers to "two clear differences between a work of art and a scientific paper." One of these, he says, is that "in the work of art the painter is visibly taking the world to pieces and putting it together on the same canvas. And the other is that you can watch him thinking while he is doing it." The scientific paper is often deficient in these respects: "It often is only analytic; and it almost always hides the process of thought in its impersonal language."[4]

Ultimately, however, the distinction between artistic and scientific endeavor is arbitrary and spurious—as Bronowski's own work so eloquently discloses. The crystal and the molecule, the spinning earth, the leaf moving in the wind are rightful subjects for both poet and naturalist: artist and scientist are not two beings, but one. When one reflects that David Rothman's *The Discovery of the Asylum*,[5] Erving Goffman's *Asylums*,[6] and Ken Kesey's *One Flew Over the Cuckoo's Nest*[7] are meditations on three faces of the same prism, that they represent three very gifted sensibilities—the historian's, the social psychologist's, and the creative writer's—brought to bear on the same "phenomena," one recognizes that Truth is many-faceted and protean, that no one tradition can claim it, that there is no last word on any subject. The walls between disciplines, between traditions, have, after all, been built by mortals. Perhaps in our own time there is a growing impatience with the light that has been shut out by their presence.

Witnesses from various fields and traditions have this in common, that they must work both inward and outward from appearances. For the writer—essayist and journalist, poet and playwright, short-story writer and novelist—as well as for the social scientist, the paths to the minds of others are well hidden. All have the same task before them: to chart a course to the inner world and to find the way back again. Throughout this enterprise, the witness must recognize and in some way account for the effect of his own presence upon that which he observes. And he is lost if he does not know from the beginning that words deceive at least as often as they reveal the truth. So do gestures and expressions and actions. All are appearances, masks that conceal, as often as mirrors that reflect the inner world. The witness must go in back of what people say and do, and around and under their words and activities; he must penetrate what philosopher Alfred Schuetz called "the-world-taken-for-granted," if he is to understand his subject's inner life.

The creative writer does this through the exercise of the literary imagination; he puts himself in the place of the other. Yet he does not surrender himself completely, because to do this is a sacrifice of one's art. The social scientist does the same thing through "participant observation." In his *Argonauts of the Western Pacific*, Malinowski wrote of the need for both the intimate and the structural aspects of life in a native community to be included in an ethnographic report:

> ... there is a series of phenomena of great importance which cannot possibly be recorded by questioning or computing documents, but have to be observed in their full actuality. Let us call them *the imponderabilia of actual life.* Here belong such things as the routine of a man's working day, the details of his care of the body, of the manner of taking food and preparing it; the tone of conversational and social life around the village fires, the existence of strong friendships or hostilities, and of passing sympathies and dislikes between people; the subtle yet unmistakable manner in which personal vanities and ambitions are reflected in the behaviour of the individual and in the emotional reactions of those who surround him. All these facts can and ought to be scientifically formulated and recorded, but it is necessary that this be done, not by a superficial registration of details, as is usually done by untrained observers, but with an effort at penetrating the mental attitude expressed in them.[8]

The social scientist must grasp the native's point of view, must reach for an understanding of the native's vision of the world. As a participant observer, Hortense Powdermaker writes, the anthropologist immerses himself in the culture in an effort to see, to feel, to think as a native would. Yet at the same time, he keeps part of himself, of his awareness, apart. "This is the heart of the participant observation method—involvement and detachment," Powdermaker says. "Its practice is both an art and a science."[9]

The sociologist must walk even more softly than the anthropologist: when one is in home territory, one assumes too readily that one is already familiar with the language, the folkways, the ceremonial round. The likelihood is very great that one may find what one is looking for, and miss what one does not expect or imagine or *want* to be there. The social scientist must take great care in phrasing questions so that the answers to them are not foreordained. He must be ever alert to the possibility that the news he brings from other worlds is not a report of what it was intended that he see and hear while visiting there. Whereas in literature the imagination is a central power, in social science it is suspect—a power to be subjected to "controls." Though both writer and social scientist serve as witnesses, their approaches to the task are quite distinctive. When the social scientist wants to find out about something, he asks questions of others. When the writer wants to find out about something, he asks questions of himself. He makes believe in order to make true.

As witness, it is the task of the social scientist to deal scientifically with nonscientific matters. The American anthropologist Clyde Kluckhohn referred to subjectivity as a *problem*, and recommended both "longitudinal and transverse methods" of research, interviews about both past and present, and multiple techniques used by multiple observers, all to cope with it. He warned:

Until anthropologists *can* deal rigorously with the "subjective factors" in the lives of "primitives" their work will be flat and insubstantial. Unless they can learn to delineate the emotional structure of societies, serious persons who wish to learn about the life of human beings in groups will properly continue to turn to literature rather than to science for enlightenment.[10]

The social scientist must report the "data" as they are actually experienced, Kluckhohn instructed; the ideal would be sound moving pictures that recorded "not only everything which informants, interpreters, and investigators said, but also all their motor activities during the interviews." Short of this, "the English words" should be "printed exactly as they were transcribed."[11]

All through his labors, the social scientist must count on the effect of his very presence on what is said and on what happens during the research study. Surveys, questionnaires, interviews, and participant observation studies all have a very human consequence. That is, once a person knows that he is being observed, that he has been singled out for an interview or for a study, he cannot help but make some adjustments in the way that he appears before others. Kluckhohn acknowledged this, that a person will be influenced by his attitude toward the researcher. There is always the strong temptation to dramatize one's life, to turn a situation of participant observation into theater, to *perform* for the social scientist. A research situation is, among many other things, an opportunity for self-aggrandizement or self-pity. Cameras, microphones, tape recorders all arouse the awareness of being noticed by others. What is natural and spontaneous is easily lost. At the very least, when one accepts the social scientist's invitation to tell his own story, he begins the gradual transformation that every research subject undergoes to some extent: he becomes a social scientist himself. Opening his life to inspection, he cannot but collaborate somewhat in self-appraisal and self-analysis. The social scientific enterprise is therefore always moral, because people are changed by the very fact that they have been discovered by researchers.

How much of another's story can the reader believe? *The Addict in the Street* is a useful document to consult in search of an answer to this question. This book is a collection of first-person stories of heroin addicts, gathered over a period of seven years with the tape recorder by Ralph Tefferteller, associate director of Henry Street Settlement. In the introduction, Jeremy Larner writes that the junkie has an urge to talk, to "verbalize," and that in each of the accounts in this book there is a hiatus between the self-portrait he offers and the actual life he leads. "Almost always," Larner observes, "the urgent flow of words enforces an utter separation between thought and actuality. The compulsive re-telling of their stories leads not to self-understanding but to rigid isolation."[12] The addict is "an indefatigable moralizer. The only trouble is, he uses his moral invention to obscure the reality of his desires. No matter what happens, it turns out that he is doing his best but fate is against him. He is right and the others are wrong." The story of Carmen Sanchez, the only woman addict portrayed in this book, illustrates this very clearly, according to Larner. He says that she presents a story of "demonic self-destruction" through her gifts of narration, that she went to every extreme to "embrace her downfall." Even so,

> after she has left school, brilliantly arranged her own seduction, run away from home, gotten herself with child four times, taken up drugs, returned again and again to her addicted husband, betrayed him with other men, gotten herself arrested, run away from Lexington and undone her cure, lost custody of her children, estranged and embarrassed her parents, turned to mugging, hold-ups, homosexuality, prostitution—after all this, she still describes each and every situation with absolute moral self-vindication. She was good, every time, and someone else did her bad.[13]

In an effort to control any biases that the listener—the transcriber—might introduce into the story-telling, Larner used certain devices so that the accounts would be presented in the distinctive styles of speech in which they were given. There are phonetic spellings of words from time to time, and the effect that is desired is that the reader will hear the accents in reading the words. Wherever they did not seem to interfere with clarity, grammatical errors were retained. The reader, so to speak, supplies his own "sic" from time to time, rather than having the social scientist or interpreter do this for him. Nor does he need the interruptions of the free flow of talk, apparently; he is left to make his own interpretations of the stories. This is "pure" reporting. The stories are indistinguishable from those that might be "told" by a fiction writer who relies on his ear and his imagination in inventing that which the social scientist and the journalist record.

It is interesting that Larner has found that heroin addicts use the jargon of sociology and psychology to explain, and even to justify, their addiction. "I would conclude," Larner remarks, "either that heroin, like travel, is broadening, or that jargon has penetrated to the very bottom of metropolitan society."[14] Larner's comment touches upon an interesting point. It is not only with the effect of his immediate presence that the social scientist must reckon; it is the very existence of the social sciences that must be taken into account when one weighs the words of first-person stories, when one tries to determine what might be made of what one sees and hears. In a strange way, social science has invented its own subjects: we guess at connections between social circumstance and consciousness, and convince others of the truth of these things even as—or perhaps even before—we convince ourselves. One does not have to be an ideologue to create one's own data: this can happen quite innocently. In an essay on American folk songs, W. Edson Richmond cites a story he found in Howard Odum's *The Negro and His Songs*, of a university dean who was sitting on a stone wall in front of his house, taking down the words of a song that the members of a road gang were singing. After a time, the dean became aware of just what it was that he was "transcribing"—

White man settin' on wall,
White man settin' on wall,
White man settin' on wall all day long,
Wastin' his time, wastin' his time.

These words were composed at that moment; they had come to life in that time and place, "and were an appropriate comment on an immediate situation, preserved by the same accident which created them."[15] Whether like this hapless dean, who all unwittingly was making his own "findings" come into being, or like a nearsighted observer who is all too literal-minded, the social scientist who is free of prejudice might commit errors, just as his doctrinaire colleague surely will. The skilled interviewer is aware of how easy it is to bring people to say, and perhaps even to think, what one wants to hear. Truth is relative to the eye and ear of the observer, always. The trick is to turn this fatal flaw to social scientific, or to literary, advantage.

The most faithful transcription, the most detailed documentary must be edited *some*where. Indeed, it was the *lack* of editing, the insistence upon including all the minutiae of day-to-day living, that was made the basis of some of the criticisms of the televised documentary of the Loud family. Virtually everything was included: the viewer yawned and drowsed through interminable nonepisodes, sucked down into a bog of domestic triviality. Of course, it is in the editing that the writer conceals and reveals his own predilections, in deciding what is to be included, and what may be left out. This is the "documentary method of interpretation" as Karl Mannheim called it: a variety of meanings are traced to a common underlying pattern. This is what the guessing of the social scientist is all about, when he reads meaning into what his "informant" tells him, and then reads meaning *out* of this into his reports. His findings, then, ought to be called *reasonable* findings, as the ethnomethodologist Garfinkel observes, although they are often presented as though they are free of interpretation.[16]

"Editing" covers a multitude of sins of interjection of opinion and attitude, Garfinkel suggests, and the exercise of judgment should be acknowledged in the presentation of research findings. When the social scientist makes a choice of subject—and of subjects—he is editing, just as he edits when he chooses his method of study. Whatever his reasons (and they were presumably excellent), Oscar Lewis chose the Sanchez family members as subjects of his first-person narrative account of the culture of poverty in Mexico City. The readers' understanding of the lives of the poor is filtered through the immediacy and individuality of each of the "children of Sanchez" and of their father, Jesus. It is not just *any* anthropologist who could have persuaded Consuelo and Manuel, Roberto and Marta, as well as their father, to speak as frankly and fully of their lives as they did to Lewis. This was his gift; he was *simpático*; he could establish and sustain rapport with them. Though he asked hundreds of questions in his interviews with them, Lewis says that he chose to eliminate his questions and to organize all that the members of the Sanchez family told him into the form of life stories. "If one agrees with Henry James that life is all inclusion and confusion while art is all discrimination and selection," he writes, "then these life histories have something of both art and life." It was his belief that this mode of presentation did not reduce either "the authenticity of the data or their usefulness for science."[17]

Each person sees the world in a unique way. For justice to be done (and Lewis himself seriously proposed this), each person should be invited to tell his own story, to write his own autobiography. Indeed, writer Joyce Carol Oates once said that everyone should write his or her own novel. (How four billion titles could be published, distributed, and read—this is another matter!) Ultimately, of course, there would have to be selection. No social scientist would find it meaningful to go on indefinitely, inviting people to talk about their lives and publishing countless transcriptions from tape of first-person stories. No matter how democratic, the social scientist cannot help but acknowledge that some people are more disposed to talk about their lives, their worlds than others are. And these are not always the same people as those who are articulate and knowledgeable.

The sociologist, C. Wright Mills maintained, is concerned with the ways in which biography intersects with history.[18] However, some historical moments, like some individuals, are more interesting than others, more eventful . . . ; there are women and men whose lives reveal what Jan Kott calls the "historical destiny of man." Tadeusz Borowski's was such a life. It not only belongs to the history of literature, Kott says, but it is literature in itself. It contains within itself the existential experience:

There are years and places, sometimes whole decades and entire nations, in which history reveals its menace and destructive force with particular clarity. These are *chosen* nations, in the same sense in which the Bible calls the Jews a *chosen* people. In such places and years history is . . . "let off the leash." It is then that individual human destiny seems as if shaped directly by history, becoming only a chapter in it.[19]

If the writer cannot find such a person, or fragments of such a person in many people, he invents him. This the social scientist cannot do. Nor does it seem likely that the social scientist could come upon someone like Borowski so long as he is engaged in the quest for Quetelet's phantom, the "average" person.

Kluckhohn wrote of the difficulties he and his associates encountered in their efforts to obtain satisfying life histories from "average" people. "There is something to the view that happy individuals, like happy nations, have no histories," he remarked, adding that, "at least they feel themselves to have none." In contrast to this are people who feel that they have led a tragic life, or who feel that they have been misunderstood, or who are in search of an audience. There are also those who think that they have led an unusually adventurous or accomplished life, and who are proud of their history. None of these, however, is an "average" person, Kluckhohn wrote. He felt that it is highly probable "that the relatively well adjusted person is less likely to be obtained as an informant and less likely to be motivated to continue through many long sessions."[20]

These considerations are as weighty today as they were thirty years ago, when the discussions by Gottschalk, Kluckhohn, and Angell of the use of personal documents in social science were first published. In *Why Survive? Being Old in America*, a book that was awarded the Pulitzer Prize, geriatric psychiatrist and newly appointed director of the National Institute of Aging, Dr. Robert Butler, suggests that it would be of great value "to have a Division of Memoirs within the National Archives to support the collection of the memoirs of both distinguished Americans and people from every walk of life about historically important aspects of American life." There should be an effort, Butler writes, to preserve the "recollections of the elders of various racial and ethnic groups" in the United States.[21] Initiated by the late Allan Nevins, among other historians, the Oral History Research Office of Columbia University was established in the late 1940s. Since that time, the United States, together with at least fifteen other countries, has experienced what may be called an oral history movement. It has been estimated that in 1977 there were about 600 oral history projects in America, and the Oral History Association, formed late in 1966, had an active membership of 1,300 persons within a decade.[22] In a review of oral history projects, John Stewart, who is assistant director of the John F. Kennedy Library in Waltham, Massachusetts, mentions the sensitivity of oral historians to the criticism "that mountains of trivia are being accumulated that will never be of use to anyone." While this would be difficult to prove, Stewart says, "the nagging doubt remains that many of these recorded memoirs are not worth preserving and that the implied value of some of these meticulously footnote [sic], bound and often microfilmed transcripts is grossly exaggerated" by those who collect them.[23] It appears that oral historians must cope with the same problems—selection of subjects, sifting of materials—as those that confront their colleagues who work with the written documents, the memoirs, letters, and diaries that it was the custom to keep in an earlier day. What is inescapable is that not everyone is inclined to reminisce, and that all too often those who are so inclined have material to offer that is too limited or extraneous to be of much value for a specific social science research project. The "subjects" of social scientific research are always selected; even if selection is random, they are drawn from some predefined social universe.

And what they have to say is always influenced to some extent by the time and place of the research. Finally, there must be interpretation of their testimony. Even Kinsey's subjects were selected, in that they were people who happened to come in contact with Kinsey and his associates and who were willing to talk about their sex lives. (Kinsey referred to them as "volunteer subjects.") One does not have to go as far as Mencken, who is said to have remarked that Kinsey's research confirmed what he always suspected, namely, that people lie about their sex lives. It is apparent that even the most spontaneous study is based upon selected remarks of selected subjects.

There are instances, though they are unusual, in social scientific research, in which the "deviant" or extreme case is deliberately chosen for study. But in most cases, a fundamental principle guiding the selection of subjects is their typicality. The social scientist searches for embodiments of social categories, for people whose circumstances and perspectives may be representative of the condition and world-view of a collectivity. Now, however tentative his study may be in the beginning, however playfully curious his attitude may be, the social scientist presupposes what moves people, and what lies behind events. He begins with appearances (what one says, how one votes, what one's marital status is, or one's criminal record or spending habits) and moves inward and outward, stitching together the predispositions and convictions, the desires and fears of inner life with the actions and interactions of the ever-changing social scene. He thinks of his subject as a creature of certain forces playing within him and upon him. There is an embarrassment of riches of these forces in the pantheon of the social sciences: the libido, the superego, guilt and aggression and fear; the will-to-power, the death wish, the profit motive; the hedonistic calculus, whether set to work in the marketplace, the polling booth, or in response to the temptation to rape or to rob, to commit murder or incest. This way of thinking, in which the human being is seen as a medium through whom the forces play, is common to psychology and psychoanalysis, to economics and political science, and to sociology. Indeed, the quarrels between representatives of the separate disciplines have to do not with the existence or nonexistence of these forces, but with the hierarchy in which they are arranged. In writings in anthropology and sociology, people are depicted as creatures of cultural systems or forces, of the social system with its functions and dysfunctions, its stratificatory scheme, its organization; from the determinist's perspective we are products, we are playthings of these gods.

The creative writer, too, has his persuasion, his point of view; he has his demons. He, too, witnesses; he waits and watches and listens. But unless he is convinced of the truth of a particular doctrine, he works with the awareness that each of us is an arena within whom these forces are locked in combat or an uneasy slumber. He sees a character as a broth of sense and nonsense, of rational thought and of emotion, of courage and cowardice, nobility and pettiness, beauty and deformity. The more effectively the writer can conjure up before us someone who is a thinking, feeling being, the more disposed we are to believe in him. The more stereotyped the character, the more aware we are that the writer sees him from the outside only, and thus that his work is a form of argument and not of the creative imagination.

Like the writer, the social scientist does not take the position of advocate—at least not openly, not officially. When we open a book written on the subject of some social type—juvenile delinquents or blue-collar workers, working women or "mother-centered families," black students or the urban poor, or an occupational study of firemen or waitresses—we are certain to be informed in an introduction or preface of the measures the social scientist has taken to ensure that what he is telling us is actually the case. He writes of the efforts he has made to neutralize his presence during the study. The controls he imposes upon himself are means by which he surrenders himself to the consciousness of his subjects. The more completely he effaces himself, the more fully he *becomes* those he is studying, the more faithful is his account. Still, he works at the mercy of his own concepts; and if he is not to find only what he began by looking for, his concepts must give way before the reality. "The longer I know this man," Robert Coles writes of one of the working people he had been studying for over a decade, "the more I hear him talk, the harder it is for me to call him this or that, and in so doing feel halfway responsive to the ironies and ambiguities and inconsistencies that I hear in his words and . . . see expressed in his everyday deeds."[24] In his remarkable paper, Coles shows us how conceptual categories—white racists, the authoritarian personality, the "one dimensional man" whose mind is held captive by "advanced industrial culture," collectivities marked off from one another by "types" of mentalities—obscure and even misrepresent the winding workings of the mind, its intricacy, its unexpected turns, its astonishing contrariness.

Human beings *act*, George Herbert Mead instructed, not merely *re*act. People observe and interpret and define; they accept or reject; they make judgments; they make indications to themselves in a social context. The Self is not a static thing, an object to be dissected for its fateful secrets, but a "process" ever moving, ever changing. We respond to others, not directly to the "stimuli" of others' words and actions, but to the meanings with which we endow them. Our relationships to others are mediated through symbols, through shared meanings; and this is what makes society possible. In Mead's teaching (and here he was in company with John Dewey and William James) we act upon the world; we confer meanings upon things; we shape our activities. Our Self, and therefore the world in which we move and act, is forever coming into being. In reflecting upon Mead's philosophy, the words of Roethke's "The Waking" come to mind:

I wake to sleep, and take my waking slow.
I learn by going where I have to go.[25]

Mead's philosophy does not inform the writings of sociologists outside the school of Symbolic Interaction. Indeed, in an essay on "Society as Symbolic Interaction," Herbert Blumer contends that most sociological views of society are deterministic, and thus at variance with Mead's teaching. Rather than seeing human societies as made up of people who have selves, Blumer writes, most sociologists "assume human beings to be merely organisms with some kind of organization, responding to forces which play upon them." The forces of status or role, social class or institution, whatever, play upon us and through us. We only imagine that we are the authors of our acts, so far as the social determinist is concerned. However, if we are to understand the actions of people, Blumer contends, we must "catch the process of interpretation through which they construct their actions." We cannot do this by arguing for the existence and power of antecedent conditions or forces; we can only catch this *process* by taking the role of the acting unit we want to understand. We must see the process from his perspective. If we remain aloof, playing the part of the objective observer, "refusing to take the role of the acting unit is to risk the worst kind of subjectivism": we will probably do our subject's interpreting *for* him.[26] This is not only unscientific; it is a violation of professional ethics. For to do this is to present oneself in the guise of presenting another person.

It is precisely this insistence upon the primacy of a view of people as thinking and feeling and acting beings, this recognition that people cannot be identified with abstract social categories without having their very humanity taken from them, that brings the symbolic interactionist very close in perspective to that of many creative writers . . . and very far from that of his determinist colleagues. For, if all that we say and do, all that we think and feel, is foreordained, and of necessity, then there are no stories to tell, no novels to write, but, rather, only descriptions of the interiors of our prisons in history and society. And philosophy, in the form of consolations.

The social scientist ought to attempt to understand the assessments of their situations that other people make, and their interpretations of their lives, without imposing his own preconceptions and point of view upon them. For many a creative writer, too, the subjects speak for themselves; but they speak *through him*. A creative writer might dismember a character; he might, as Proust did, create a character who is a composite of many beings. He might invent a character out of the cloth of his imagination if he feels that such a person *should* be in that place at that time. The writer reads minds, puts words in people's mouths and feelings in their breasts, fills them out from within, reaches around appearances. For the social scientist, this is license, the taking of outrageous liberties. For the writer, this is a natural exercise of the literary gift. Yet both, coming around by way of different paths, perform the art of interpretation. Writing of his ten years of field work as a child psychiatrist in both the North and the South, among Appalachian, migrant farm, and ghetto families, Robert Coles speaks with sensitivity of how he has interwoven literary and social scientific insights:

I have learned to question a number of medical and psychiatric tenets I had never before doubted. I have learned to give "ordinary" people more credit for courage, guile, discretion and, yes, those "higher things" like sensibility, restraint, tact, generosity. I have learned to draw upon a book like Ellison's *Invisible Man* instead of a book called *The Mark of Oppression* . . . . I have learned that one does not have to be a political or social or philosophical "romantic" to comprehend and appreciate the kind of truth that binds a Faulkner to a Tolstoy, an Agee to a Bernanos, a Simon[e] Weil to an Orwell. I think that more than anything else I have learned to *know* what social scientists know, but *see* what a Eudora Welty, a Flannery O'Connor, a Richard Wright, a Robert Penn Warren, a Walker Percy demand and suggest and hint and urge one like me to see. What a far from tragic poet has called "the things of this world" defies all categories, man-made and inborn.[27]

The significance of art, Helen Vendler writes, is basically nonreferential, even though art may refer to many subjects. In reviewing Coles's book on William Carlos Williams, Vendler says that Coles uses Williams to conduct crusades of Coles's own, "setting himself (by implication) and Williams up as defenders of the mute forgotten folk ignored by intellectuals in the ivory tower and shrinks in the air-conditioned office." Williams himself had said in his essays, Vendler recalls, that art "is not a dray horse carrying something for an alien purpose." But Coles, she maintains, is using literature as a critical measure of his own discipline:

. . . in taking Williams as a prop to bolster his theories of art, psychiatric practice, and social attitudes, Coles is simply transforming literature into a vehicle for his own propaganda. Coles misapprehends, as do other "interdisciplinary" users of literature for their own ends, the many functions of art—functions of pleasure, vicarious experience, imaginative reconciliation, fantasy, escape, and so on. He thinks that if you are poor you want to read about the poor.[28]

Williams knew, Vendler writes, that the poor more often want deliverance from a preoccupation with their condition. Only one of the purposes of art, Vendler reminds us, and, at that, one of its lesser purposes, is mimetic.

Though no one is in a position to speak with authority on what the final purpose of either art or social science may be, it is clear that there is a tension, sometimes even a clear conflict, between engagement in literary and social scientific work. In a review of the film critic Pauline Kael's book *Reeling*, Richard Gilman says that he finds himself wincing "at her blindness to how imagination works or ought to." The dialogue in the film *Shampoo*, he remarks, is not transcribed but created. Fiction, whether in film or in any other form of art, "is, or . . . ought to be, an increment to experience not a mirroring." Gilman writes that he does not go to the movies to find what the "real" psyche or voice of a Los Angeles hairdresser is: "the truth of any art . . . lies in itself, not in its fidelity to the various surfaces of the world."[29] Though there are writers who would not agree with this distinction, many would. And many social scientists would agree that the truth of *their* work lies in its fidelity to the surfaces of the world.

Yet distinctions and resolutions are always much more clear in theory than in practice. Writers and social scientists alike must wrestle with the same demons. No witness can be completely separated from that which is witnessed. The "surfaces of the world," as Machiavelli noticed long ago, are deceptive. And human nature is intricate and protean. In his preface to Malinowski's *Argonauts of the Western Pacific*, James Frazer praises Malinowski for seeing man "in the round and not in the flat," for appreciating that man is a creature of emotion as well as a creature of reason. Not only scientists, but writers as well, Frazer remarks, are too quick to make abstractions:

The man of science, like the man of letters, is too apt to view mankind only in the abstract, selecting for his consideration a single side of our complex and many-sided being. Of this one-sided treatment Molière is a conspicuous example among great writers. All his characters are seen only in the flat: one of them is a miser, another a hypocrite, another a coxcomb . . . not one of them is a man. All are dummies dressed up to look very like human beings; but the likeness is only on the surface, all within is hollow and empty, because truth to nature has been sacrificed to literary effect. Very different is the presentation of human nature in the greater artists, such as Cervantes and Shakespeare: their characters are solid, being drawn not from one side only but from many.[30]

Literature celebrates life; social science seeks to understand and explain it. Yet, in the finest works of social science and of literature, all three are achieved.

Unless he masquerades as one of the people he is studying, the social scientist must find some way to engage their cooperation, or at the very least their tolerance of his presence. "Field work by its very nature is at heart a collaborative enterprise," Casagrande writes. One must be bold, to "come as an inquisitive stranger to live among an alien people . . . . At the very least the anthropologist's presence on the scene must be condoned and his impertinences suffered." However, the anthropologist needs more than this; he needs people's active cooperation.[31] What has the social scientist to offer in return for revelations of the subject's life, for baring one's circumstances and thoughts? How are people persuaded to become "subjects"? There are a number of devices that social scientists might use. Kluckhohn mentioned appeals to pride and *amour-propre*, the giving of gifts, the offering of rides in a car or of writing letters or interceding for the person with a court or Indian Service officials. He also suggested the swapping of anecdotes.[32] In his study of aging among the Highland Maya living in Chiapas, the psychologist David Gutmann invited his "respondents" to interview *him*. In turning the social science tables on himself, he promised that he would be as candid in his answers as he counted on them to be.[33] In some cases, the subjects are told a likely (or unlikely) story about the objectives of the research. In still others, the social scientist impersonates someone. Or he reveals his purposes gradually, allowing people's curiosity about him to lead the way. In the very decision that is made about explaining his presence, the observer weaves himself into that which is observed.

A collection of anecdotes about the adventures and misadventures by which cooperation is won in field research has yet to be gathered together.[34] There are many reasons why people choose to work *with*, rather than *against*, the social scientist. Kluckhohn reported that he knew Indians who genuinely wanted whites to "know the truth, not some of those lies about us that are in books." An anthropologist might, therefore, appeal to tribal honor. There is also personal vanity to be considered, although for non-Western people, Kluckhohn observed, "personal immortality through the printed word seldom has the place it occupies" in Western societies. (On the other hand, there is compensatory advantage, in that, while Europeans may withhold important facts for fear of bringing embarrassment to their families, people in nonliterate societies are not concerned about the possibility that what they disclose may become common knowledge among their people.)[35] It is this need "to leave something behind, to give a little gift, to create an illusion of immortality" to which Elisabeth Kübler-Ross appeals when she talks with dying patients. She writes:

We acknowledge our appreciation for their sharing with us their thoughts about this taboo topic, we tell them that their role is to *teach* us, to help those who follow them later on, thus creating an idea that something will live perhaps after their death, an idea, a seminar in which their . . . fantasies, their thoughts continue to live, . . . become immortal in a little way.[36]

A social scientist may sometimes count on this, too: that, like the Indians Kluckhohn referred to, there are people who think that the attitudes and opinions about social issues and social problems presented in the media are distortions of reality. These people may welcome the opportunity the social scientist offers them when he requests their cooperation in a study, in order to correct what they believe to be misrepresentations of public opinion.

Yet for all that, the very suggestion that one's views might be made public will repel certain people just as it will attract others. Research is always in some measure an invasion of privacy. Like the anthropologist's natives, certain people in the United States today—the very poor, or victims of a disaster, or the recently bereaved or divorced, for example—may feel demeaned or offended by the suggestion that they reveal their feelings, open their lives to a team of researchers, and, through them, to unknown publics. To the vulnerable or the sensitive, an interview is an interrogation, and a study is a violation of one's right to privacy as well as of one's sense of dignity. Kluckhohn made an interesting point in remarking that in nonliterate societies, the subject need not fear that what he says will become known to others in the community, since they will never read the anthropologist's book. Kluckhohn suggested that the fact that the field worker is, in part, a stranger might be capitalized upon. But the social scientist cannot offer this protective anonymity to those living in contemporary society.

It may be that, given the way so many are behaving lately, we are inclined to assume that everyone is prepared to be an exhibitionist. One's ears are so dinned by the shrill voices of those of every persuasion. And there seems to be another debut, another "coming out" on the part of someone of this or that social category every day. It is easy to forget that there are those who have the gift of silence. But there are reserved people; there have always been. And those who "speak out" should not be taken as representative of the population. Some people have no interest in social science, or even think that it is in some way subversive. Some may not be in the mood to cooperate in a study because they are preoccupied with personal problems. Others distrust anyone they do not know, or are paranoid or very secretive by nature. Whatever the reasons may be for refusal to become involved, the fact remains that *all* research findings are prejudiced somewhat because of the absence of certain people. Too often, this is airily dismissed by a statistical statement about the percentage of returns from a sample.[37]

A study in social science is always a testing of certain notions against the sayings and doings of particular people living in particular places at particular moments in time. And, without this individuality, the documents and testimony would be lifeless. It is through particular people that one reaches for the universal; individuals are the medium, and they lead (or mislead) the way. Those who refuse to participate in research must be taken into account—those who did not fill in the boxes on the questionnaire, those who did not consent to grant an interview, those who remained in the shadows while a participant observation study was underway. Even if volunteer subjects do speak honestly, they can never be presumed to be speaking for those who elect to remain silent.

There is another reason why the truths of research should not be taken to be unassailable. That is the fact, for which we can be everlastingly grateful, that there are no means by which people's stories about themselves can be absolutely verified. All oral testimony, all first-person narratives, are appearances. When the late Jules Henry set out to study five families in which a child had become emotionally ill, he took care to observe them directly "in their native habitat, going about their usual business." He had his own room in the Rosenbergs' house, where he lived for a week. When studying the Jones, Metz, and Wilson families, he arrived at breakfast time every morning, and did not leave until bedtime. And a student, "Susan," stayed through the day at the Keen home. Henry contended that experimental studies of human behavior are artifical, and wrote that because of this they repelled him. They divorce human behavior from its surroundings, he maintained, and therefore render it meaningless. "I require the actuality of . . . the 'existential human being' as he lives his real life," Henry declared. "I have to see *that person* before me; and what I cannot see as *that actuality*, what I cannot hear as the sound of *that voice*, has little interest for me. Human life fills me with a wild, intoxicated curiosity."[38]

Henry evinced a strong skepticism of fixed response as well as of open-ended surveys and of statistical studies. His witnessing is of extraordinary value because of his "wild, intoxicated curiosity," because he looked through appearances. In his chapter on the Jones family, he wrote that Mrs. Jones was "too miserable to tell the truth" when she gave him her case history. Therefore, "she had to describe their relationship as good. *Thus direct observation contradicts twelve hours of interview.*"[39] When writing of the Metz family, he tells the story of a visit by Mrs. Metz's son, reconstructing it from his notes in order to show the reader the contrast between her play-acting and her actual relationship to her son. He says that he took care to allow us to see how he himself was taken in by Mrs. Metz, convinced of her love for Albert because of her successful performance as a loving mother. But when she can no longer control her hostility, "the scenery folds, the houselights go up," and she stands before us "without make-up or costume, in the ordinary clothes of a mother who cannot stand her child." There is nothing in his notes, Henry remarks, that gives "any more convincing proof of the value of firsthand observation."[40] No questionnaire or interview could possibly disclose that which was revealed through Henry's keen participant observation: the rough-housing between the Jones boys and their father . . . the gory nursery tales and bedtime songs Dr. Jones told and sang for his sons . . . the meaning of soda pop in the relationship between Irving Rosenberg and his mother . . . the canned peas Mrs. Rosenberg was forever serving up (she "was marooned in a sea of packaged soup, trapped in a can of peas!").

The witness must pierce the veil of testimony to achieve understanding. Like the creative writer's, the social scientist's eyes and ears are informed by an awareness that transcends even as it encompasses what is immediate and given. Henry brought all that he had learned from his training as an anthropologist to bear on what he observed in the daily round of these families' lives. In his detailed discussion of food, he showed how food is used in expressing pathological relationships within the family. Particular instances brought to mind the universal: he discussed his findings in terms of the "configuration of eating" in the United States. He wrote of the "doctrine of fluids"—which fluids may be mixed, and which may not—and the "doctrine of bodily positions" at the table, and the "doctrine of quantity" as it is applied to the partaking of meals. He reminded his readers that it is taboo, so far as middle-class norms are concerned, to put food directly on the table. Indeed, he suggested that the measure of the significance of the occasion, or of social status itself, may be the frequency with which food is put directly on the table: "To put one's bread on the table is, perhaps, pardonable, to do it with corn on the cob is outrageous, but to deliberately pour milk on it is unthinkable."[41]

The Germans say, *Am Tische scheiden sich die Klassen*. What happens at mealtime is always telling, and reveals far more than distinctions made between social classes. These are matters about which little can be learned through interviews; one must break bread with others to know what, in fact, does take place. But participant observation is not enough; one must have a grasp of the symbolic significance of actions and words if one wants to make what one has observed meaningful for others. Like the writer, the symbolic interactionist perceives the universal in the particular. On "Ward B" in the public mental hospital where he was a participant observer, Erving Goffman writes that bad demeanor, as this would be measured by middle-class standards, was very common. He describes how a patient might snatch at extra food, and how patients would take all their share at one time instead of waiting until they had eaten a serving of food. There were occasions when a patient appeared at the table half-dressed; "One . . . frequently belched loudly at meals and was occasionally flatulent . . . . Swearing and cursing were common . . . . Loud sounds were sometimes made by sucking on straws in empty pop bottles."[42] Such behavior ought to be studied, Goffman suggests, if we are to learn what it is that we take for granted in the way of *good* demeanor.

Social scientists and writers alike are foragers, engaged in an unending search for the reasons why people act and think and feel as they do. There are fragments of research reports that read much like an excerpt from a drama or a short story, and in reading them one appreciates how many gifts are shared in common by both social researcher and artist: curiosity, intellectual alacrity, a sharp eye, a keen ear. In his essay on the forging of a self-image in a "Negro lower-class family," Lee Rainwater finds that family arguments are a key, perhaps even a master key, to the understanding of how the personality is shaped. In his report of this research, which was part of a broad community study that included participant observation and interviewing of the residents of the Pruitt-Igoe housing projects in St. Louis, Rainwater writes that "As the child tries on identities, *announces* them, the family sits as judge of his pretensions. Family members are both the most important judges and the most critical ones."[43] Rainwater shows how the dynamics of socialization are revealed in quarrels. He narrates a bitter argument, and discusses the themes appearing in it that dominate identity problems in Negro slum culture:

The argument represents vicious unmasking of the individual members' pretenses to being competent individuals. The efforts of the two girls to present themselves as masters of their own fate are unmasked by the mother. The girls in turn unmask the pretensions of the mother and of their two brothers. When the thirteen-year-old daughter expresses some amusement they turn on her, telling her that it won't be long before she too becomes pregnant. Each member of the family in turn is told that he can expect to be no more than a victim of his world, but that this is somehow inevitably his own fault . . . . in Negro slum culture growing up involves an ever-increasing appreciation of one's shortcomings, of the impossibility of finding a self-sufficient and gratifying way of living. It is in the family first and most devastatingly that one learns these lessons. As the child's sense of frustration builds he too can strike out and unmask the pretensions of others. The result is a peculiar strength and a pervasive weakness . . . . Family members become potential enemies to each other . . . .[44]

Social scientists are very explicit about the reasons why a particular place and particular people were chosen as a site and subjects for research. E. E. Le Masters, for example, writes of his study of his conversations with about fifty men and women, regular patrons of "The Oasis" tavern in the Midwest:

. . . it would be difficult to find a more interesting community than Lakeside. All of the problems facing America are facing Lakeside—pollution of their beautiful lake, white-collar invasion of their blue-collar town, drugs in the local high school, rising taxes, urban sprawl, the war in Indochina, inflation, the revolt of youth, the desire of women for a better deal . . . . The tavern is a good vantage point from which to study these problems.[45]

Sometimes a social scientist, like a writer, finds a place and people near at hand. But there are occasions when the researcher goes to great lengths to research a problem or an issue. Robert Buckingham, a medical anthropologist and director of research for the New Haven Hospice, had his cousin bring him to the emergency room of the Royal Victoria Hospital in Montreal as a young man (under an assumed name) who was said to be dying of cancer of the pancreas. Convinced that he could not gather data about the lives of the dying by observing them, Buckingham obtained the cooperation of the physicians and the director of the hospital in arranging to live as a patient among hopelessly ill patients. He "took copious notes during the 10 days in the hospital, telling anyone who asked that he was writing a book and 'wanted to finish before [he] died.'"[46]

Whatever the researcher's mission, and wherever it may bring him, all share certain problems; and this is best appreciated by a study of witnessing of widely different localities and events. Robert Coles, in writing of "The Observer and the Observed," says that he wonders "how often we give those we 'study' credit for sensing our struggles, wanting to help *us*, and . . . having in mind some of the same conflicting interests or aims we do."[47] He writes of the limitations of studies of crisis situations—that people can weary of talking about the same critical issue over and over again, that there is "a larger context to the lives observers like me encounter at a certain moment of 'crisis.'"[48] And he makes the remark, which could well be taken as good counsel for all writers and researchers, that he decided to seek out many people of diverse backgrounds because of "a streak of rational skepticism in me, and as well an aversion to ideology, *all* ideology."[49]

In these researches, a distinction between anthropology and sociology is rather academic: participant observation can be practiced anywhere in the world, and for quite some time anthropologists and sociologists have been trespassing on one another's turf. A consequence of this is that the resemblances of the two disciplines to one another have become more clear, along with an appreciation of the fact that they have a common origin. But there is a fundamental difference in method between them, due, perhaps, to the distinction that has always been made between the "cultural" and the "social." This difference has to do with the attention that anthropologists have traditionally paid to the objects, the things of which the humans' material world is made. The anthropologist, close kin to the archaeologist, comes to know people and their ways through a close examination of their "material culture." Indeed, in *La Vida* Oscar Lewis compares the anthropologist's interest in material possessions to that of the archaeologist.[50] The anthropologist learns much about a person by noticing what he keeps and uses, what he throws away, and what he wants to have buried with him in his grave. Except for such matters as "status symbols," objects are infrequently mentioned in sociological literature.[51]

Of course, if things are mass-produced, "instant," plastic, prepackaged, there is little about one that can be learned from them beyond the amount of wealth one can claim and one's spending habits. Very few of the objects of a person living in contemporary society have sacred significance, value that extends beyond the monetary, the utilitarian or the reputational. For the ancients, for those living in tribal societies, there was a sense of kinship with things that we, perhaps, could never fully appreciate. Objects were invested with a part of one's very being. They were a link to the ancestors and a bond with those yet unborn. In a letter to his Polish translator on the meaning of the *Duino Elegies*, Rilke wrote of the intimacy of a house, a well, a cloak for his grandparents. These were vessels "in which they found and stored humanity," and now they were being crowded out by things from America—things that were empty, indifferent, false, forms of "dummy-life":

*A house, in the American understanding, an American apple or vine, has* NOTHING *in common with the house, the fruit, the grape into which the hope and meditation of our forefathers had entered . . . The animated, experienced things that* SHARE OUR LIVES *are coming to an end and cannot be replaced.* WE ARE PERHAPS THE LAST TO HAVE STILL KNOWN SUCH THINGS. *On us rests the responsibility of preserving, not merely their memory . . . but their human and laral worth . . . . The earth has no other refuge except to become invisible.*[52]

The sense of urgency, of having little time to rescue and preserve that which is disappearing—this the anthropologist shares with the poet. Things that are privately owned and cherished unlock the meaning of lives from within, of relationships leavened by the insults and the mercies of moving time. Objects are the crystallization of meanings, values, personal histories. They have a cultural, but also a psychological significance, a historical as well as a poetic meaning. Rilke bade us to take within ourselves "this provisional, perishing earth" with such passion that it may take root in inner life. Those who fulfill this mission are "the bees of the invisible." How much can any writer tell of lives, of people, that has meaning and that will endure, if he does not take his readers beyond the words they speak and write, the accounts they give of isolated actions, into their worlds and the things of which those worlds are made? Taken from their surroundings and the objects that are part of their lives, people are hollowed out, faceless, historyless. The research "subject" whose voice is recorded on tape, whose words are recorded in transcriptions of "responses" is a hollow man, stuffed with the straw of sociological abstraction. One must know more, if one is to know him. Witnessing is a quest for what Jules Henry called the actuality of the existential being, a quest fired by a "wild, intoxicated curiosity."

It may have been more than mere chance, and the accessibility of a site for a research project, that drew Malinowski to the Trobriand Islands, Raymond Firth to Tikopia, Peter Freuchen and Edmund Carpenter to the Eskimo, Oscar Lewis to Mexico and Puerto Rico. In many a work in social science, the writer tells us how he came to be fascinated with his subject. Robert Butler writes "a personal note" in the opening pages of his book *Why Survive? Being Old in America.* He says that it was love for his grandfather and for an elderly family physician who cared for him when he had scarlet fever that led him to the study of medicine. And it was his grandmother's spirit and endurance through the harsh years of the Depression that brought him to specialize in gerontology and geriatric psychiatry.[53] Le Masters, too, discusses the personal reasons for his attraction to "The Oasis," where the construction workers congregated in late afternoons to talk about their lives. "I have always overlapped two social worlds—that of the blue-collar worker and that of the white-collar worker," Le Masters writes. "I have been a 'marginal' person in the sociological sense. The men at The Oasis reminded me of the blue-collar aristocrats I had known as a youth—they were (and are) proud and independent."[54] In *Blackberry Winter*, Margaret Mead says very frankly that she loathed the culture of the Mundugumor, while her husband, Reo Fortune, was both repelled and fascinated by the people. Working with them brought out certain aspects of his personality, she remarks, with which she felt no empathy.[55] The seasoned social scientist appreciates the full challenge of witnessing. One must enter the lives of others so completely that one can see with their eyes, hear with their ears. At the same time, one must withhold a part of the self. If one surrenders to one's subjects completely, if one allows oneself to become possessed by others, to *become* the Other, then a tribe has lost an anthropologist and can adopt a new member; then there are two subjects, and no longer an observer and the observed. Participant observation demands both involvement and detachment, Hortense Powdermaker wrote. It is both a science and an art.

It was the *science*, the *detachment* that was attacked passionately, repeatedly, furiously by James Agee in *Let Us Now Praise Famous Men*. This work, he wrote in the preface, was intended "as a swindle, an insult, and a corrective." He and Walker Evans meant to deal with their subject "not as journalists, sociologists, politicians, entertainers, humanitarians, priests, or artists, but seriously."[56] Both men came to the tenant-farming families in Alabama not as strangers, but, in Agee's bitter word, as spies. In his list of Persons and Places, Agee calls himself "a spy, traveling as a journalist," and Walker Evans a "counterspy, traveling as a photographer." Agee writes of his mission with an anger turned as much against himself as against those who sent him on his "assignment":

It seems to me curious, not to say obscene and thoroughly terrifying, that it could occur to an association of human beings drawn together through need and chance and for profit into a company, an organ of journalism, to pry intimately into the lives of an undefended and appallingly damaged group of human beings, an ignorant and helpless rural family, for the prupose of parading the nakedness, disadvantage and humiliation of these lives before another group of human beings, in the name of science, of "honest journalism" . . . of humanity, of social fearlessness, for money, and for a reputation for crusading and for unbias which, when skillfully enough qualified, is exchangeable at any bank for money.[57]

What brought James Agee to these people was a sense of kinship with them that was deep and abiding. But more than this, it was love for them, unabashed love that he felt, and this he came to recognize himself, keenly and painfully. In the "Second Introit," he recollects how he had happened to stay with the Gudgers. As he accepted the food a sleepy Annie Mae prepared for him—more food than he could eat, but food he *does* eat nonetheless, so that they will not think he feels superior to them or to their food—the feeling grew within him that he had come home. The Gudgers seemed to him to be his sister and brother, but then more than that, his own parents: "all that surrounded me . . . was familiar and dear to me as nothing else on earth." It came to him at that moment "that this was my right home, right earth, right blood, to which I would never have true right. For half my blood is just this; and half my right of speech."[58]

For Agee, the "assignment" from *Fortune* magazine had been a homecoming, a reunion with a part of himself that he felt was most vital and true, and that he had in some way betrayed during the years of his education at Phillips Academy and Harvard, and in the artistic and social circles of New York City. He was, Walker Evans wrote, a fugitive from the magazine editorial offices in New York, from social-intellectual evenings in Greenwich Village, "and especially from the whole world of high-minded, well-bred, money-hued culture, whether authoritarian or libertarian." The writing in this book, Evans said, reflects Agee's rebellion, a rebellion that was private and very powerful.[59]

Agee and Evans spent part of a summer among these people. One might think that part of a summer would barely afford an anthropologist enough time to unpack his gear, set up his tripod, and arrange his books and papers in his tent. But the number of days and nights spent in witnessing matter very little when measured against the sort of person the witness is, what is in *him* and not in his methods. Between Agee and Evans, Robert Fitzgerald says, they "made sure that George and Annie Mae Gudger are as immortal as Priam and Hecuba, and a lot closer to home."[60]

Again and again, Agee speaks of himself as a spy, once as "a reverent and cold-laboring spy." He wanted his text to be read aloud, and, if possible, continuously; he wanted his readers to become as involved as he and Evans were. Like a social scientist, Agee intended to write of what was *there*, to rid himself of any preconceived notions of what he ought to find. And he wanted to write without being deceived by the allurements of the literary imagination. A person exists, he says, "as no character of the imagination could possibly exist."[61] He speaks of the "immeasurable weight" of a human being "in actual existence."[62] If it were possible, he says, he would not write at all. There would be photographs, and "the rest . . . fragments of cloth . . . . A piece of the body torn out by the roots might be more to the point."[63] These people have their meaning not through the writer, as in a work of fiction, but *in themselves.*

The reader is reminded of Jules Henry's insistence upon the actuality of the existential being. It was the social scientific way of knowing a person that Henry would not accept. It was the literary imagination that Agee said he found so wanting. Both art and science fail before life. These people were sacred for Agee, Walker Evans said. Agee's feeling for their holiness is expressed in the very choice of a title for the book, and in so many passages. In "Colon," Agee asks, "For one who sets himself to look at all earnestly, at all in purpose toward truth, into the living eyes of a human life: what is it he there beholds that so freezes and abashes his ambitious heart?"[64] The reverence and love Agee felt both blinded him and gave him sight. In his paper on "Understanding White Racists," Robert Coles reflects that Agee "had a hard time commenting upon the darker, less generous side of the Alabama tenant farmers he grew to love so much." He knows from his own work in Alabama, Coles says, how "racist" such people can be, and he does not doubt that "in 1965 the road between Selma and Montgomery was lined by people not unlike Agee's friends."[65] Agee became, as many a witness becomes, whether he wills it or not, champion and defender of "his" people. Still, the champion did not sacrifice, did not wholly consume, the poet in him—*or* the anthropologist.

That summer of 1936, Walker Evans was, to use the words of Roberta Hellman and Marvin Hoshino, "an anthropologist with a camera." Indeed, Hellman and Hoshino find it uncanny that Claude Lévi-Strauss records in his *Tristes Tropiques* exactly what is recorded in

Evans' photographs. Evans was far more than "just another '30s liberal photographer." His formative influences are to be traced to the avant-garde of the late 1920s; he "took from the School of Paris not aestheticism (which is basically asocial) but a method for examining society clinically." Like an anthropologist, Evans studies "the customs, artifacts, myths, architecture, and rituals of a culture to see how its need for order corresponds to his own."[66] And Evans' companion, whose fascination for the possibilities of the camera is woven through the pages of this book as it was through the days of his life, wrote in word portraits, not only of the people, but of the *place* the two men haunted together. Hellman and Hoshino find that the passion of Agee and the reticence of Evans contradict one another. It is difficult to arrive at any final judgments about this. It *is* clear, however, that Agee wrote of the film as at least equal to literature. "The camera," he said, "seems to me, next to unassisted and weaponless consciousness, the central instrument of our time."[67]

Unassisted and weaponless consciousness . . . and the eye and ear of the poet and the anthropologist. Agee and Evans came upon a church, and Agee wrote that he saw "the light so held it that it shocked us with its goodness straight through the body."[68] Lying down to sleep, he sees "the still inviolate, lyric body of a child."

> . . . it is . . . very close to dark, with daylight scarcely more than a sort of tincture on the air, and this diminishing, and the loudening frogs, and the locusts, the crickets, and the birds of night, tentative, tuning, in that great realm of hazy and drowned dew, who shall so royally embroider the giant night's fragrant cloud of earthshade: and so, too, the talking is sporadic, and sinks into long unembarrassed silences; the sentences, the comments, the monosyllables, drawn up from deepest within them without thought and with faint creaking of weight as if they were wells, and spilled out in a cool flat drawl, and quietly answered . . . . and George says, Good night Louise; good night George; night, Immer; night, Annie Mae . . . .[69]

Objects are alive; Agee is one of Rilke's bees of the invisible. A trunk is "elderly, once gay, now sober." The chairs in the kitchen "sit in exact regiment of uneven heights with the charming sobriety of children pretending to be officers or judges." The light is sometimes white, and sometimes silver. The poet-photographer's eye follows its shifting moods. In the front bedroom, "When one of the shutters is opened," it is "new and uneasy in the room, as if the objects were blinking, or had been surprised in secret acts." Agee finds the shoes "silent"; he finds "an old black comb, smelling of fungus and dead rubber, nearly all the teeth gone," on the bureau. He does not miss that, "At the right of the mantel, in whitewash, all its whorlings sharp," there is "the print of a child's hand." And on the edge of the mantel, he finds "a broad fringe of white tissue pattern-paper which Mrs. Gudger folded many times on itself and scissored into pierced geometrics of lace, and of which she speaks as her last effort to make this house pretty."[70]

Agee opens Louise's schoolbook, *Around the World with the Children*, and enters the child's world. We know little things about her— *Louise, Louise* is written in pencil on a calendar on the wall. We know them all, we know their lives with a hurting intimate knowing. Agee devotes an entire page to their beds. At times, he says, they look almost level, even though the springs are sagging. But, "At other times, the bed, neatly made though it is, looks like an unlucky cake." Our senses "are crudely woven," he reflects, and "swarms of immediacy slide through these nets at best, assisted though they be by dream, by reason." But our senses and our reason are what we have; and whatever we know of others is sifted through them. Agee writes of the odors— odors of pine lumber and of woodsmoke and of cooking; of sweat and sleep and staleness; of corn . . . and of

another and special odor, very dry and edged: it is somewhat between the odor of very old newsprint and of a victorian bedroom in which, after long illness, and many medicines, someone has died and the room has been fumigated, yet the odor of dark brown medicines, dry-bodied sickness, and staring death, still is strong in the stained wallpaper and in the mattress.[71]

Poet and social scientist . . . now and again, one gives way to the other. Agee writes on and on of clothing. He introduces us to George Gudger on Sunday, and his wife on Saturday, and to the Rickettses and the Woodses in their Sunday-best. He writes of overalls ("They are pronounced overhauls"), of shoes, of hats. There is a meditation on three women's dresses that, in a few pages, tells us more about poverty than the most meticulous survey ever could, because we understand it from within ourselves.

Just as any anthropologist might, Agee explains how cornshuck hats are made. He notices that the women often use fertilizer sacks in place of calico to make their dresses, and that, because of this, one company began to make its fertilizer sacks in calico patterns. Then he becomes a poet again. The sadness, the proud sadness of the poor, in putting on the face they want the world to see! For Annie Mae, decent clothes count second only to food in a list of life's necessities. Margaret's ready-made dress, an imitation of the "basic black dress" of the well-to-do, middle-aged woman, has transparent crepe sewn over with small, jet beads, many of them lost now, or hanging loosely from their threads. And the cloth is "sweated open irreparably and alarmingly at the armpits, so that when the arms are raised, there is in this somberness the sudden bright dreadfulness of twin yawning cats."[72] These are the clothes, Agee reminds us, that the girls must wear to attract men, to find a husband. In one passage, Mrs. Woods stands in the drugstore waiting for a doctor to attend to her abscessed tooth. She stands under the gaze of the men at the soda fountain, bareheaded, barelegged, barefoot, in her thin dress that is torn, and in the sweat and the dirt, and with her dark, sweated nipples showing through the thin materials of her slip and dress. And the men keep staring. In this passage, Agee brings us mercilessly, even ruthlessly, to an awareness of the humiliation and the helplessness that being poor can sometimes mean. Reading it now, those vast numbers of us who have lost touch with rural America and with the Depression and the poverty that are at once part of our history and our present lives, are reminded of how, for so many, being barefoot and sweaty and dirty and wearing "overhauls" have become no more than a costume for a dress-down party, how, for so many, poverty became a role to play.

Agee has the power to awaken within the reader long-forgotten and deeply buried understandings. He reminds us that what we know of others can never be more than what we bring to them of ourselves. We know "not merely with the counting mind, nor with the imagination of the eye," he writes, but "with the whole of the body and being, and in translations of the senses so that in part at least they become extrahuman."[73] As a child who goes to his mother's closet and buries his face in her dresses to catch their musk, Agee seeks out the "hidden places." He takes out garments and holds them, and then puts them away again "so reverently as cerements, or priest the blessed cloths." He suffers shame and sorrow that he has intruded upon the privacy of these people, that he has violated their little world so as to bring it to others. To us. He is so ashamed; to Fred Ricketts, he writes, "you could not get it out of your head that we were Government men, who could help you."[74] He and Walker have intruded upon these lives, and he cannot forgive himself for that, remembering Mrs. Ricketts standing before the camera

> naked in front of the cold absorption of the camera in all your shame and pitiableness to be pried into and laughed at; and your eyes were wild with fury and shame and fear, . . . and so there you stood, in a one-piece dress made of sheeting, that spread straight from the hole where the head stood through to the knee without belting, so that you knew through these alien, town-dressed eyes that you stood as if out of a tent too short to cover your nakedness: . . . and Walker setting up the terrible structure of the tripod crested by the black square heavy head, dangerous as that of a hunchback, of the camera . . . a witchcraft preparing, colder than keenest ice, and incalculably cruel.[75]

One is haunted by the thought that the cost may have been too great; that others may distort or make light of, or remain indifferent to this vision, or reduce it to some arid ideology. Perhaps it would have been the better part of love to have left this little world alone, inviolate. Agee is angry, not so much at *Fortune* magazine, nor even at the "criminal economy" in which these people are "social integers," as at himself—for having come there, for having trespassed upon these lives. In some way, he felt, in having discovered them, he had betrayed them. Coles writes that he wonders if not only Agee but also George Orwell in *The Road to Wigan Pier* and Simone Weil in *The Need for Roots* expressed their irritation with intellectuals out of a growing feeling that the work they had undertaken—as observers and writers, as witnesses—was, after all, impossible.[76]

In spite of his impassioned claim that this could not be, Agee's literary gifts have brought us an understanding of these things that perhaps nothing else, not even the camera (though he would vehemently attack this suggestion) has it within its power to do. *How was it we were caught?* we read, these the words of Agee's literary imagination working. He writes of how each family in the world is apart from all the others, and "inconceivably lonely, sorrowful, and remote." And this is how it is. He writes of how men and women are drawn together, and then a child is born, and then other children . . . of how the beginning of this was "before stars," and no one knows where it will all end. Some years ago, I assigned this book as one of several for a course I taught in Social Problems; and my students read this passage with me, aloud, as Agee had wanted it to be read, as if we were at a prayer meeting: *How was it we were caught?*[77]

Agee writes about the army worms, what they sound like when they have invaded a field. He tells us about the snakes, the wildlife, as any anthropologist with a naturalist's bent would do; and about the Johnson grass, and how tired you come to feel and where it aches most after you've picked cotton for hours. He writes of the light and heat, "this brilliant weight of heat" which "is piled upon you more and more heavily in hour after hour so that it can seem you are a diving bell whose strained seams must at any moment burst." And of how your eyes "are marked in stinging sweat" and how your head roars gently, "like a private blow-torch." After weeks of working with Walker, he is alone and free one Sunday afternoon, and he writes of what a "terrible event" it can be in summer, in a small town in the South, when nothing stirs, not a human being or an animal, "nor even the leaves of the trees and the crops except in the slow twisting of some white and silent nightmare." He brings us there in Ageean prose that is like no other prose, that cannot be paraphrased without a sacrifice of its very heart—prose we learn to trust because, as Fitzgerald writes in his memoir, even "the weariest river of Ageean prose winds somewhere safe to sea"[78]—he brings us to that Sunday afternoon. We drive down main street with him, knowing that

every last soul in all these shaded, jigsawed, wooden houses must be dead asleep under the weight of the hot greasy sunday dinner in shaded rooms, not even a sheet over them, whose added weight would break them open; and the houses themselves, withdrawn in their dark green, half-bald, twiggy lawns, were numb with sleep as ruins in the dappling and scarce twisting of their tree shade. All the porches were empty, beyond any idea of emptiness.[79]

In this huge book, with its meditations on shoes and light, odors and porches, bedbugs and the philosophy of education, this "young man's book" as Dwight Macdonald calls it, "exuberant, angry, tender, willful to the point of perversity," we have an American classic—a broth of poetry and photography, anthropology and literature, social science and journalism, satire and philosophy. From it, Macdonald writes, a truth emerges that takes in and yet "goes beyond the truth about poverty and ignorance in sociological studies (and 'realistic' novels)," and the truth is that these lives, when they are "imaginatively observed, are also touched with the poetry, the comedy, the drama of what is unexpected and unpredictable because it is living."[80] This astonishing achievement, *Let Us Now Praise Famous Men*, is social-science-become-art. We need this kind of book—not another survey, another report of the findings of a study done with questionnaires or interviews or even participant observation, but *this* kind of book, the kinds of books, as Kafka wrote in a letter to Oscar Pollack, "that act upon us like a misfortune, that make us suffer like the death of someone we love more than ourselves, that make us feel . . . lost in a forest remote from all human habitation—a book should serve as the axe for the frozen sea within us."[81]

In is entirely fitting that William Stott devotes Part Four of his book *Documentary Expression and Thirties America* to *Let Us Now Praise Famous Men*, presenting a chapter on the photographs and a chapter on the text. In Stott's lucid and comprehensive book, a work that brings our past to life and thereby restores it to us, he writes that in passages where Agee discloses "the unacknowledged sexuality of everyday experience: the random small liaisons that happen all the time but that one doesn't talk about nor even, sometimes, realize," he brought us to the truth of (in this case) Emma as a human being, a full woman, "and not merely an integer in a criminal economy." When one admits the possibility of such encounters "between a social 'victim' and the reporter documenting his or her life," then one can "bridge the social and economic gulf between them and severely weaken the idea that hardship is the *basic* fact of the victim's life."[82] Agee "strips himself to have the right to report their nakedness," Stott says, and in so doing challenges the reader to strip himself as he turns the pages of the book. Agee was—and Evans insisted upon this, Stott reports—a moralist; he demands of his readers no less than to "establish real relation" with these people, to "fall in love with them."[83] The form of *Let Us Now Praise Famous Men* is an imitation of the workings of consciousness, Stott brilliantly perceives, "wherein perception is sudden, inexplicable, quickly lost, and always beginning again. What one feels constantly behind the words on the page is a consciousness laboring toward the world, Nature, the truth." The book opens the way to reality.[84]

Stott's book is absolutely indispensable as a guide to understanding what Agee and Evans were trying to accomplish. It is also an excellent source book for interdisciplinary courses in American studies, American literature, popular culture and film, humanistic social science and qualitative sociology. Social scientists will find his chapter on "Social Science Writing" especially illuminating. In this chapter, Stott reports that W. Lloyd Warner thought of social science reports that are made up of facts, without any mention of the process by which they were garnered, as "sham objectivity." He reminds us of the distinction that Cooley drew between the "statistical method" and that which Cooley favored, the "life study method," and of the sociologist Thomas Minehan's insistence upon the "literary" (Stott uses the term "documentary") as opposed to the "scientific" method as the only acceptable approach to social reality. He reminds us, too, that although the statistical approach was widely practiced in the thirties, it was severely criticized as well. Vital statistics were very hard to come by at that time, and those that were available were not only doubted, but censured because of their lack of a human quality. "It is clear," Stott writes, "that the journalists most sensitive to the hardships of the time felt a quantitative description of society traduced the reality it tried to convey."[85]

Stott has found that most social scientists of the thirties, like Warner, were attracted to the use of the documentary rather than, or as supplementary to, the statistical method. Still, some "were troubled at using a strategy which reported particular experience rather than quantitative generalization." John Dollard spoke of the "bad conscience" that troubled him on the issue of what method to adopt for *Class and Caste in a Southern Town*. He felt that the statistical method, the basis for the credibility of social scientific research, could not be satisfactorily applied to his needs. The sociologist who coined the term "participant observer," Edward Lindeman, felt that a quantitative interpretation of social reality was inadmissible, Stott reports. And Thomas Minehan, who collected over 500 case histories of runaway youth for his *Boy and Girl Tramps of America*, came to reject the statistical method of description and analysis as not only inadequate, but untrue.[86]

In his chapter on social science writing, Stott examines the methodological considerations that went into a number of works, among them Allison Davis' *Deep South,* Thomas and Znaniecki's *The Polish Peasant in Europe and America,* Louis Wirth's *The Ghetto,* John Landesco's *Organized Crime in Chicago,* Harvey Zorbaugh's *The Gold Coast and the Slum,* E. Wight Bakke's *Citizens without Work,* Mirra Komarovsky's *The Unemployed Man and His Family,* Robert C. Angell's *The Family Encounters the Depression,* and Eli Ginzberg's *The Unemployed.* Of the case study method, he recalls that in 1940 Lazarsfeld suggested that its most judicious application "'may lie in the analysis of exceptions to general trends, which should be ascertained by crude statistical procedures.'"[87] Perhaps, Stott suggests, it was the intention of social scientists who presented case histories that the people all would sound so much alike: "Redundancy and obviousness were virtues. In a time of trouble, the confirmation of what the audience already knew could be exactly what a social scientist . . . *wanted* to achieve, and the case-study method the perfect means." Ginzberg, in *The Unemployed,* demonstrated "that the unemployed were like everybody else." Stott writes of "consensus social science" that "it uses the case-study method to efface individuality." Representative cases only are selected for the purpose of portraying a united community.[88] But Stott concludes from his analysis of case studies that, when the method is used seriously, it will always uncover concrete, particular experience, that which resists abstraction.

According to Stott, the participant observer method, pioneered by those of the Chicago school of the 1920s, dominated social science research in the thirties. This was also the decade, he notes, when anthropologists adopted participant observation in their studies of the "natives at home." In his judgment, the sociologist Thomas Minehan was the participant observer par excellence: he "spent two years in boxcars and hobo jungles collecting information" for his book *Boy and Girl Tramps of America.* Minehan decided to become a vagrant among vagrants after concluding "that he could not learn 'the inner mind of the man on the bread line' as a middle-class investigator in a good suit talking to 'social cases.'"[89]

Stott's account of the uses of the case study method, of participant observation, and of the first-person narrative in the thirties provides rich evidence of the moral and intellectual challenge that witnessing ever presents to both social scientists and writers. One of the great gifts of this book is an appreciation of the fact that, although it is often enough imagined to be otherwise, none of the difficulties encountered by the witness is particularly new. Lewis Hine, a sociologist, and Jacob Riis, who was a police reporter, are identified as pioneers of "socially committed photography." Both thought the camera to be a stronger weapon against poverty than the pen. "Word-men both, they nonetheless felt images more telling than words." Hine said that he would not need a camera if he could tell the story in words. Riis's work in the 1880s and 1890s, and Hine's in the first decades of the twentieth century were, Stott comments, the works of people a generation ahead of their time.[90] Social scientists, in reading of their rich heritage, are startled into a sudden flash of self-awareness: how much one absorbs, through some subtle alchemy, of the traditions of a discipline! And how little some things change over the decades! Minehan suffered from an excess of empathy, in Stott's judgment, as did Whyte. At the conclusion of his chapter on social science, Stott observes that, although "the participant-observer approach brought thirties social scientists into close relation with what they studied, and enabled them to convey its felt life," it also "lent itself to the engagé emotionalism characteristic of writing at the time."[91] Then as now—and, indeed, as always—in witnessing there is the struggle for balance between detachment and involvement, objectivity and empathy. Whatever the witness may discover about others in his work, through it he discovers the reaches of his own humanity. Full witnessing is not only an intellectual and aesthetic, but also—and perhaps most of all—a moral engagement.

Telling it "like it is," narrating one's "own story" as in Clifford Shaw's *The JackRoller*; having people express their own understanding of things as in Studs Terkel's *Working* or Larner and Tefferteller's *The Addict in the Street* is thought by some social observers to be the most certain path to another's inner life. It is as if, by offering the subject the tape recorder, the socal scientist does away with himself. There is no intermediary between speaker and listener; there is no interpreter.[92]

The tape recorder, Oscar Lewis said, "has made possible the beginning of a new kind of literature of social realism." Because of it, uneducated, even illiterate people can tell us of their experiences, their thoughts and feelings—spontaneously, naturally, without inhibition. Indeed, Lewis thought of this sort of verbal testimony as superior to the novel in its possibilities for revealing the inner lives of poor people. "The slums have produced very few great writers," he wrote in his introduction to *The Children of Sanchez,* and those who *do* become great writers "generally look back over their early lives through middle-class lenses and write within traditional literary forms."[93]

Lewis contended that it was in the nineteenth century, when the social sciences were very young, that the impact of urbanization and industrialization on the lives of people everywhere was the subject of novels and plays, and the preoccupation of social reformers and journalists. But in our time, he claimed, though these upheavals are found in societies throughout Latin America, Africa, and Asia, there is "no comparable outpouring of a universal literature which would help us to improve our understanding of the process and the people." Our need for this understanding is urgent, he wrote, and he believed that the social sciences, and particulary anthropology, are well suited to creating this literature. He criticized middle-class sociologists, who were pioneers in the study of urban slums, for neglecting the poor and turning their interests to suburbia (as, indeed, some of them did until the momentum of the sixties carried their attentions elsewhere). Most novelists too, he charged, "are so busy probing the middle-class soul that they have lost touch with the problems of poverty and the realities of a changing world."[94]

This is not the place to look more closely into that word "most" either in terms of the late 1950s when these words were written, or in terms of today's very complex literary goings on. To respond to Lewis' charges would require a separate work. It is clear that they were made out of a deeply felt commitment to the kind of anthropology he practiced as much as preached. The literature on the theme of the upheavals caused by social change in Latin America, Africa, and Asia is rich and diverse, though perhaps there was not the "outpouring" that Lewis felt there should have been. Furthermore, though the social scientists may have turned in great numbers to "probing the middle-class soul" in the 1950s, all that changed dramatically in the decade that followed. Whatever the ultimate consequences of the impact that the 1960s had upon social science may be, no social scientist will ever be quite the same again.

Like Agee, Lewis never lost the awareness that he had in some way intruded upon the lives of poor people, for whom he had a strong affection. To redeem his sin, he elected to have these people speak for themselves as much as possible, rather than through a "middle class North American mind." Unlike *Let Us Now Praise Famous Men*, Lewis' *The Children of Sanchez* is the work of a man who believed in the value of the "first person story," of verbal testimony. For Lewis, the people's *talk* is central; we know them each and all through what they say about their lives. For Agee, the people are known intuitively, through the little traces they leave of themselves here and there, through their expressive faces, the way they walk . . . and through their silences. We reach toward them, as Agee did, through the sense of place. Lewis describes the *vecindad*, the Sanchez home, as a playwright might describe the stage on which his drama unfolds. The streets, the courtyards, the shops are located for us precisely and objectively. To Agee, the landscape breathes and moves; it is alive, a living presence.

For the social scientist, "place" is a setting. Indeed, Oscar Lewis referred to La Esmeralda, the slum in San Juan in which he gathered materials for his study of poverty, as just that—a *setting*. In *La Vida*, we read of the 900 houses in which 3,600 people live, houses that run in rows from east to west; the slum is built on a steep embankment between the ancient fort walls of San Juan and the sea. We see the slum from the wall above, and from this distance, Lewis wrote, it almost has the look of prosperity. But then, moving closer in, we see its subdivisions. Though the heart of the city can be reached from La Esmeralda in ten minutes' time, the slum is marginal to it, separated visibly from it by the wall. "From the wall down to the sea," Lewis wrote, "the physical condition of the houses becomes poorer and poorer" and the social status of the people declines. The poorest live on the beach, which is a dangerous place because of the continuous threat of high tide. Lewis found the beach to be the dirtiest part of the slum. "Several large conduits, broken in places, carry sewage down to the sea, and the beach swarms with flies and is littered with trash—

garbage, human feces, beer bottles, condoms, broken beds and rotted pieces of wood. It is a refuge for dope addicts." Even so, those who live in La Esmeralda find uses for the beach—for making love, and for fishing, for bathing, "and, when hungry, for collection of snails and crabs."[95] After this description, we read very little else about the place; it is the *people* of *La Vida*, now, who step forward from these pages to claim our attention. It will be their words, their voices, that will haunt us, and not La Esmeralda, nor the apartments in New York City where some of them go to live.

In *Soulside*, Ulf Hannerz presents a few sketches of places—Ruby's apartment, the look of the buildings along the main street of Washington's ghetto.[96] And in *Blue-Collar Aristocrats*, Le Masters describes the Oasis, again much as the dramatist describes the stage.[97] In Elliot Liebow's *Tally's Corner*, too, it is as if the physical milieu must be described—saluted in passing—a people's space in the world located and its features roughly outlined before one gets down to the "real" business. Liebow writes of the New Deal Carry-out shop on a corner in downtown Washington, D.C., where he "made like an anthropologist," studying Negro streetcorner men. He tells us that "The air is warmed by smells from the coffee urns and grill and thickened with fat from the deep-fry basket." He writes of the jukebox and the pinball machine and the advertising posters. Above the telephone on the wall, there is a "long-legged blonde in shorts and halter" who "smiles a fixed, wet-lipped smile of unutterable delight at her Chesterfield cigarette, her visage unmarred by a mustache or scribbled obscenities." And in the background there is an ocean liner riding "a flat blue sea." This is the *setting*—and Liebow uses this very word for it—this, and the corner walk in front of it, where twenty men are drawn together for "effortless sociability."[98]

Liebow, like Frederick Thrasher, author of *The Gang*, who worked as a participant observer for seven years, studying boys' gangs in Chicago; like William Whyte and Herbert Gans and Jules Henry, like Erving Goffman in his research for *Asylums*, and like Le Masters, had to find a way to gain acceptance and the cooperation of others, so that their world might be made known to us, made a part of our experience. Their books, and the many others of this genre, have both a literary and a social scientific value. Indeed, the distinction between the two seems in certain passages to be merely academic. Where does the poet begin and the anthropologist or journalist end in *Let Us Now Praise Famous Men?* In his foreword to *Tally's Corner,* Hylan Lewis writes that Liebow's book is "as akin in preoccupation and point" to Ralph Ellison's *Invisible Man* as it is to Whyte's *Street Corner Society,* to Eugene O'Neill's *The Iceman Cometh* as to Lee Rainwater's "Crucible of Identity: The Negro Lower Class Family," or Kenneth Clark's *Dark Ghetto.*[99] And Oliver La Farge, in his foreword to Oscar Lewis' *Five Families,* which was published before *The Children of Sanchez, La Vida,* and *A Death in the Sanchez Family,* wrote that the *nouveaux riches* Castro family in the book is one that would "dismay Chekhov" and "stand Zola's hair on end." The technique Lewis used in *Five Families,* La Farge observed, represents a resolution of a difficulty that confronts the contemporary social scientist. Traditionally, he recalled, the anthropologist studied small and highly cohesive communities, and could present discussions of his findings which were scientifically acceptable, that is, fairly free of his own biases. However, if the society which is being studied is large and complex, it cannot be fully seen by the "humanistic, face-to-face method" because it comes up "against firm limits of numbers, variety, or usually both." Therefore, the social scientist uses statistics and tests. In following Tepozteco families who migrated to Mexico City, Lewis presented a portrait of countless numbers of people through a kind of "sampling in depth," using the technique of studying a day in the life of five families. This, to La Farge, meets the requirement of scientific objectivity without reducing human beings to ciphers.[100] Lewis reached for a way of uniting a form of social science with a form of literature. Because of this, his works have a catholicity of appeal and significance such that they lend themselves to many courses of study—in Latin American studies programs, in cultural history and literature, in anthropology and sociology, in history and social psychology. So it is with *Let Us Now Praise Famous Men,* and with the writings of Robert Coles, of Loren Eiseley and René Dubos, of Lewis Mumford and J. Bronowski, among others: they are works that are the seedlings of Hesse's Bead Game.

To each his gifts . . . and his weaknesses. Every work ought to be judged and appreciated in its own terms, as well as in terms of its contribution to a particular intellectual discipline. The social scientist is taught to hold himself at one remove from those he studies. The writer must do this too, if he is not to be overwhelmed by his "characters." If, however, one is too scrupulous about this, something very vital may be sacrificed. Agee tells us something about Alabama tenant farmers and their families in the 1930s that we can learn in no other way. And this is precisely because he surrendered himself so completely to them. He sanctified them. It is clear that these people can be very mean. The Woods family believe that the water in the spring they use is "full of fever" because it is used by a family of Negroes who live under them in the hollow. And when the Negro children appear, or their parents, Pearl Woods throws rocks and bits of wood at them. The animals are cared for and given food in proportion to their usefulness. The cow and the mule and the hogs come first, and then the dogs and cats. And if the children mistreat the kittens, the reproof is only casual. If the dogs are slow or clumsy, they might be kicked so hard that their ribs are cracked. Agee never dwells on the cruelty of these people, as he dwells on their beauty. He does not ever seem to think in terms of judging them, but only of judging himself (and his readers). His love blinds him, so that, as Coles has remarked, he found it difficult to comment on their darker, less generous side. The poet and the lover in him dominated the social scientist he was talented enough to become; he reveled in his biases. Still, the reader need not embrace these people as Agee did (though he would find this heresy) to come to see and know them. It was Agee's love that brings us here, yes. But it is his power of literary evocation that holds us—that, and his sense of place, a sense so keen that it transforms the place into something alive and enduring on this "provisional, perishing earth."

There are many passageways to the lives of others. Ruth Cavan studied diaries to write her book on suicide. W. I. Thomas read letters to the *Forward*, excerpts from the records of the Girls' Protective Bureau, and autobiographies as sources for *The Unadjusted Girl*. In his essay on "The Historian and the Historical Document," Louis Gottschalk reminds us of the many types of documents available to the social scientist: contemporary records, confidential reports, public reports, memoirs and autobiographies, official histories, questionnaires (which, he says, are hardly a recent innovation), and government documents. He says that many historians, as well as some political scientists and sociologists, "have altogether too respectful an attitude" toward government documents. Many of them

> are not even primary sources. To be sure, many statistics—vital, actuarial, census, fiscal—are available nowhere but in government publications and therefore have to be derived from them or not at all. Yet the responsible editor upon whose authority they ultimately rest was probably not the compiler, and the compiler probably had to depend upon enormous staffs of less responsible people ... sometimes remarkably inexpert census-takers, surveyors, examiners or assessors.[101]

Social scientists more often than historians, Gottschalk observes, tend to an uncritical acceptance of government documents and official histories. And they are too quick, at times, to use secondary historical writings without inquiring into the sources of information upon which they are based, or weighing different schools of thought.[102] (At the other extreme, they may overlook historical materials altogether.) They do not, Gottschalk contends, make sufficient allowance "for the egocentrism of compilers and enumerators of quantitative data," whereas they are more aware of that of the authors of qualitative documents. When one looks into quantitative measurements, one finds they are actually largely qualitative. Why does this escape some social scientists? One reason may be that one only questions what one does not want to accept. Another may be the insistence upon "scientific method" and the confusion of scientific method with quantification. Whatever the explanations may be, social scientists need to think twice before dismissing literary sources as "impressionistic," when nothing could be much flimsier than the "scientific" sources used as a basis for some research studies. It is sobering to read Gottschalk's remark that, in spite of "the amazing achievements of epigraphers, papyrologists and paleographers, the historian of the social behavior, attitudes, and cultural patterns of Biblical, Greek, Roman and medieval times still has few sources better than the contemporary works of fiction, drama, and poetry."[103] Of course, Gottschalk adds that a historian would use the literary works as sources of information only if he can confirm this information by observations made elsewhere.

Sociobiology, psychohistory, photojournalism . . . the worlds of thought are merging. It is clearer than ever that the social scientist and the writer are often laboring in the same vineyard. Not that this ought to be celebrated unreservedly: "Historians, psychologists, sociologists," Helen Vendler remarks, "anthropologists, theologians, and philosophers can all return from the same novel carrying different bones." And these bones "bear odd and hardly accidental resemblances to the retrievers."[104] Vendler makes a strong statement about the fundamental differences between literature and social science. There is no question but that there are many mansions in the house of human experience, and that neither literature nor social science would be well served if the one were simply merged with the other. It is clear that, although they are both "about" Newburyport, Massachusetts (albeit in different decades) and "about" the social classes in that community, Warner and Lunt's Yankee City series and J. P. Marquand's novel *Point of No Return* are two very different works. So are the novels *Poorhouse Fair* by John Updike and *Celebration* by the late Harvey Swados different in purpose and effect from Butler's *Why Survive? Being Old in America*. One learns different things and in quite a different way from reading the Lynds's books on Middletown and Sinclair Lewis' *Main Street; Let Us Now Praise Famous Men*, and any social science study of poverty in the rural South during the Depression; Dan Wakefield's *Island in the City* and Piri Thomas' autobiographical work, *Down These Mean Streets*. Still, there are qualities in the literary works that many social scientists found absent from the works in their own disciplines—qualities they did not want to do without in classroom discussion of certain social issues and social problems. So it happened, more markedly in the sixties than in any previous decade, that many social scientists included fictional works in the readings lists for their courses. What qualities did they find in these works that persuaded them to assign them as reading for their social science students?

In a paper on "The Future of the Humanities in General Education," literary critic I. A. Richards wrote of the juncture of the humanities with the sciences—a juncture being a convergence, but also a crisis—as a head-on confrontation between "two unreconciled ways of conceiving man and his good and how to pursue it." He drew a distinction between the physical and social sciences, in which men are viewed as subject to forces emanating from the outside, and the humanities, in which individual man is still conceived of as ideally autonomous.

Socrates claimed, Richards recalled, that he who is least able to be changed from the outside is happiest—a spirit, not an object to be manipulated (however benevolently), who learns by exercising his innate freedom. Quoting a passage from Warner and Havighurst's *Who Shall Be Educated?* in which "learning how to behave" is said to mean "acquiring the proper responses to the batteries of social stimuli which compose our social order," Richards asks if learning to behave should mean anything resembling this. "To a humanist (or a Platonist)," Richards declared, "it should mean learning the *what's* and *why's* of human good—what man's duties and responsibilities and his right relations to his fellows are, and learning how to stick to them under the terrible pressures of pleasure and pain . . . which forever try to force us from them."[105] If the humanities decline, he wrote, this means that a person is becoming ever more vulnerable to exploitation and manipulation, for the "humanities are his defence against emotional bamboozlement and misdirection of the will." And a student of science, "without the support of that which has been traditionally carried by literature, the arts and philosophy—is unprotected; the main doctrines and positions which keep man humane are insusceptible, at present, to scientific proof." No true humanist, Richards concluded in this essay, can accept the claim that scientists have inherited the task of the humanities, any more than he can truly despair of man.[106]

There is something that the humanities have to offer the student of social science that cannot be found elsewhere. Without it, the subjects of surveys and interviews, questionnaires, and even of participant observation studies, may remain wooden, mechanical, nonhuman. It is the obsession with quantification—with the "hardware" that is truly Ambition, Distraction, Uglification, and Derision—the drunkenness with ideology, and the bogs of unrelieved positivism and rationalism in which some social science is still mired, that account for the atrocities against language and the presentations of masks for human faces and stylized, conventional responses for the blaze that full experience is, that are still found in so many social scientific works. Even if (and this is a gigantic If) the social scientists could prove beyond doubt that they have discovered what most people actually do, and what their opinions and sentiments are about social issues and social problems, it does not follow that this would then constitute the Good.[107] In any case, what constitutes the Good is to be sought not through the study of social science, but through the study of its source, philosophy.

The thrust of this plea for the restoration of the tradition of humanism to social science is the recommendation that social scientists apply for a final decree of divorce from rigid and simpleminded determinism, a divorce that, ironically, the natural sciences have already been decreed. Social scientists need to attend to what Blumer taught many years ago, what was ignored at our peril, that a "variable" is a "complex, inner-moving process," that the mind and the actions of any human being defy all categories and all prophecies. Each of us, Jung said, has his or her own story to tell . . . a story that continues to unfold so long as each of us lives. In an earlier period in our national history, Paul Lazarsfeld called for a "maximum of concreteness," and social scientists attempted to realize this through participant observation studies, detailed case histories, and oral and written first-person narratives. The quest for reality will go on so long as there is social science. Our mission is clear; Stott has stated the matter with brilliant conciseness: "An imagination that seeks the texture of reality must fix upon particulars."[108]

In *The Coming of Age*, Simone de Beauvoir quotes passages from diaries, notebooks, personal documents, to present the "being-in-the-world," the view from within, of the experience of aging. Yet in this impassioned book (which reads so often as a manifesto), she says that our understanding of aging is imperfect because "the evidence, the opinions and the books concerning the last stage of life have always been a reflection of the state of the upper classes: it is the upper classes alone that speak, and until the nineteenth century they spoke only of themselves."[109] Most old people, Beauvoir says, are poor and neglected and in despair; and when we compare the praises of old age with this reality, much of the writing on old age looks "like mere intellectual elucubrations for the sole use of . . . the eupatrids, the highly-privileged." A deficiency of using personal documents, she contends, is that they represent the writing of the privileged minority who had the leisure and the means to keep these records. Yet these writings of the privileged minority—of Cicero, Montaigne, Schopenhauer, Victor Hugo, Michelangelo—have so much to give us. How much we lose, in the way of appreciation of them, by thinking of them only as writings of those of a privileged caste! It should never be assumed, furthermore, that if the writings of the *under*privileged were available, they would be a single voice raised in a single cry. How often, in the name of humanitarianism, a people's full humanity is taken from them! To subject literary work to the scrutiny of a mind that is already made up about the purpose and meaning of human life, to judge it in other than its own terms, is to fail to receive it.

In a letter to Andrea Caffi, Nicola Chiaromonte wrote feelingly of his rejection of the dogma that it is "our moral duty to accept certain notions about the class struggle or private property, under pain of being classified with outcasts and monsters." He quotes a passage from Marx in which there is a contemptuous contrast drawn between *appearances* and a *final explanation*. In social reality, Chiaromonte maintained, men's illusions about their situations are as real as their final explanations. And a final explanation is no more real than dreams and religions, fear and cowardice, weaknesses and vices. Only if we exclude "all awareness of psychological reality," he reminded us, can "the individual and *individuals* . . . be made to fit into a type or a class." There is always human freedom; there is always "the contingency of the facts—their ambiguity, their 'polyvalence,' and their individuality." Chiaromonte argued in this letter that the mystical appeal to facts beyond the limits of appearances is at the root of modern fanaticism, whatever guise it may take. He knew that human beings cannot be forced into symbols or numbers without losing their humanity; and he knew, too, that we cannot presume to know the historical reasons for human events until after they have taken place (if even then!).[110]

The vision of the witness may be clouded, on the one hand, by a naïveté that brings him to look only at the surfaces of things, or, on the other hand, by a dogmatism that compels him to read certain predefined, unalterable meanings into appearances. The social scientist needs, far more than training in methodology or doctrine, reaffirmation of the bonds between social science and the humanities. To insist that there is but one path to Truth, to close the doors to all systems of ideas but one, is to forfeit everything—compassion, intellectual curiosity, the chance for discovery. The language of the ideologue is newspeak; it carries within it, perhaps more than we know, the power to destroy all that makes us human. In the shaping of judgment, all books must be opened, all documents read, all possibilities explored. The mark of the most gifted witnesses, those whose works will endure if any endure, is a curiosity, a seeking, that awakens our own. When James Agee wrote about film director John Huston, he said,

> Most movies are made in the evident assumption that the audience is passive and wants to remain passive; every effort is made to do all the work—the seeing, the explaining, the understanding, even the feeling . . . . Huston's pictures are not acts of seduction or of benign enslavement but of liberation, and they require, of anyone who enjoys them, the responsibilities of liberty. They continually open the eye and require it to work vigorously; and through the eye they awaken curiosity and intelligence. That, by any virile standard, is the essential to good entertainment. It is unquestionably essential to good art.[111]

To awaken curiosity and intelligence. What higher purpose could social science have than this? In this, at least, good social science is good art.

# SIX

## On the Uses of the Imagination

> *Masterpieces are not single and solitary births; they are the outcome of many years of thinking in common, of thinking by the body of the people, so that the experience of the mass is behind the single voice.*
>
> —— Virginia Woolf, *A Room of One's Own*

In *The Sociological Imagination*, a work of the late 1950s, C. Wright Mills wrote that if it is true that serious literature, the "essence of the humanistic culture," has become a minor art, this is a consequence not only of the development of the mass media and of mass publics. It is owing, too, to the quality of contemporary events, "and the kinds of need men of sensibility feel to grasp that quality." Mills asked—rather, *demanded*— "What fiction, what journalism, what artistic endeavor can compete with the historical reality and political facts of our time? What dramatic vision of hell can compete with the events of twentieth-century war?" People want to understand social and historical reality, Mills declared, and contemporary literature does not often provide them with adequate means for that understanding. People want facts; they want to know the meanings of facts; they want "'a big picture' in which they can believe and within which they can come to understand themselves. They want orienting values too, and suitable ways of feeling and styles of emotion and vocabularies of motive." And these they do not readily find in contemporary fiction. Perhaps, Mills granted, all these *may* be found there. But what matters for his argument, what he claims is significant for us, is that people "do not often find them there."[1] To know what is the case, and what to make of that, and even by what we ought to live—all this, Mills contended, requires the exercise of the sociological imagination. And this, he seems to imply in "The Promise," the energetic first chapter of this influential book, supplants—indeed, may have already supplanted— the literary imagination.

Mills gave voice to a judgment that may have been quite prevalent in the 1950s. It was at that time, Hortense Calisher recalls, that younger writers were gravely told, as if it were a law,

that the novel was dead, poetry dying, and all verbal art shortly to follow, since imagination, against the violence of the present world, had no force worth considering. The world's disorders were now of such magnitude that there was no point in replicating them on the page in any way except one. All the power was now in the miserable fact. From now on, this would be all that serious people wanted to hear.[2]

Teaching English to three survivors of Hiroshima, whose flesh "rotted visibly," Calisher felt that every time they left, bowing as they moved backward through her porch door, they seemed to take with them her right to speak, to create. And she remembered that, when she worked in the slums, "when you're staring at the mangled child, or the starved one," it is really of no help at the moment to listen to Mozart's *Requiem*.

However, Calisher goes on to remark, a recital of a litany of the facts is of no help, either (though she had not then yet come to that realization). Now, she says, she would not give up writing, even if she were assured that by so doing she could solve some world problem. For, she says,

It takes us a long time to understand the difference between communication and thought. Even in an age when news was pallet-sized and a mind's meditation could remain intact before the evils of the day, I doubt that the best minds did. Now that we know all the horrors at once, guilt and responsibility are everywhere—and the Babel of bloody facts. But nobody's obliged merely to duplicate these, on the coprophiliac page. We're not compelled to imitate or outdo chaos, but to consider it.

The fact is that the facts we live by never stay quite the same.[3]

That which *does* stay the same, Calisher reminds us, is the mysteriousness of things, and the possibility of our knowing, and our consciousness of this possibility: the verbal arts are "Ways of pointing with the calipers of thought, under that small eternal light, consciousness." She states that she has no more intention of giving them up than painters had of giving up their art when they saw what Daguerre was doing.

The question of the relationship of art to life is timeless, and it is encapsulated within the issue concerning the relationship between literary and political activity. In the twentieth century, writers have been given terrifying occasions for agonizing about the purpose and meaning of their creativity. In his study of *Documentary Expression and Thirties America*, Stott reports that between the beginning of the Depression and the bombing of Pearl Harbor, Theodore Dreiser did not publish any fiction, and wrote very little of it. "How can one more novel mean anything in this catastrophic period through which the world is passing?" Dreiser asked, and went on to say, "No, I must write on economics." Dreiser was not atypical of the writers of that period, according to Stott: "Even Wallace Stevens, that most aesthetic of writers, felt the tendency." Stott quotes Wallace Stevens as having declared in 1936, "The social situation is the most absorbing thing in the world today." It was Stevens' feeling that the Depression, and later the war, had shifted people's attention "in the direction of reality, that is to say, in the direction of fact," and he favored this trend. "In the presence of extraordinary actuality," Stevens is quoted as having stated, "consciousness takes the place of the imagination." Stott cites Daniel Aaron's judgment that most writers of that period believed that writing fiction was "too frivolous an activity for a time of social cataclysm," and that they turned from artistic activity to what Dreiser wrote—"journalistic ephemera." Proletarian fiction, which Stott finds to have been part of the documentary movement of the thirties, represented the efforts of many novelists to write work that appeared to be straight journalism.[4]

Writing in the 1950s, C. Wright Mills implied that the novel, the short story, the poem, the critical essay had all abdicated the vital center of our consciousness, our knowing of social and historical realities. And it was his forceful argument that sociology, once it renounced the obfuscation, the wind, of "grand theory" and the hollowness of "abstracted empiricism," could fulfill its promise—to make our lives, our world intelligible. Presumably, this was to be done through the excellent old ways of systematic examination and informed analysis. This, the relentless pursuit of what is the case, of the "miserable fact," was, for Mills, the exercise of the sociological imagination. Though it is nowhere acknowledged in his book, Mills was restating an issue that many writers had struggled with in the thirties, an issue, indeed, that has its origins in antiquity. And Mills was making the proposal that the sociological imagination works in a way superior to that of the literary imagination, that fact—reality—is superior to fiction.

But, as Morroe Berger remarks in his *Real and Imagined Worlds*, if one asks which is the superior genre, history (and in this case, social science in general, and sociology in particular) or fiction, one must follow this with the question, Superior for what purpose? "The case for the superiority of fiction," Berger notes, "goes back at least to Aristotle and has not changed much since then." Berger observes that the case for the superiority of history does not have advocates as staunch as those who contend that fiction is superior; still, "the novel has had to rely on history as a record and as a genre. The earliest modern novelists sought to give the status of truth and historicity to their stories."[5]

What is the nature of art, the nature of social science? What is the meaning, the purpose, of art? Of social science? And how can it be said that those in the world of letters treat of fiction and those in the world of social science treat of fact, when we do not know the difference between fact and fiction, when, in our own time we are recognizing (as it has surely been recognized in earlier times) that there are many fictions in fact, and many facts in fiction?

In his postscript to his work on *Fact and Fiction: The New Journalism and the Nonfiction Novel*, John Hollowell writes:

The best new journalism is a reflection of our unusual self-consciousness about the historical importance of our times. The assumption underlying most of the books of nonfiction I have discussed is that future historians will find these years unique, perhaps even part of a fundamental watershed in human consciousness. The nonfiction novels of Capote, Mailer, and Wolfe are deeply colored with the mood of perpetual crisis that pervaded the sixties.[6]

Mills's was an untimely death. Had he lived, he might have found that the "new journalists" and "nonfiction novelists" were exercising what he called the "sociological imagination" in their work. For, of all the social scientists, sociologists are the most engaged in the quest for living reality, for understanding of the present moment, of history as it is coming into being. Without historical perspective, however, the social scientist may, in his fascination with contemporary issues, fall into the error of what Bierstedt calls "temporocentrism" which, he says in *The Social Order*, he has elsewhere defined as "'the unexamined and largely unconscious acceptance of one's own century, one's own era, one's own lifetime, as the center of sociological significance, as the focus to which all other periods of historical time are related, and as the criterion by which they are judged.'" Sociologists, Bierstedt writes, are in need of "the deepening sense of time" that the study of history offers. In his judgment, "Much of contemporary sociological research . . . especially in the United States, is concentrated upon the 'specious present' and neglects an extended temporal orientation." Temporocentrism may be the affliction of many contemporary fiction writers, as well as of many sociologists, for both are tempted to place what Bierstedt calls "an exaggerated emphasis" upon present reality. We tend, Bierstedt comments,

> to ascribe a unique importance to the problems of our own era and to regard them as more complex than the problems that faced the man of imperial Rome . . . , or the man of the Renaissance. We are afflicted with a sense of urgency, a feeling that these tasks need to be undertaken, these problems solved, this action accomplished before it is too late. . . . it is impressed upon us, in sermon, commencement address, and daily newpaper, that we are living in an age of transition. So Adam might have remarked to Eve on the occasion of their departure from the Garden of Eden.[7]

In *The Sociological Imagination*, Mills devotes a chapter to the "Uses of History," in which he declares that the social sciences are historical disciplines:

To fulfill their tasks, or even to state them well, social scientists must use the materials of history. Unless one assumes some trans-historical theory of the nature of history, or that man in society is a non-historical entity, no social science can be assumed to transcend history.[8]

Indeed, Mills borrows Paul Sweezy's depiction of sociology as the attempt to write "the present as history." This, of course, is the same effort as that in which many contemporary writers are engaged, an effort that has often led them to renounce the writing of fiction for the writing of "faction," a combination of social fact and make-believe. Yet writers, as well as sociologists, reach for universal truths, for that which lies *sub specie aeternitatis*. When Mills exhorted his colleagues to turn away from the wasteful pursuits of "grand theory" and "abstracted empiricism," and to exercise the sociological imagination in quest of the "big picture," he was expressing the belief that sociologists could do what great writers have, in Walter Bagehot's opinion, always been able to do, namely, to "seize on the public mind." For this, Bagehot said, was the source of the originality of the literary giants. It would not be enough, then, to report on the facts, however meticulously. One would have to know how to make sense of what one discovered, how to make the facts speak to us of our condition. For this, one needs imagination. Henry James put the case very clearly when, at the age of thirty, he asked his friend Sarah Wister, "What's the use of writing at all, unless imaginatively? Unless one's vision can lend something to a thing, there's small reason in proceeding to proclaim one has seen it. Mere *looking* everyone can do for himself."[9] But is not the imagination the same, whether it is used in literary creation or in sociology?

"How different things would be," Robert Nisbet muses, "one cannot help reflecting, if the social sciences at the time of their systematic formation in the nineteenth century had taken the arts in the same degree they took the physical sciences as models."[10] This is a fascinating suggestion, leading at least *this* writer to extravagant flights of fancy. Imagine turning the pages of the sociological journals, and finding there, in place of the often dull and stilted prose, cartoons and couplets, prose poems and dramas, excerpts from novels, short stories, haikus! But what is done, is done; when Nisbet writes of the difference between the portraits drawn by the artist and those drawn by the sociologist, he finds it to be, in essence, "the higher degree of attention paid by the arts to individuality, to qualities intended to be and to seem unique in the subject, for in sociological writing a certain level of abstraction and generalization is inescapable."[11] The "sociological portraits"—of the bourgeois, the worker, the bureaucrat, the intellectual—are general, abstract. The "role-type" is, Nisbet says, "stripped . . . of all that is merely superficial and ephemeral," until "only what is central and unifying" remains. But in the novels of Dostoevski, Tolstoy, Balzac, and Dickens, where the conditions of societal life are vividly portrayed, "we are dealing with a distinct, unforgettable *individual*."[12]

When one has something to say, one must choose the form in which it is to be expressed. This choice in itself is fateful. The thought, the emotion, the tale to be told, take shape through the mode of expression chosen by the writer. A scribbler since childhood, I have written poetry, essays, short stories, novels, "articles" in social science, prose poems, original satires, fables, and plays. I learned very early in writing that, though there are many ways to say something, what is said in a poem cannot be translated into a short story, a play, an essay, without changing its nature, without irrevocable loss. And my long apprenticeship in the house of social science has taught me, too, that I am working in a different way when I think sociologically than when I think as a creative writer. Perhaps what Mills meant by the "sociological imagination" is not so much imagination as a form of consciousness, of reasoning and analysis. Today there is thought to be a division within the human brain between these powers of analysis and artistic imagining.

Sir Charles Sherrington has called the human brain "an enchanted loom where millions of flashing shuttles (the nerve impulses) weave a dissolving pattern, always a meaningful pattern, though never an abiding one; a shifting harmony of sub-patterns." Recent studies suggest that there is a duality in ways of thinking, between abstract and analytical thought, as expressed in logic and mathematics (and social science), on the one hand, and fantasy and dreaming, imagery and music and intuition, on the other. This duality reflects the localization of different mental abilities in the left and right cerebral hemispheres. It is thought that the left half of the brain is the locus of scientific modes of thinking, and the right half is, so to speak, inhabited by the artist, the poet, the dreamer dwelling within each of us.[13] The question is haunting: Must one faculty be exercised only by sacrificing the use of the other? Is it not possible that the two hemispheres could work together harmoniously?

In the chapter "World within World" in *The Ascent of Man*, J. Bronowski wrote of the intellectual breakthrough which heralded the age of modern physics, the passage, with the discovery of the electron, from thinking about atomic weight to thinking about atomic number, that is, atomic structure. Modern physics, he said, became the greatest collective work of science, but more than that, the great collective work of *art* of this century. He referred to it as a work of art because the idea that there is an underlying structure in the atom, a world within the world, was one that captivated the artistic imagination immediately. After 1900, Bronowski claimed, art underwent a fundamental change. And this is because it began then with the same ideas that fired the imagination of modern physicists. There was a shift from the fascination with the colored surfaces of things to a quest for the structure. The task of the artist remained what it had always been, to make that which is hidden, visible, to make us *see*. But now we were invited to look *through* the surfaces:

Since the time of Newton's *Opticks*, painters had been entranced by the coloured surface of things. The twentieth century changed that. Like the X-ray pictures of Röntgen, it looked for the bone beneath the skin, and for the deeper, solid structure that builds up from the inside the total form of an object or a body. A painter like Juan Gris is engaged in the analysis of structure, whether he is looking at natural forms in *Still Life* or at the human form in *Pierrot*.[14]

Though the two ways of working, the way of the scientist and the way of the artist, are clearly distinct, there are moments when artist and scientist are working together inside the same head. Bronowski wrote here of the Cubists who, inspired by the families of crystals, expressed a scientific fascination in an artistic way. And he wrote of Niels Bohr as a "consummate artist" who conceived of the stained-glass window in the atom, its spectrum, and grasped from this the idea that every element has a spectrum of its own, which "has a number of bright lines which characterise that element."[15]

The Cubists went one way, and the physicists another. Today we speak of the *two* worlds, the *two* cultures, not only because each has its own perspective, but because each conveys its truths distinctively. In social science, the world is known through systematic examination of all that is "out there," of the "given." In literature, what comes to be known is known through intuition, through the solitary journey into the regions of the writer's soul. For social scientists, literature was "the road not taken."

In a paper reprinted from *Antioch Review* and incorporated into a collection of readings for Introductory Sociology, Bennett Berger echoes Weber's celebrated phrase about the disenchanted state of the world. The social scientist, Berger writes,

is perceived as challenging that tradition of humanism and art which has subsisted on the view that the world *is* enchanted, and that man is the mystery of mysteries. To the carriers of this tradition, every work of art and every poetic insight constitutes further proof that the world is enchanted, and that the source of man's gift to make art and to have poetic insight is a mystery made more mysterious by each illumination. The power of this tradition should not be underestimated; it is well rooted in the thinking of modern literature, with its antiscientific temper and its faith in the recalcitrance of men to yield up their deepest secrets to the generalizations of science.... Intellectuals in this tradition seem to believe that the fulfillment of the goals of social science necessarily means that the creative powers of man will be "explained away," that his freedom will be denied, his "naturalness" mechanized, and his "miraculousness" made formula....[16]

Berger finds it inevitable that those who hold a view of social science that is this "fearsome" will have the conviction that "a science of society is both impossible and evil." Sociology, which he says is of all the social sciences the "most successfully maligned," is cast in the role of "*upstart*." Not completely acknowledged by either of its parents— the humanities "from which it gets its subject matter" or the sciences "from which it gets its methods"—sociology is seen by many to be engaged in the effort of making "the enchanted data of the humanities yield up their mysteries."[17]

In this paper, Berger suggests that, so long as sociologists are committed to the scientific tradition and address their work to the community of their colleagues rather than "to a general literate audience," criticisms leveled at the quality of their writing are irrelevant. Scientific writing ought not to be expected to be aesthetically pleasing, Berger maintains, and scientists ought not to be expected to be literary stylists. It is his belief that to apply aesthetic criteria of evaluation to a pursuit that is nonaesthetic is tantamount to denying sociology the status of a science. Berger perceives the traditions of humanistic study as those that conduce to "the apprehension of cultural wholes; they encourage commentary and interpretation" of the "backgrounds" of the subject matter in which one claims expertise. In contrast, he remarks, since empirical sociology is committed to the scientific method, it is often rendered "incompetent to deal with the 'big problems,'" and often its practitioners find themselves with a "trained incapacity" to make statements about matters for which no scientific proof can be adduced.

The man of letters is conceived of as the intellectual of our time, Berger reflects,[18] not because he is a writer or a critic, but because, through the literary works and criticism he creates, he comments on contemporary culture and interprets contemporary experience. People in the world of letters can assume the role of intellectuals, according to him, because they are free "from the parochial demands of technical specialization," free to "make large and uncompromising judgments about values," and free (they enjoy, he says, a "maximal freedom") from "institutional restraints."[19] Now, it is this role, the role of commentator on and interpreter of contemporary life, that Mills assigned to sociologists in his work on the sociological imagination. Through the exercise of this faculty, Mills believed, the sociologist could reveal the larger design, the "big picture," of societal structure and historical movement. For Mills, the sociologist who realizes the "promise" of the discipline could do *both*—make sense of the lives we live, and make sense of the ways in which our lives are lived.[20]

The issues raised in Berger's paper are compelling for both social scientists and humanists. The paths those in these two worlds take seem to meet and then diverge and then meet again. Both social scientists and humanists have some of the same problems to resolve: the question of the measure of moral distance to be maintained between themselves and those they study, and the knotty problem of what constitutes evidence or proof of what they take to be true. Furthermore, Berger's portrayal of humanistic endeavor, the active encouragement of "evaluation, the development of point of view, and heterogeneity of interpretation," is one that many a social scientist would accept as the purpose of his service in the classroom. It is undeniable that the sociological enterprise, for all its origins in that intuitive leap in the dark that propels us to discovery, to new knowledge, is an engagement in gathering facts and assembling them in accordance with the canons of the scientific tradition. But what of the larger design? How is that to be apprehended?

In a passage in *Suicide*, Durkheim remarked that not everything of social reality is to be found in a material, an external form; not all the aesthetic spirit of a nation can be embodied in the works it inspires, nor is all morality contained in laws and precepts. Much of it is scattered about, lying in wait for the discoverer:

> There is a large collective life which is at liberty; all sorts of currents come, go, circulate everywhere, cross and mingle in a thousand different ways, and just because they are constantly mobile are never crystalized [sic] in an objective form. Today, a breath of sadness and discouragement descends on society; tomorrow, one of joyous confidence will uplift all hearts . . . . And all these eddies, all these fluxes and refluxes occur without a single modification of the main legal and moral precepts, immobilized in their sacrosanct forms.[21]

That is why life in Imperial Rome could never be understood through a study of its laws only. One must enter into an age, as Dilthey taught us, to apprehend it more fully; and its literature, its drama and poetry, open the door to us. Precepts, Durkheim instructed, express the underlife, but they do not supplant it.

Durkheim's approach was that of the *erklärende* strategy; he moved inward from the surfaces. No matter how individualized a person may be, he believed, there will always be something collective about his character. It was this aspect to which Durkheim's attention was drawn, this little mirror in the soul where the collective conscience is reflected, whereon it is engraved, however faintly. This is the site where sociological excavation is to begin. And Durkeim was led there by the "social facts," those manifestations of the collective conscience. The social facts were his divining rod. They led him to the wellsprings of the Zeitgeist.

There is another way to this place. Perhaps it may be called the way of intuition. Shortly after he was awarded the Nobel Prize for Literature, Saul Bellow was interviewed by Joseph Epstein. Asked if he imagined a perfect reader for his novels, Bellow replied,

> Well, I do not start out assuming that I am *sui generis*. What I think I might have, apart from the techniques that I have learned about my craft over the years, is a certain clairvoyance about discovering issues, questions, problems before they are seen by most others—sometimes in a general, sometimes in a quite particular way. After publishing "Herzog," for example, I was interested to learn that all sorts of people wrote letters to the famous that they never sent, à la Moses Herzog. More generally, I find that the things that agitate, confuse and sometimes indeed frighten me about our time agitate, confuse and frighten a great many others. As a novelist, it is a good part of my job to attempt to formulate as dramatically and as precisely as I can, the pain and anguish that we all feel. Now more than ever, it seems to me, it becomes the writer's job to remind people of their common stock of emotion, of their common humanity—of the fact, if you will, that they have souls.[22]

It is given to very few, this gift of prescience. Through a strange blend of concentration and abandonment, of heightened self-awareness, and yet self-forgetfulness, one may become a medium through whom the forces of an age make themselves known, through whom the Zeitgeist speaks. George Eliot once said, "My predominant feeling is—not that I have achieved anything, but that great, great facts have struggled to find a voice through me, and have only been able to speak brokenly." In his *Sociology as an Art Form*, Nisbet says that this is just as possible for the social scientist to achieve as for the artist. Creativity, Nisbet reminds us, by way of a passage he cites from Livingston Lowes' study of *Road to Xanadu*, is universal. "What else is imagination," Nisbet asks, "but the moving around in the mind, restlessly, compulsively, so often randomly, of *images* with which to express and to contain some aspect of perceived reality?"[23]

In the act of creating, one receives this protean flow and reaches for form within the chaos, both at once. For sociologists, this encyclopaedic grasp of reality eludes us still, this realization of the Comtean vision of the possibilities of the discipline. As the "social facts," the events are broadcast even as they happen, those who examine their lives, those for whom it is a moral imperative to make sense of this world, narrow their sights, looking here or there because one cannot look everywhere at once. Auden once spoke of the danger for modern man as one of "paralysis in the void of infinite possibilities." Many contemporary thinkers have spoken of how impossible it seems to explore the past fully or to keep pace with present reality, and of how our rationality, as well as our creativity, suffer from the massive efforts we make to assimilate the constant barrage of information directed at us. The truly wise know more surely than anything else what they do *not* know. Whatever one's chosen field of endeavor may be, one reaches for Truth through the understanding of little truths, for the miraculous through appreciation of the little miracles in everyday experience, coming to understand with Tennyson's Ulysses,

Yet all experience is an arch wherethrough
Gleams that untravelled world whose margin fades
For ever and for ever when I move.

Those who counsel us to hold to our sense of our limits, of our finitude, can scarcely be heard in all the din. The few who know this, know us as we do not begin to know ourselves. And future historians who would understand us would do well to attend to our silences.

To make our condition intelligible, even to teach a moral lesson now and then—these both a literary work and a work in social science can, and sometimes do, achieve. Always this has come from working within an enclosed space, a clearly demarcated compass. How, then, can the imagination—by *any* name—scan what Mills called the "big picture"? It should never be forgotten, Nisbet writes, "that no genuinely good or seminal work in the history of sociology was written or conceived as a means of advancing theory—grand or small. Each has been written in response to a single, compelling intellectual problem or challenge provided by the immediate intellectual environment."[24] Decades ago, Max Weber gave a clear forewarning to social scientists and writers alike, as well as to political and religious leaders. It is our fate, he wrote, that the world has become disenchanted, that

the ultimate and most sublime values have retreated from public life either into the transcendental realm of mystic life or into the brotherliness of direct and personal human relations. It is not accidental that our greatest art is intimate and not monumental, nor is it accidental that today only within the smallest and intimate circles, in personal human situations, in *pianissimo*, that something is pulsating that corresponds to the prophetic *pneuma*, which in former times swept through the great communities like a firebrand, welding them together. If we attempt to force and to "invent" a monumental style in art, such miserable monstrosities are produced as the many monuments of the last twenty years. If one tries intellectually to construe new religions without a new and genuine prophecy, then, in an inner sense, something similar will result, but with still worse effects. And academic prophecy, finally, will create only fanatical sects but never a genuine community.[25]

It might be instructive to consider in what measure Mills's exuberant vision of the possibilities of the sociological imagination may be rooted in the expansive spirit of the 1950s—that fateful decade that spawned so many sociological studies *and* so many sociologists. It might be instructive, too, to consider in what measure the lore of sociology, a discipline that ever reaches toward the universal, is firmly rooted in a particular time, in a concrete place.

As one who came of age in the 1950s, I remember a time when the distinction between the literary and the social scientific imagination seemed very clear to me. A poet more than any other sort of writer then, I did not look for strong connections between my creative endeavors and the sociology, history, and philosophy courses I was taking, preparatory to entering law school in my senior year. Having held various jobs since the age of fourteen, and having been entirely self-supporting since the age of eighteen, I knew from the very beginning that I could not hope to earn a living as a writer. But I knew, too, that writing would be my life. College opened a vast horizon to me: I was the first member of my family to go, and I had to make my own way. This I did, by working twenty or twenty five hours a week, along with carrying the same number of courses as any full-time student. There was no time for play; from the beginning I knew I had to decide upon a vocation, a profession. Social science intrigued me, but I imagined then that I had been elected to a life of action, as much as to a life of thought. I enrolled in the pre-law curriculum, and took sociology as my major field.

Every student has illusions about courses before taking them; I was not prepared for the realities of law school. The courses in real property and contracts, torts and constitutional law were the very apotheosis of abstract, analytical thinking. And in law school there were no countervailing currents, as are found in liberal arts, to such specialization. Some weeks after I began my studies, I dropped the course in real property and enrolled in a course in play writing. After my first semester in law school, I transferred back into the college of liberal arts, and graduated with an A.B. and a major in sociology. From that time on, through the Master's degree and then the doctorate, I worked, both as a poet and as a sociologist, writing—when the words came—on the margins of leaves in notebooks fattening with the lore of social science. I was aware of a difference between the social scientific and the literary imagination; and the brighter the one grew in intensity, the more shadowed the other became. On holidays and between semesters, when I read poetry and fiction rather than the works of the masters in Sociology—these were the most fertile periods for writing poetry, and the occasional play, and even, once, a libretto for an opera a composer friend was writing of *Lysistrata*.

If there *are* turning points in our lives, one was, for me, in 1960 during the spring semester, after I resigned from my teaching post to await the birth of my first child. Free for the first time in years from academic demands, I began to write fiction, and discovered what seemed at the time to be inexhaustible literary energies. After that, month upon month and then year upon year, I went on writing—short stories and novels, original satires and essays and, though ever more rarely, poetry. What had happened was just the reverse of what Thomas Babington Macaulay remarked of the course of intellectual development. In the brief time I spent in law school, and after that, all through graduate school and beyond, it was the left hemisphere of the brain, the locus of the faculties of abstract thinking and analysis, that was called into play. My taste for the theoretical, for generalizing, was very keen. In the second half of life (to use Jung's apt phrase), I find the images and dreams, all that is particular and concrete, subtle and detailed, most compelling. I become ever more vexed with the taxonomic approach to things, ever more impatient with abstractions, ever more critical of the general statement.

Not that the old fascinations die—far from it. One cannot forget what one has learned so well. Habits of thought, instilled through years of intellectual labor and dedication, become part of the self, of the mind's very activity. The social-scientist-self knows that many a private trouble is joined to a public, a social issue, and that the condition of manifold selfhood and of the schisms within the soul is societally grounded, foreordained by the accident of birth into these times that are our own. Claude Lévi-Strauss has stated the first principle of social science perfectly: "Whoever says Man says Society." Yet the writer-self knows that every human being lives and feels, thinks and acts as a creature of will and passion as well as of intellectual understanding, and is Subject over and above Object of study. It is always the Subject, moving and changing, perverse and willful, now crude or weak, and again compassionate and generous, we need to know if we would know ourselves.

One makes choices, or at least imagines one is choosing. From a choice other choices flow, a lifeway is shaped, one that, so long as it is being lived out, eludes any final judgment. Once one takes the literary veil, one learns that one cannot dedicate one's full energies and hours to academe. Writers, who are so often English majors, cannot both write and teach full time, cannot serve two masters. If one chooses the academic life, chooses to commit oneself to teaching, to service in the intellectual discipline taken as one's calling, the artist-self remains subordinate to that of the teacher and the scholar. Energies released in a classroom where there is vitality, laughter, argument, communal searching—these are restored only very slowly. Nor does the dedicated teacher turn students away. If one is truly and fully a scholar, a social scientist by day, one cannot truly and fully be a creative writer by night. And if one chooses the literary life—in the face of the indifference, the silences that can last a lifetime and beyond it, that await one, in the face of a struggle that can only intensify in time, and of the self-doubt that afflicts even the most confident, and of the unending uncertainty and the rejection, knowing the obscurity that is the fate even of many of very great gifts; if one takes that risk despite all this—one must give up one of the most prized rewards the academic life offers the committed and the persevering: continuity. Continuity in working with students, in working within the growing and changing, many-faceted intellectual discipline—this must be sacrificed if the artist-self is to be ascendant. It has been said that half a loaf is better than none. But here, one must make do with two halves of two loaves.

In *Blackberry Winter*, Margaret Mead writes a retrospective of her student days. For years she had written poetry (and short stories, as well) as did some of her classmates. Indeed, she had gone to DePauw with the thought that she might become a writer. And when she transferred to Barnard, she continued to major in English. But, she writes, "Although I could write well, I realized that creative writing would not provide a central focus for my life." Above all else she wanted to make a contribution to the world. She weighed the possibility of a career in politics, and decided against this, too. She came to feel that science "is an activity in which there is room for many degrees, as well as many kinds of giftedness" and so she chose it—social science, and ultimately, anthropology.[26]

Ruth Benedict, too, was a poet as well as an anthropologist. She had been Boas' teaching assistant when Margaret Mead first took the course in anthropology offered by Boas in her senior year at Barnard. Benedict had come to the study of anthropology in her thirties; she had been writing poetry for years before that. One nom de plume she assumed was Anne Singleton. Looking back at her life now, at her achievements, and reflecting upon the great influence of her work—particularly that of *Patterns of Culture* and *The Chrysanthemum and the Sword*—it might seem to us, with the sagacity so often assumed by those of later generations, that she chose wisely, that her talent lay in the road she *had* taken, that the poet she might have become could never have achieved the stature of the anthropologist she was. Yet once a life has ended we see it as so much more *finished* than any life ever really can be. This is the fiction underlying all biography. In her introduction to *An Anthropologist at Work: Writings of Ruth Benedict*, Margaret Mead writes of these things with eloquence and feeling:

What happens on the growing edges of life is seldom written down at the time. It is lived from day to day in talk, in scraps of comment on the margin of someone else's manuscript, in words spoken on a street corner, or in cadences which lie well below the words that are spoken. Later it lives on, reshaped and reinterpreted, in the memories of those who were part of it and finally slips, like a child's leaf boats after a long journey down a stream, into the unrecognizing hands of one's spiritual descendants who do not know the source of the water-soaked treasures which have landed on the shores of their lives. In any generation there may be a group of people who find meaning in just these unrecorded parts of life, who can read a book the better for knowing what the author meant to write while writing something else.[27]

Each of us has her or his own ghosts . . . or are they Muses? For one, it is Gertrude Stein, and for another Sylvia Plath; who is to decide for someone else who one's ghosts should be? In my ghost-warren Ruth Benedict hovers about, she who had been able, in her own way, to weave poetry and anthropology together in books that, as Margaret Mead has said, "would be read as often by future poets as by future anthropologists." Ruth Benedict seems to have been haunted, too; perhaps, in her own way, she was a precursor of those who are at work now, in the last decades of this century. "The sense of living different lives," Margaret Mead reflects, "of incompatibility between her own temperament and any particular version of American culture, never left her."[28] I offer my own experience of the consonances and dissonances between the currents of the imagination set to work in the literary and social scientific quest, for the record of both that is continually unfolding.

The moral aspect of relationships between people has always been a subject of great fascination for me, and I chose as the subject of my doctoral dissertation the history, nature, and application of professional codes of ethics.[29] In this 444-page tome, I wrote of the relationship between the study of sociology and the study of ethics, and of the history of the learned professions. I inquired into the meaning of the term "profession" and of the idea of "professionalization," a word that was much in vogue in the 1950s. Once I had surveyed the literature on the nature of the professions and of professional life, I traced the history of the code of ethics of the American Medical Association and the American Association of University Professors and then compared the academic and medical professions in terms of the many dimensions of practice to which professional ethics pertain. I conducted a number of interviews (25 members of each profession was the number eventually settled upon) of physicians and professors teaching in the southern community where I was then living. I did not use a tape recorder, but took notes as the interview went along in my own variation of the Gregg shorthand system. Undecipherable to anyone else, this form of note-taking had been used with great success for years in classroom lectures, and I had become so proficient at it that I could do a good bit of writing without glancing down at the notebook. Often I had the strong impression that the speaker had forgotten that I was recording his or her words. However, when it became apparent that note-taking was intrusive, I put my pen away and committed what I heard to memory. I had so arranged my schedule that I transcribed interview notes immediately after the hour or hour and a half was over. And, blessed with an unusually retentive memory and strong powers of concentration (these have been tested and proven reliable to me in other connections, on other occasions), I recreated the interview in typescript that I am quite sure is faithful to what had been said.

In requesting interviews, I sent around a long letter describing the nature and purpose of my research to a number of professors and physicians in the community. These were selected with an eye to obtaining as many perspectives as I could of the meaning of professional ethics in theory and in day-to-day practice. I requested interviews of women and men, of blacks and whites, of teachers in a university medical school as well as of academicians who were actively serving as consultants for business and industry, of practitioners of many specialties and professors of many disciplines, of those in both professions who had administrative experience as well as of those who, by every indication, were working as "free" professionals. I was not, of course, granted an interview with every person of whom this was requested; there were a few refusals. And I knew, without the grace of any remarkable intuition, that a few of the people who *did* grant me an interview were initially very guarded, suspicious of me and of my motives. I was, after all, thrice damned, as a woman, a Yankee, and a social scientist. And I spent many hours chasing physicians around the city, mending broken appointments; and many more in waiting rooms and outer offices, hoping that perseverance would win out (it almost always did).

Under the guidance of my major professor, I had drawn up a very ambitious schedule of interview questions, open-ended and accompanied by many probe questions. The purpose of my research was twofold. On the one hand, I wanted to draw a collective portrait of the ethical ideal of the professional for each of these two groups, the physicians and the academicians. On the other hand, I wanted to compare the two professions, to find the resemblances of one to the other and the differences between them in their perspectives on professional ethics. My attention was drawn in several directions at once. This is, of course, the nature of human experience, as the symbolic interactionists well know. When I reported my research "findings" in the dissertation, in conformity with the canons of social science, I sifted each theme or topic from the "data" and discussed it separately. The presentation reads as though each consideration had been taken up separately, turned over in the mind, and then put aside in order to move on to the next. This is how the sociologist shapes order out of what is chaotic. But I was alive to all that was happening in these interviews, which wavered so often on the very edge of conversation. As I listened, and spoke, the writer-self was busily creating stories, fragments of plays, puns, *bons mots.* Flashes of character irrupted through the talk that wandered, sometimes breaking off and then circling back again to one theme or another. Indeed, how could it be otherwise? We were, after all, talking about moral issues. The writer in me made things up, filled in spaces, using imagination in a way that is inadmissible in science. I was writing two very different sorts of work at once, though at the time the dissertation was the one that was put down on paper. The stories, the plays, the satires, and prose poems were consigned elsewhere. When one has been a house divided for so long, one knows when it is expected that the doors to separate rooms be kept closed.

I had been employed as a research assistant in a study of hospital administration the year before I conducted my interviews with the physicians, and had become somewhat familiar with their world because of this research experience. I knew that it would be advisable to seek an interview with the president of the local medical society (the white one, from which the black physicians, who had established their own because of this, were excluded), since this would give me entrance to the offices of many other physicians who might otherwise have turned me away as some sort of spy. I requested, and was granted, an interview with this physician first; and more than once I assured other physicians at the outset that I had talked with him. I used this whenever I needed to, and in all cases where I did, it was very helpful. One physician, who was a self-appointed spokesman for the medical confraternity in the city, volunteered to help me locate the doctors he thought I ought to interview, and furnished me with a list of names. I accepted this gratefully although, of course, I made a very different use of it from what he had intended. He cautioned me: Some physicians might refuse to see me, he said; "They might think you're necking with some federal agency."

The physicians I interviewed were very curious about me. Some asked me how old I was, others what my religion was, or if I could tell them what I was *really* after. "I thought your questions would *really* be rough," one physician commented at the end of our interview. When I asked him what he meant by "rough questions," his reply was, "Colleagues." He looked at me in a puzzled way, as if to ask what other meaning the phrase could possibly have.

How preoccupied these physicians were with colleague relationships! A few of them seemed to half hope that I would carry tales from one interview to another, and appeared to be disappointed (although in other ways quite relieved) that I could not be persuaded to violate the seal of confession. When I asked a physician to tell me what he or she thought ethical or unethical behavior on the part of a doctor really *is*, more often than not this was translated to mean that I wanted them to explain the code of etiquette governing the medical confraternity. "Colleague" meant a fellow physician to most of the doctors I interviewed; they did not confine the term to those who were practicing in their own specialty. When I first mentioned "ethics," doctors usually talked to me about the intricacies of the referral system, about the norm prohibiting the passing of judgment on another physician *particularly* in the presence of a patient, and other matters pertaining to colleague relationships. This was in striking contrast to the interpretations made by professors of the term "professional ethics." It is not that professors advocated or invited criticism of colleagues (although some of them may as well have), but that the professors most often thought of their relationships to *students* when they talked about ethics. There were a few who mentioned falsification of research findings or default in meeting obligations to the university or community, in addition to violations of the code governing their relationships with students. But, whereas physicians seemed to equate ethical concerns with relationships with colleagues, professors equated them with just about everything else first.

I gave very specific examples when asked to do so, and I found what I expected to find here, that what was a sensitive area for one person was uninteresting to another, or, for still another, an occasion to hold forth, to make a little speech. One might laugh when I mentioned fee-splitting; another might shrug; a third would say he was certain there were no cases of it in the community. Some thought I wanted to talk about advertising and they told me, trying to be helpful, that this was no problem, they had learned all about it in medical school. A few of them talked about abortion, and a very few about physicians who take on surgery cases without having adequate training. Many physicians said they were irritated with patients who have a smattering of knowledge about medicine and yet who talk to them about it as if they were professional peers. "Sidewalk diagnosticians," one physician called them; they seemed a thorn in everybody's side. The 1950s were the time when "miracle" or "wonder drugs" came of age; and many physicians spoke to me about how aggravating certain people can be, expecting there to be an instant cure for every ailment. "People just can't understand why fat doesn't melt away," one doctor said. "What they *should* understand is that if they would quit feeding their fat faces, they might lose a little weight." The professors, too, expressed exasperation with clientele. Some spoke of the student who does no work, who just occupies space in the classroom, as the least desirable sort of client; others spoke of the student who is disruptive or hostile in the classroom. Many professors said they were distressed about open admissions or about mass education. "I am honestly convinced," one professor told me, "that liberal arts education is not for the masses." Though he did not appear to be aware of this, he was speaking for many of his colleagues.

All this was grist for the mill of sociology. I was after a portrait of the ethical ideal of the academic and medical professions. I was looking for general characteristics, for "the" professor and "the" doctor, as well as for contrasts between the two. These did emerge from the "data." Unlike their compeers in medicine, few academicians seemed to be preoccupied with colleagueship. Of course there were exceptions: a mathematician, in talking about the issue of academic freedom, said that although he did not feel it in his own work, he was sure that his colleagues in political science or history must experience this as a very real issue in their lives. But the sensitivity that physicians showed toward one another's situation, their awareness of problems that are common to all members of their profession, could not be found in the interviews I had with professors. It so happened that I talked with these people in 1957, and the salaries of professors at that time and in that particular place were very low—in fact, downright abysmal. Many professors talked with me about their financial problems. One said that, to enter academe, "we almost have to take a vow of poverty." Yet these people thought of their economic plight as a personal problem and on an individual basis at that time. Indeed, one academician denied that professors were poorly paid. I would hear some professors say this, he advised me, but this sort of talk was unfounded. "Of course," he went on to comment, "my wife and I have always had an independent income." He seemed completely unaware of the connection between this and his lack of concern about academicians' salaries. In some cases, professors spoke of people in other disciplines and other colleges of the university with active dislike. "The arts people," one commented, "affect university policies more than the science people. They have less to do and they spend more time talking about these things."

For all their differences, there was a consensus among the professors (although this went unrecognized by them) that the "public" lacks an understanding of the actual meaning, in terms of hours of work, of a twelve- or fifteen-hour teaching load. This provided another striking contrast between members of the two professions. When physicians spoke to me of the false "public image" of doctors, they nearly always talked about money, about the layman's misconceptions about the wealth of doctors. And when they spoke about the sacrifices one has to make to be a doctor, they nearly always talked about the lack of time for leisure activities. While the professors were sensitive about having a generous amount of "free" time and suffered from want of a good income, for the physicians it was just the other way around.

Only a very few professors seemed to regard their obligations to, and their relationships with, the university as a sensitive subject. "I owe the university what any employee owes his employer," one of them said, and he might have been speaking for most of the academicians I interviewed. In the house of academe there are many mansions; and these are often divided against one another. But physicians, too, work within the context of institutional life. Most of them spend a good many hours in the hospital. And they appeared to be very preoccupied with their relationships to the two hospitals in the community. One hospital was Baptist, and the other Catholic, each with a distinctive *modus vivendi*—and this, of course, I knew something about, because of my work as a research assistant in a study of hospital administration. The matter of how emergency cases were handled, particularly charity cases, was a sensitive topic. "We don't need a charity hospital here," one physician told me, "but we'll *get* one." At the time I was conducting these interviews, there was a movement afoot to apply for funds to build a charity hospital in the city. The local (white) medical society was opposed to this. "The politicians are pushing one just to get votes," one doctor explained to me. The impression one would get from reading official statements made by members of the local medical society would be one of unanimity among the physicians in their opposition to having a charity hospital built in the parish. But that this impression would be false is clear from reading the remarks made in my interviews. "I do feel that we have many more charity cases going to New Orleans than we *think* are going there," one physician commented, adding, "a lot of doctors would disagree with me." While one doctor said he simply did not believe the official estimate that had been made of the number of indigent patients in the community, another stated flatly that the local hospitals did not accept many charity cases. "I oppose a charity hospital not as a doctor, but as a taxpayer," one physician told me. Another came out with the remark, "I definitely think we need a charity hospital, but it wouldn't do anything but harm me if I was quoted directly." One physician voiced his approval of the movement to build a charity hospital in the community (the movement was ultimately defeated), describing the need as nothing short of desperate. Again, the contrast between the two professions was striking. In academe, though professors work under a single roof, the attitude was, Every man for himself. Among physicians, who spoke of themselves so often to me as "the last of the rugged individualists," there was great care taken to present a united front to the lay world.

Each of these interviews was an event in itself; each had its own distinctive quality. "I almost refused to see you," one physician confided to me. "A lot of doctors will, because they figure—*you* know, the commercial side of it—they would be losing money. They *might* accept because they're curious. They want to see what you look like, and what your questions are. A doctor's time, though, is very valuable." One physician barely granted me forty minutes for the interview, and responded to many questions with sarcastic laughter and criticism of their wording and intent. I scribbled the aside in my notes that, during this interview, his telephone rang, and when he talked over the wire his manner changed completely. I could tell from the conversation that he was talking with a colleague. One professor wrote checks and busied himself with the papers on his desk as he answered questions. Another was visibly impatient, more interested in criticizing the questions asked of him than in giving his attention to them. Still another opened the interview by announcing that he could not give me much of his time, and by warning me that he was not "typical."

There was one physician who kept me waiting an hour and twenty five minutes past the time he had established for our appointment, and did not apologize at all for this. His manner was brusque, and his answers were cryptic. Finally he burst out with, "I might talk to other doctors about this, but not to somebody with a pencil in their hand." At this, I put away my pen and notebook, and at once he became more responsive. And there was the physician who had his receptionist phone me and ask me to leave a copy of my questions at his office so that he could prepare his answers to them beforehand. Occasionally, a professor or a doctor would say, "Don't write this down, but . . . ." These words alerted me to the good chance that I was about to hear something of particular importance in that person's life. As soon as they were spoken, I put aside my pen, in order to free the tongue that had been intimidated by it, and I concentrated on memorizing all that was said thereafter. Often, after an interview was over I would dash around a corner and, leaning against a building I would write furiously while my spouse, who usually drove me to these appointments, waited, whistling, contemplating the southern sky. When a professor or a doctor cautioned me, "You ought to drop that question," I did forthwith, taking care to come around to it from another path later in our talking, knowing that I had touched on some vital nerve.

Most of the interviews lasted from between an hour to an hour and a half. I remember one physician who was very taken by the whole project. "Mercy!" he exclaimed once, "you *do* ask hard questions!" He had planned the interview in such a way that I knew he thought it would take much less time than it actually did. My impression was that he became intrigued with the research in spite of himself. Another physician scheduled the interview for late afternoon when he would be finished working for that day. He offered to get me a Coke, got one for himself, and then put his feet up on his desk and talked about his life and work with genuine enthusiasm. "Who thought up these questions?" he asked me. "They're really *good*! They're hard to *answer*!" Time and again he would ask me, "How'm I doing? Did I digress too much?" He told me that his wife had taken some sociology courses and that he had looked at her books and had the impression that it is a broad and interesting field. He confided that, if his life had gone a bit differently, he would have become a musician or a writer. He asked me endless questions about my research. "You're killing us off first, and then the professors, eh?" he asked. When I left, he thanked *me* for having interviewed him!

It was clear that some of these people had been thinking about the things we discussed for a very long time, and others very little, perhaps not at all. When I asked one professor to tell me what he thought an ideal professor is like, he replied, "You have to have read Goethe's *Faust* to understand my answer. He would be a one-to-one combination of Faust and his servant. He has to know rules and principles, and have a respect for tradition, but also he has to have the courage to try to change if tradition is wrong. And he should be able to read through the dust, and see the humanity that *created* the manuscript." Some of these people were deeply in love with their work.

The contrast between the worlds of the professor and the physician emerged once more when I looked over what was said in my interviews about the ideal student and the ideal patient. There was a collective portrait of the ideal student; one professor's depiction was much like another's. But what was an ideal patient for one doctor was pure poison for another. Some said they preferred to treat men, others women. Some said they liked intelligent patients, while others preferred to treat "the most ignorant person around." One physician said that the most difficult patient to treat is the geriatric patient: "The difficult thing is—don't write this down—when some old crock comes in and you have to separate the social narrative from the physical one." Others preferred to treat the older patient.

According to the canons of science, it should have been possible for my study to be replicated by any other sociologist. I have many doubts about this. There is an electricity between any two people; the sort of charge depends very much upon who each of them happens to be. Establishing rapport is as much a matter of this, perhaps even more so, as of a command of interviewing skills. I am certain, too, that there were occasions when things would have gone differently if I had been a man, or a southerner by birth, or much older, or working on a project funded by some prestigious foundation. Then, too, I am rather short and very slender, and people have a way of thundering at me sometimes. There is also the matter of familiarity with the worlds into which one enters as a researcher. That I know the world of academe too well goes without saying. I had been a "participant observer" of it for many years, so much so that it is almost second nature, say, to read an advertisement in the newspaper of a vacancy in an institution of higher learning, and to see under and through it enough to know whether such a job actually exists, and to predict fairly accurately if it does, how it will eventually be filled. One has to look sharp when one is working in home territory, for then one tends to presume too much and can easily become careless. So far as the physicians were concerned, my work as a research assistant in the hospital administration study helped me in knowing their world somewhat better, and also in being able to separate fact from fiction every so often. For example, when I asked the doctors if they thought physicians kept up their medical records, and dutifully jotted down the occasional "No" or the usual "Yes, they are very faithful in doing this," I knew (and sometimes the physician knew that I knew) perfectly well what the actual situation was.

But the replication of research involves much more than this. There is a very real sense in which all research results in social science are fixed in time and place. These interviews were conducted in 1957 in a community in Louisiana. My "findings" are anchored in that very particular (and, for me, still very living) reality. During the time I was working on my dissertation, there was that movement to build a charity hospital in the community and this affected the subject matter of the interviews. That was the time, too, when the "wonder" drugs were widely prescribed. Many physicians talked about their ethical perspectives in terms of the use of these drugs and in terms of their relationships to the "detail men" from the pharmaceutical companies who came around to their offices to "brief" them on what was new. At that time, too, the hysterectomy was an operation very much in vogue. One physician told me, "The uteruses fly around this town too much." This, too, became the axis on which talk about ethical behavior turned for some physicians.

These particulars about concrete situations could, of course, be sifted out of the "data" by the sociologist who is after only one thing, the refinement of the concepts of "profession" and of "professional ethics." But this would mean the forfeiture of the heart of the research enterprise, at least for me. This is because it seems to me that everything turns on the truth that human beings can only find the meaning of ideas or of principles by working them through particular situations in which they are involved. As it was for the physicians, so it was for the professors. These interviews were held, after all, in the aftermath of the McCarthy era. One professor had the witch hunt very much on his mind when, in quick reply to a question I asked about the nature of unethical activity in academe, he said, "Twenty years from now, a person might find that a club he joined today made him subversive." Another, in response to a question about whether or not he felt the freedom of the professor was restricted in any way, replied, "Not if he's a decent human being. I wouldn't want to see any Communist get on the faculty."

Furthermore, these interviews were conducted only three years after the Supreme Court ruling on the *Brown* v. *Board of Education* case. Many professors talked about the consequences that might befall those who publicly opposed segregation—consequences which, in those particular years, could have been very grave indeed. One professor spoke of how much he resented the fact that he was not free to associate with his colleagues at the Negro university nearby. Still another said he felt he could not express his honest opinion about the local Citizens Council without imperiling his position at the university. And there were those—doctors as well as professors—who talked about sexual behavior or drinking when I brought up the issue of professional morality. "If you took students in your house and served mixed drinks," one professor told me, "you could easily lose your job." And a physician said, "A professional man has to conduct himself next to God. He can't put himself in a situation where he gets censured. You let a *doctor* get taken in for drunken driving, and his reputation falls off like petals from a dead rose. People expect a doctor to be like a preacher or priest."

During the final examination on my dissertation, one of my professors (as I recall, it was Professor Heberle) asked me, "If you interviewed a hundred doctors and professors rather than twenty-five, or, for that matter, five hundred or a thousand, wouldn't you find that their responses fell into certain patterns? Wouldn't you be able to establish categories of perspectives on professional ethics?" He was reminding me, of course, that this would be my business as a sociologist, that the very fact that this study was conducted by a candidate for a doctorate in sociology meant that I went about my work in a certain way, used an approach distinctive from that which might be taken, say, by a philosopher or a psychologist. He was drawing my attention to what it means to think sociologically.

This was, like all good questions, one that stimulated a lively exchange between the members of the examining committee and their victim. And, like all good questions, it was one that I shall never have done answering. As a sociologist—and that was the self presented at this gathering—I addressed myself to those working within a certain intellectual tradition, and opened my methods of study and my analysis of what I found to examination by a jury of my peers. I had traced the history of the professions and the development of a code of ethics by physicians, as well as the attempts on the part of university professors to formulate such a code. Then I had talked with members of both professions about the meaning of ethical standards in their day-to-day practice; and I had discussed the similarities and differences between the practitioners of medicine and of university teaching. I had studied the literature on professions and professional ethics, and in my empirical work I had looked for, and found, certain patterns. I had made general statements, and explained why I thought they could be justified. The dissertation was an offering, with all the ritual that accompanies such endeavors in academe, to the "body of knowledge" of sociology, and an invitation to colleagues and future students of sociology for further exploration. As such it transcended all that was unique and particular and concrete about professional life. It represented knowledge learned through systematic study of what was *out there*, in the world, rather than knowledge achieved by looking within, by the exercise of the literary imagination. Its language was the language of description and analysis, not the language of symbolism and dreams, intuition or narrative.

But the South has changed, the times have changed, and so have I; there have been transformations. If I were to conduct this study today, I probably would not find as many physicians ruminating about the effects of the policies of Roosevelt and Truman on their profession, as they did twenty years ago. Their thinking about socialized medicine would probably be differently phrased today. They would have, no doubt, much to say about Medicare and Medicaid, programs which have now been in existence for a good ten years. The issue of the charity hospital, which preoccupied so many of them in 1957, is no longer salient. And, too, their thinking about "wonder" drugs and about "unnecessary surgery" has surely been modified in the past twenty years. The situation of the Negro doctors in the community has changed, too. I do not drive a car and, as a consequence, my husband often drove me to my appointments for interviews. Sometimes he went away and returned to pick me up an hour or an hour and a half later; sometimes he waited for me in his car, or in the outer office. I remember very well that when I interviewed a Negro physician, my husband happened to be free to wait for me that day, and did so in the outer office. The receptionist must have told the doctor this, because, when I entered his office, he said before we began talking, "You can bring your husband back here, too." I still feel to this day the shame I felt then, knowing all that went into this invitation. It was one of the many moments of truth I experienced in the ten years I lived down there, coming face to face with the *apartheid* of the Deep South. All that made up the "social system" was quietly spoken, in those few words. And as I told him that I preferred to talk with him privately, and that my husband often accompanied me because I do not drive, there was in the look between us a common and a grievous suffering. I like to think that could not happen now, that today a black man and a white woman could sit and talk together alone without the atmosphere being charged with sexual innuendo. The times were very much with us, in all these interviews. "A friend of mine contributes to the Citizens Council," one physician confided, "which is a bane to me. They should take out all his blood and fill him up with Negro blood."

There have been changes, too, in the university. The doctrine of "interposition"—Calhoun's argument to the effect that a state can interpose its sovereignty to resist and even nullify the effects of what it sees as an intolerable and unconstitutional federal ruling—had been resurrected at that time. In fact, there was one semester when I did not register as a graduate student because I chose not to comply with the transparent new (and short-lived) directive of the university that I had to write to my high school (in Chicago!) for a letter testifying that I was "of good moral character." Professors can meet socially with their Negro colleagues, now, both on and off the university campus. And the issue of desegregation of the schools, a burning issue then, has been carried some distance in the direction of resolution. As an alumna of this university, I receive the alumni newsletter, and I think the composition of the faculty has changed more than it would have under ordinary circumstances. I simply would not be talking with the same people today as I did then. For many reasons, the faculty was far more cosmopolitan, far more ethnically mixed than it is today. My "sample" in 1977 would not have the ethnic diversity it had in 1957.

There would, I suspect, be some things that have remained much the same. In both professions, there are people who speak of their work with a joy, a fascination that one lifetime is too brief to realize fully. The doctors would, I imagine, still talk with me about the marvels that have been accomplished in the conquest of infectious diseases in this century. They would remind me today, as they did then, of the toll they once took, and of how people take our good fortune too much for granted. There would still be irritation at "sidewalk diagnosticians," I suppose. And the professors, now more than ever before, would have occasion to talk about the issue of education for the masses. The doctors would still be loathe to criticize their colleagues. I know this, if by no other means of documentation, because I have been a patient many times since, in the Midwest and East as well as in the South. Too, I know after having lived out a quarter of a century in the groves of academe, that the professors' engagement in internecine warfare is livelier than ever. Ostensibly a community of masters and disciples, academe is a condition in which each professor tends to go his or her own way, muttering or shouting under some private shell or in the interminable meetings that now seem to be called around the clock. Gathered together under one roof, and given what may be the most severe crisis the profession has yet experienced, academicians are now locked in very real combat.

Nor has there been a radical change in the stereotype professional people say the public has of them—of the physician as too rich, and of the professor as a dilettante. Now, as then, there would be members of both professions who would receive me in richly furnished, deeply carpeted offices, and others who would be hard at work in humble, even shabby quarters. I learned much about these physicians by studying their patients in the waiting room, by eavesdropping as I pretended to read a magazine (the social scientist, like the wiriter, is an incorrigible spy). I used my eyes as well as my ears: I did not miss the picture of the Sacred Heart in the modest office of one physician, or the Catholic literature in his waiting room. There were physicians who pointed proudly to the licenses on their walls as they talked to me, and one who showed me that he kept the Hippocratic Oath framed above his desk, and told me that he often looked at it. There was a professor who waved his arm, taking in the four portraits on the walls of his office, who said to me, "These are the four greatest teachers I ever had." While I was waiting for people, I jotted down items about the look of inner offices. There were signs on desk blotters, and on the wall: I HAVE NO QUARREL WITH THE MAN WHO CHARGES A LOWER PRICE, one doctor had posted, HE KNOWS THE VALUE OF HIS WORK BETTER THAN ANYONE. And another: BLESSED ARE THEY THAT RUN AROUND IN CIRCLES, FOR THEY SHALL BE CALLED WHEELS. Everything has meaning; everything is part of a larger design.

But that design, that *sociological* design, that tapestry that is called a dissertation, if of necessity silent about much that I remember of those years, of the South as it was then. The sociologist does not describe his "interviewees." He does not write that this one is thin, that one has a lisp, or another a distracting facial tic. Such matters are, to put it mildly, extraneous. I might have had an impression of one person as a deep voice coming out of a bushy beard, or of another as a pair of dark-framed glasses carrying around a haggard-looking man, or of still another that he had about himself an air of rabbinical sadness. If I wrote these things in my dissertation, members of my examining committee might have recommended that I take a long rest. But it *was* expected of me that I notice the interviewee's sex and probable age, and certainly his or her ethnic affiliation. The "socioeconomic status" of a physician's patients can, of course, be rather accurately estimated by a careful observer. So can a professor's attitude toward the university or toward his students. One learns some things without needing to ask questions, and other things by asking the right questions and then listening to what is said and what is left *un*said. Still, as I reread these pages of "data" (there was a flood, and these, along with many of my manuscripts, crumble in my hands) I am astonished at the lucidity of my memory as it restores to me this one's face, that one's voice . . . I can hear the harsh, staccato delivery of this one, the soft southern speech of another. I can hear the laughter of one or another; laughter is as individual as a thumbprint. When I hold these papers in my hands, something of the very air of that place is restored to me, of the South, which has become a part of my very being—the steaming heat, the ruthlessly brilliant sun, the haunting fragrance of jasmine, and of sweet olive, and of ligustrum. It all returns—the late fifties style of dress, too . . . the extravagant coiffures of the women, the "man in the gray flannel suit."

All that it is foreordained by the traditions of sociological research would be shorn from this "material," all that returns. And my imagination works in two directions at once. As I was writing these essays, the half-finished manuscript lay on my desk beside them, the manuscript of short stories about that place in just those years. I have been writing two books, this one and a literary work this year, just as I did then, when I was writing a dissertation and at the same time a book of poems. Memory is sometimes so keen,memory with its powers of trickery and of sudden revelation, that one cannot but smile over the social scientific constructs even as one writes about them. I feel a certain self-mockery when I speak of "the fifties" or of "Eisenhower's America" or of "the South" because I know that these are the fictions, these are the phantoms conjured up by the sociological imagination. We have made them up so that we can make true.

Above all else, looking through these papers again is an encounter with my former self, not only with the sociologist coming of age but with the writer coming into her own as well. The gods, Max Weber often said, are at war with one another. Yes, and they wage their battles through the mortals. The very point of social science is that the observer, "trained" to conform with the canons of the discipline, will see things anyone else working within that same tradition would see. This would be death to a literary work. All that glimmers on the periphery of the sociological enterprise is grist for the creative writer's mill.

Each interview, I was keenly aware, was an interruption in an ongoing life. And each life was many-sided, and infinitely complex. And these people were talking *at* me and *through* me, as often as or even more than they were talking *with* me. One physician could not get past the feeling that he was speaking *for* and *to* the medical community. After talking with me for over an hour, with a waiting room full of patients, he dismissed me. I left, and heard him calling me. He chased me down the hall, wanting me to scratch out something he had said, wanting to rephrase a statement he had made. It was clear that he did not think of his works as destined for the pages of a dissertation in sociology. He was so upset by the whole business, I wondered why he had not rejected my request for an interview in the first place. He had been so late for the appointment—almost two hours late—that I decided to leave and to try again later. I met him in the elevator, and we went back in for the interview. He was angry with me for doing this work, and flustered that he had been asked to be a part of it. But he could not let me go very easily. There was something he wanted to say, not *to* me, but *through* me, *through* the research project. Some of these people were talking to the American Medical Association, or to their spouses, or to an anxious client, or to the "public," or even to themselves, mulling things over aloud, some of them for the first time in many months, or perhaps in many years. The distractions that enter into what we call the "ecology of the interview"—the sudden, shrill ring of the telephone, the knock on the door—and those of inner life that I intuited from slight, barely perceptible shifts in an expression, a tone of voice, were interwoven with the "responses." Some of these interviews were not really interviews but soliloquies. Others approached a true dialogue. Some of these people were indifferent, others amused, still others *be*mused by the study. All this entered the region of my mind that, for want of any other name, I call the literary imagination.

Literature, C. Wright Mills wrote, may have become a minor art. Perhaps this is true of social science as well. Indeed, it may be that in this age (and Weber intimated this) there can be only minor arts. Mills suggested that works created by the use of the sociological imagination could fill the place abdicated by literature because, he thought, fiction could not compete with social fact. Yet in much contemporary literature (and this may have always been so; it may be that we are only coming to recognize what has always been the case), fiction is interlaced with nonfiction, with social and cultural and historical fact. And in these facts there is much of fictional, of mythological significance. In *Fact and Fiction*, Hollowell notes that Tony Tanner, in a discussion of Capote's *In Cold Blood*, refers to a statement in Thoreau's *Walden* in writing of "Capote's creation of myth from a passionless presentation of 'facts'":

Thoreau wrote: "I would so state facts that they shall be significant, shall be myths or mythologic" and Capote is in something of an old American tradition when he tries to get at the "mythic" significance of the facts by simply stating them. . . . It is a tradition based on the belief that "if men would steadily observe realities only" they would discover "that reality is fabulous."[30]

Events may be unnoticed or, at the other extreme, may overwhelm us. It is not what happens that matters so much as what we make of it, and to make sense of things we need both reason and imagination. In the United States today, there appears to be a distrust of fiction, of the workings of the imagination through the social facts. Evidence for this is all around us: books of nonfiction are published and sold at a ratio that has been estimated as between 7 and 10 to 1 to books of fiction. Editors and readers appear to cast a colder eye on fiction than on "reality." In his review of García Márquez' *The Autumn of the Patriarch* and Alejo Carpentier's *Reasons of State*, Michael Wood suggests an intriguing reason as to why this may be the case. Latin American novelists, according to Wood, have "a strong sense of reality as fiction. Reality is full of fictions in Europe and North America, too," he goes on to remark, "but I think we imagine the truth can be found, in most cases, if we really need it. In Latin America the truth is often not only unavailable, it is unimaginable, and unwanted." Thus, García Márquez' patriarch learns at last that "a lie is more comfortable than doubt, more useful than love, more lasting than truth."[31]

But who is to have the final word about the truth of things? On the basis of what "evidence" can this claim be made? A character's action, a combination of circumstances may seem to one reader to be completely unbelievable, and to another a painfully exact imitation of life. Our experiences, the influences that play upon our actions, the shape our intelligence takes are all so various that a moment of true communication is all but miraculous. Every person, Kierkegaard said, is an exception. So must it be with the stories each of us has to tell.

And so must it be with the portion of ourselves represented by the social fact, the statistic. The opinions we state about social issues, the way we vote or spend our money, the decisions we make about marrying and divorcing, the number of children we have, if we have any at all (demographers refer to this as our "reproductive behavior"), the design of our work life, and all the rest—these are surfaces, manifestations of thought and feeling, of fabulous experience that must be explored if we are to understand what any of it means. Appearances are not reality. Appearances are not truths.

To explore and to excavate, one needs an appreciation of what the humanities have to offer us. But today many humanists are suffering a failure of nerve. "Utilititarians and their enemies are at each other's throats again in American colleges and universities," Benjamin DeMott writes. Referring to the decline in the numbers of students planning to major in English and the humanities, fine arts and mathematics, De Mott says that the money crisis in higher education is at the root of the conflict on the campuses between "purists" and "utilitarians." The era of expansion in academe is over, now: "In the mid-70's, the safety valves are gone, and one academician's success is perceived as another's imminent budget cut."[32] In another item, De Mott discusses a symposium in which reference was made to the widening gulf between humanistic enterprises and common human concerns, and quotes Frederick Ness, head of the Association of American Colleges, who said that the reason why "a student can get an English major and know absolutely nothing about literature" in some departments, is because many members of that department "feeling as if the world has passed them by, decided the only way they could be heard was to become political and social scientists." De Mott suggests that one reason for the "negative self-images" of people in the humanities "is the incompatibility between humanistic studies and the spirit of the present." He observes that the foundation of the humanities is the Word, the "print culture," which is losing the central place in our lives.[33] This may well be so; surely it can be argued successfully that film is the emblem of our time. But if that is the case, people in the humanities and social sciences ought to lay down their arms in recognition of the fact that they have a common enemy.

Just as Mills felt, in the 1950s, that sociology was not fulfilling its promise, so there are contemporary thinkers whose judgment it is that this may be said of literature. In his Nobel Prize address, Saul Bellow spoke of the patience of the intelligent public, which "endures disappointment after disappointment, waiting to hear from art what it does not hear from theology, philosophy, social theory and what it cannot hear from pure science." There is a longing, immense and painful, Bellow said, for an account that is more full and coherent and flexible "of what we human beings are, who we are, and what this life is for." He spoke of European writers of the nineteenth century "who would not give up the connection of literature with the main human enterprise" and said that this very idea would have shocked Dostoevski and Tolstoy. But today, Bellow said, there is this distance between the public and great artists. For whatever reasons, literature moved ever further away from the vital center. Now we wait, we who "are much more limber, versatile, better articulated," for the writer who can begin to build a bridge. Bellow expressed the fervent wish that writers "would come back from the periphery." The center, he said, is still open to them—to those who will take heart, to those who will take the dare.[34]

In much this same spirit, Mills exhorted sociologists to lay the ghost of a rigid scientism for good, to weave the social facts into a coherent, all-encompassing design, to address themselves to the central issues of our time. Though separated by nearly twenty years, and by two traditions whose fates seem, for all the differences between them, to be strangely and wonderfully intertwined, both these thinkers intuited a vital center of meaning and truth, to be apprehended by those who write the best of literature and the best of social science. For both—one who died just as he was coming into his own as a major thinker in social science, the other who lives on, his powers increasing, now with the mantle of greatness placed upon his shoulders—there is this radiant vision of what social science, what literature could offer us in our quest for the essential meaning and truth of our lives. In their words, impassioned and aware, there is a challenge to both worlds, one that remains open, that could still be met.

Perhaps there has been a retreat of the literary imagination from social and historical reality. Fiction, Michael Wood writes,

serves to complicate the world—like a character in Julio Cortázar, it understands by complicating—and perhaps we should distinguish between cultures which still need to understand their world in that way and cultures which have had all the complication, and perhaps even all the understanding, in some senses, they can take. Thus the old novel is alive and well in India and Latin America (or was when last heard from) while it totters toward anemia in North America and England. I don't think that this tottering is solely a question of literature being edged out by history and sociology. It is a question of a major withdrawal of our imaginations from the historical world. Proust speaks somewhere of the faith that is needed for the creation of reality. We should ask, perhaps, about the faith that is needed for the creation of realistic fiction.[35]

Weber wrote that it is no accident that our greatest art is not monumental, but intimate. This may be true of our greatest social science as well. To try to say too much is to risk saying nothing. "Within one mind an advance in knowledge generates more thought, more knowledge," philosopher Stuart Hampshire writes. He reminds us in this essay on "The Future of Knowledge" that the *philosophes* of the Enlightenment "saw the need of putting modern knowledge together in an encyclopaedia small enough to be the stored contents of a single enlightened mind," and on this basis they hoped there would be an advance in the socal sciences and in social planning, one that would parallel the advances that had been made in physics and in engineering after Newton. Hampshire writes of two respects in which these hopes have been disappointed. One is that "after two centuries we have still not come anywhere near to any exact understanding of human behavior and of social change." Except for economics, Hampshire says, the social sciences do not have any useful laws of nature. And the other is that "we still cannot design a new town, or even a housing development . . . as a center of pleasure in living and as a fully human environment." Calling our attention to the fact that we do not have, despite the great advances in the common good which have been made, and which we too readily dismiss, the optimism about the future of our society that earlier thinkers had, Hampshire asks, "Why?" and says,

> One reason is a mistake in the theory of knowledge . . . : of its nature knowledge advances by the division of labor, by ever-increasing specialization. Every inquiry subdivides into new disciplines requiring separate investigation. It is also true that new knowledge depends on ideas from different disciplines being connected within a single mind. This contradictory requirement, not to be avoided, is a principal wound in modern culture, and it has been a topic for political theorists, poets, and philosophers ever since the Enlightenment. The most beautiful and most productive research, both in historical scholarship and in the physical sciences, is often the most minute and exact and the most remote from immediate common interests. . . . Beauty is often in detail, in science as in the arts.[36]

It is in their use of the *verstehende* method that social scientists are drawn into adopting the humanistic perspective. Indeed, it is instructive to read Hampshire's statement that "The best anthropologists have been, and still are, careful in moderating their claims to be scientific in explaining, as opposed merely to describing, social forms."[37] It cannot but happen that, in the quest for meaning, the social scientist and the writer and literary critic meet time and again. The humanities, it has been said, bring us the best that has been thought and written. Well, the social sciences bring us the latest, and the whole of it, from the ridiculous to the sublime. Each nourishes the other. And both are needed—the depth of the one, the breadth of the other—for a fuller understanding. Novelist Carlos Fuentes once said in an interview that literature overtakes history in that it offers us more than one life. To form our identity, Fuentes said, we are in need of many experiences, and this is what literature offers us. To this it may be added that the best of social science offers many experiences, and the possibility of more than one lifetime. Perhaps Clyde Kluckhohn said this best: "*Anthropology holds up a great mirror to man and lets him look at himself in his infinite variety.*"[38] The poem, the essay, the interview, the short story, the field study, the novel: all ways of seeing awaken us to the myriad possibilities within ourselves. In good fiction there is living reality. And in good nonfiction, in the works of social science that are well crafted, thereby hangs a tale—many a tale. Through reading of the lives of others, we come to know ourselves. Through examining our own souls, we come to know others—their worlds, their souls. No word sent forth from any one pathway of the imagination can be the last, the final word. Whatever form it appears to take, and whichever of the two traditions—the literary or the social scientific—that may claim it is of only momentary importance. If it is imaginative, it will endure if anything endures. It may even be thought of one day as a seedling of Hesse's *Glasperlenspiel*, of the Bead Game.

# Biographical Notes

Agee, James. Twentieth-century American poet, novelist, film critic, and screenwriter. His works include *A Death in the Family* and *The Morning Watch*. He is the co-author of *Let Us Now Praise Famous Men*. He died in 1955.

Algren, Nelson. Contemporary American novelist and short-story writer. His works include *The Man with the Golden Arm; The Neon Wilderness; A Walk on the Wild Side;* and *Notes from a Sea Diary*.

Alvarez, Alfred. Contemporary British poet, novelist, screenwriter, literary critic, and essayist. His works include *The Savage God: A Study of Suicide; Under Pressure;* and *Beyond All This Fiddle*. He edited *The New Poetry: An Anthology*.

Aron, Raymond. Contemporary French sociologist, historian, and political journalist. His works include *German Sociology; Introduction to the Philosophy of History; Democracy and Totalitarianism;* and *The Elusive Revolution*.

Auden, Wystan Hugh. Twentieth-century English-born poet, dramatist, essayist, and literary critic who lived in the United States after 1939. His works include *The Age of Anxiety; The Dance of Death; The Dyer's Hand;* and *The Shield of Achilles*. He died in 1973.

Auerbach, Erich. Twentieth-century German-born philologist, scholar, and critic who lived in the United States. His works include *Mimesis: The Representation of Reality in Western Literature; Literary Language and Its Public in Late Antiquity and the Middle Ages;* and *Scenes from the Drama of European Literature*. He died in 1957.

Bagehot, Walter. Nineteenth-century English economist, political analyst, sociologist, and author. His works include *The English Constitution; Physics and Politics; Lombard Street;* and *Economic Studies*. He died in 1877.

Beauvoir, Simone de. Contemporary French philosopher and author of fiction and nonfiction. Her works include *The Second Sex; The Mandarins; The Blood of Others;* and *She Came to Stay.*

Bellow, Saul. Contemporary American novelist and short-story writer. He won the Nobel Prize for Literature in 1976. His novels include *The Adventures of Augie March; Henderson the Rain King; Herzog;* and *Humboldt's Gift.*

Benedict, Ruth. Twentieth-century American anthropologist, educator, and author. Her works include *Patterns of Culture; Zuni Mythology; Race, Science, and Politics;* and *The Chrysanthemum and the Sword.* She died in 1948.

Berger, Bennett M. Contemporary American sociologist, educator, and author. His works include *Working-Class Suburb* and *Looking for America.*

Berger, Morroe. Contemporary American sociologist, educator, author, and translator. His works include *Bureaucracy and Society in Modern Egypt; Equality by Statute;* and *Real and Imagined Worlds.* He is co-editor of *Freedom and Control in Modern Society.*

Berger, Peter L. Contemporary Austrian-born sociologist, educator, and author now residing in the United States. His works include *A Rumor of Angels; The Precarious Vision;* and *Invitation to Sociology.* He is co-author of *The Social Construction of Reality.*

Bettelheim, Bruno. Contemporary Austrian-born psychologist, educator, and author now residing in the United States. His works include *Love Is Not Enough—The Treatment of Emotionally Disturbed Children; The Informed Heart; The Empty Fortress;* and *Children of the Dream.*

Bierstedt, Robert. Contemporary American sociologist, educator, and author. His works include *The Social Order; Power and Progress: Essays in Sociological Theory;* and *Emile Durkheim.* He is editor of *Florian Znaniecki: On Humanistic Sociology.*

Blumer, Herbert. Contemporary American sociologist, educator, and author. His works include *Symbolic Interactionism: Perspective and Method; Movies and Conduct;* and *Public Opinion and Public Opinion Polling.* He is co-author of *Movies, Delinquency and Crime.*

Boorstin, Daniel J. Contemporary American historian, educator, and author. His works include *The Americans: The National Experience; The Landmark History of the American People; The Sociology of the Absurd;* and *Democracy and Its Discontents.*

Borges, Jorge Luis. Contemporary Argentine novelist, short-story writer, poet, and critic. His works include *Labyrinths: Selected Stories and Other Writings; Ficciones; The Book of Imaginary Beings;* and *The Aleph and Other Stories.*

Borowski, Tadeusz. Twentieth-century Polish poet and short-story writer. His works include *Farewell to Maria* and *Stone World.* He committed suicide in 1951.

Bronowski, Jacob. Twentieth-century scientist, philosopher, educator, and author, born in Poland and raised and educated in England. His works include *The Common Sense of Science; Science and Human Values; The Identity of Man;* and *The Ascent of Man.* He died in 1974.

Burns, Elizabeth and Tom. Contemporary British sociologists, educators, and authors. Co-editors of *Sociology of Literature and Drama.* Elizabeth Burns is author of *Theatricality.* Tom Burns is author of *Local Government and Central Control,* co-author of *The Management of Innovation,* and editor of *Industrial Man.*

Butler, Robert N. Contemporary American psychiatrist, educator, and author. His works include *Why Survive? Being Old in America.* He is co-author of *Human Aging; Aging and Mental Health;* and *Sex after Sixty.*

Calisher, Hortense. Contemporary American novelist and short-story writer. Her works include *In the Absence of Angels; Textures of Life; The New Yorkers;* and *Herself.*

Cameron, J. M. Contemporary British critic, educator, and author, now residing in Canada. His works include *The Night Battle* and *Images of Authority.*

Capote, Truman. Contemporary American novelist and short-story writer. His works include *Other Voices, Other Rooms; The Grass Harp; Breakfast at Tiffany's;* and *In Cold Blood.*

Cary, Joyce. Twentieth-century British novelist and author of political works. His books include *Herself Surprised; A Fearful Joy; The Horse's Mouth;* and *A Prisoner of Grace.* He died in 1957.

Chiaromonte, Nicola. Twentieth-century Italian critic, educator, and author. His works include *The Paradox of History; La Situazione Drammatica;* and *The Worm of Consciousness and Other Essays.* He edited *A Critique of Violence.* He died in 1972.

Clausen, John. Contemporary American sociologist, educator, and author. His works include *Sociology and the Field of Mental Health.* He edited *Socialization and Society.*

Coles, Robert. Contemporary American psychiatrist and author. His works include *Erik H. Erikson: The Growth of His Work; Children of Crisis I: A Study of Courage and Fear; Migrants, Sharecroppers, Mountaineers;* and *The South Goes North.*

Coser, Lewis. Contemporary American sociologist, educator, and author. His works include *The Functions of Social Conflict; Men of Ideas; Georg Simmel;* and *Political Sociology.*

De Mott, Benjamin. Contemporary American journalist, educator, novelist, and short-story writer. His works include *The Body's Cage; Hells and Benefits; Surviving the Seventies;* and *Scholarship for Society.*

Dollard, John. Contemporary American psychologist, educator, and author. His works include *Caste and Class in a Southern Town.* He is co-author of *Personality and Psychotherapy; Children of Bondage;* and *Scoring Human Motives.*

Durkheim, Emile. Nineteenth- and twentieth-century French sociologist, educator, and author. His works include *The Division of Labor in Society; The Rules of Sociological Method; The Elementary Forms of the Religious Life;* and *Suicide.* He died in 1917.

Eastman, Max. Twentieth-century American poet, critic, educator, essayist, historian, and translator. His works include *The Enjoyment of Poetry; Reflections on the Failure of Socialism; Poems of Five Decades;* and *Love and Revolution.* He died in 1969.

Ehrenpreis, Irvin. Contemporary American critic, educator, and author. His works include *The Personality of Jonathan Swift; Literary Meaning and Values;* and *Swift: The Man, His Works, and the Age.* He is co-editor of *The Familiar Letter in the 18th Century.*

Eiseley, Loren. Twentieth-century American anthropologist, educator, and author. His works include *The Immense Journey; The Unexpected Universe; The Night Country;* and *Darwin's Century.* He died in 1977.

Eliot, George (Mary Ann Evans). Nineteenth-century English author of novels and journals. Her works include *Adam Bede; The Mill on the Floss; Silas Marner;* and *Middlemarch: A Study of Provincial Life.* She died in 1880.

Ellison, Ralph. Contemporary American novelist and essayist. His major work is *Invisible Man.* He has also written *Shadow and Act.*

Erikson, Kai T. Contemporary American sociologist, educator, and author. His works include *Everything in Its Path* and *Wayward Puritans: A Study in the Sociology of Deviance.* He is editor of *In Search of Common Ground: Conversations with Erik H. Erikson and Huey P. Newton.*

Escarpit, Robert. Contemporary French critic, educator, and novelist. His works include *Sociologie de la Littérature; Hemingway; La Faim de Lire;* and *The Book Revolution.*

Etzioni, Amitai. Contemporary German-born sociologist, educator, and author now residing in the United States. His works include *A Comparative Analysis of Complex Organizations; Modern Organizations; Studies in Social Change;* and *The Active Society: A Theory of Societal and Political Processes.*

Evans, Walker. Twentieth-century American photographer, educator, and author. His works include *American Photographs; Message from the Interior;* and *Many Are Called.* With James Age, he wrote *Let Us Now Praise Famous Men.* He died in 1975.

Faulkner, William. Twentieth-century American novelist and short-story writer. He won the Nobel Prize for Literature in 1949. His works include *The Sound and the Fury; As I Lay Dying; Light in August;* and *Intruder in the Dust.* He died in 1962.

Feinberg, Leonard. Contemporary American critic, educator, and author. His works include *Introduction to Satire; The Satirist;* and *Asian Laughter.*

Fiedler, Leslie. Contemporary American critic, educator, novelist, and short-story writer. His works include *An End to Innocence; Back to China; Love and Death in the American Novel;* and *The Jew in the American Novel.*

Fitzgerald, Robert. Contemporary American poet and translator. His works include *A Wreath for the Sea; In the Rose of Time: Poems 1931-56;* and translations from Latin, Greek, French, and Spanish.

Foucault, Michel. Contemporary French philosopher, educator, and author. His works include *The Order of Things; Madness and Civilization; Les Mots et les Choses;* and *Histoire de la Sexualité* (3 vols.).

Frazer, Sir James George. Nineteenth- and Twentieth-century English anthropologist, educator, and author. His works include *The Golden Bough: A Study in Magic and Religion; Totemism and Exogamy; The Belief in Immortality and the Worship of the Dead;* and *Folk-Lore in the Old Testament.* He died in 1941.

Frye, Northrop. Contemporary Canadian educator and critic. His works include *The Stubborn Structure; Anatomy of Criticism: Four Essays; Fables of Identity;* and *The Critical Path: An Essay on the Social Context of Literary Criticism.*

Fuentes, Carlos. Contemporary Mexican novelist and critic. His works include *Where the Air Is Clear; The Death of Artemio Cruz; Change of Skin;* and *Terra Nostra.*

Garfinkel, Harold. Contemporary American sociologist, educator, and author. His works include *Studies in Ethnomethodology.*

Glazer, Nathan. Contemporary American sociologist, educator, and author. His works include *Affirmative Discrimination: Ethnic Inequality and Public Policy* and *American Judaism.* He is co-author of *The Lonely Crowd* and *Beyond the Melting Pot.*

Goffman, Erving. Contemporary American sociologist, educator, and author. His works include *Encounters; Asylums; Behavior in Public Places;* and *Stigma.*

Goldmann, Lucien. Contemporary French philosopher, sociologist, and author. His works include *The Human Sciences and Philosophy; Immanuel Kant; The Hidden God;* and *The Philosophy of the Enlightenment.*

Gorer, Geoffrey. Contemporary English-born psychological anthropologist and author. His works include *Exploring English Character; Himalayan Village: An Account of the Lepchas of Sikkim; The American People;* and *Death, Grief, and Mourning.*

Gottschalk, Louis R. Twentieth-century American historian, educator, and author. His works include *Lafayette and the Close of the American Revolution* and *Understanding History: A Primer of Historical Method.*

He is co-author of *Toward the French Revolution* and editor of *Generalization in the Writing of History*. He died in 1975.

Gouldner, Alvin M. Contemporary American sociologist, educator, and author. His works include *The Coming Crisis of Western Sociology; Patterns of Industrial Bureaucracy;* and *For Sociology*. He is co-author of *Notes on Technology and the Moral Order*.

Hampshire, Stuart N. Contemporary English philosopher, administrator, educator, and author. His works include *Spinoza; Thought and Action; Freedom of the Individual;* and *Freedom of Mind and Other Essays*.

Hannerz, Ulf. Contemporary Swedish anthropologist and author. His works include *Soulside: Inquiries into Ghetto Culture and Community; Palaverland: Nigerianska Bilder; Caymanian Politics: Structure and Style in a Changing Island Society;* and *Tropiska Akvariefiskar*.

Hardwick, Elizabeth. Contemporay American critic and novelist. Her works include *The Simple Truth; A View of My Own;* and *Seduction and Betrayal*. She is editor of *The Selected Letters of William James*.

Harrington, Michael. Contemporary American social scientist, educator, and author. His works include *The Other America; Toward a Democratic Left; Socialism;* and *The Accidental Century*.

Heberle, Rudolf. Contemporary German-born sociologist, educator, and author now residing in the United States. His works include *From Democracy to Nazism: A Regional Case Study on Political Parties in Germany; Social Movements: An Introduction to Political Sociology;* and *The Labor Force in Louisiana*. He is co-editor of *Ferdinand Tönnies on Sociology*.

Henry, Jules. Twentieth-century American anthropologist, educator, and author. His works include *Jungle People; Culture against Man; Pathways to Madness;* and *Jules Henry on Education*. He died in 1969.

Hesse, Hermann. Twentieth-century German-born novelist, poet, short-story writer, and critic. He won the Nobel Prize for Literature in 1946. His works include *Demian; Siddhartha; Steppenwolf;* and *Magister Ludi (The Bead Game)*. He died in 1962.

Hollowell, John. Contemporary American educator and author. He has written *Fact and Fiction: The New Journalism and the Nonfiction Novel*.

Huxley, Aldous. Twentieth-century English novelist, short-story writer, and critic. His works include *Ape and Essence; Point Counterpoint; Brave New World;* and *Antic Hay*. He died in 1963.

James, Henry. Nineteenth- and twentieth-century American novelist, short-story writer, dramatist, critic, and essayist. His works include *The Portrait of a Lady; The Wings of the Dove; The Golden Bowl;* and *The American Scene*. He died in 1916.

Jung, Carl G. Twentieth-century Swiss psychiatrist and author. His works include *Contributions to Analytical Psychology; Modern Man in Search of a Soul; Man and His Symbols;* and *The Integration of the Personality.* He died in 1961.

Kazin, Alfred. Contemporary American critic, educator, and author. His works include *On Native Grounds; Contemporaries; Starting Out in the Thirties;* and *Bright Book of Life.*

Kermode, J. Frank. Contemporary English critic and editor. His works include *The Sense of an Ending; Continuities; D. H. Lawrence;* and *The Classic.*

Kluckhohn, Clyde. Twentieth-century American anthropologist, educator, and author. His works include *Mirror for Man* and *Navaho Witchcraft.* He is co-author of *The Navaho* and co-editor of *Personality in Nature, Society, and Culture.* He died in 1960.

Kramer, Hilton. Contemporary American art critic and author. His works include *The Age of the Avant-Garde.* He is editor of *Perspectives on the Arts.*

Kroeber, Alfred. Twentieth-century American anthropologist, educator, and author. His works include *Anthropology; Configurations of Culture Growth; Nature of Culture;* and *Cultural and Natural Areas of Native North America.* He died in 1960.

Kübler-Ross, Elisabeth. Contemporary Swiss-born psychiatrist and author now residing in the United States. Her works include *The Psychology of Dying* and *On Death and Dying.* She is editor of *Death: The Final Stage of Growth.*

Ladd, Everett C. Contemporary American political scientist, educator, and author. His works include *Negro Political Leadership in the South; American Political Parties;* and *Ideology in America.* He is co-author of *Professors, Unions, and American Higher Education.*

La Farge, Oliver. Twentieth-century American anthropologist and writer of fiction and nonfiction. His works include *The Enemy Gods; The Door in the Wall; Laughing Boy;* and *Santa Eulalia.* He died in 1963.

Larner, Jeremy. Contemporary American writer of fiction and nonfiction, and screenwriter. His works include *Drive, He Said* and *The Answer.* He is co-editor of *The Addict in the Street* and *Poverty: Views from the Left.*

Larsen, Eric. Contemporary American critic, educator, and writer. He is the author of fiction and articles on American literature.

Le Masters, E. E. Contemporary American sociologist, educator, and author. His works include *Parents in Modern America; Blue-Collar Aristocrats;* and *Modern Courtship and Marriage.*

Levin, Harry. Contemporary American critic, educator, and author. His works include *James Joyce: A Critical Introduction; The Power of Blackness; Contexts of Criticism;* and *Grounds for Comparison.*

Lévi-Strauss, Claude. Contemporary French anthropologist, educator, and author. His works include *Structures of Kinship; Structural Anthropology; The Savage Mind;* and *Mythologiques* (4 vols.).

Lewis, Oscar. Twentieth-century American anthropologist, educator, and author. His works include *Five Families: Mexican Case Studies in the Culture of Poverty; The Children of Sanchez: Autobiography of a Mexican Family; Pedro Martinez: A Mexican Peasant and His Family;* and *La Vida: A Puerto Rican Family in the Culture of Poverty—San Juan and New York.* He died in 1970.

Liebow, Elliot. Contemporary American anthropologist, educator, and author. His works include *Tally's Corner: A Study of Negro Streetcorner Men.*

Lienhardt, Godfrey. Contemporary English anthropologist, educator, and author. His works include *Social Anthropology; Divinity and Experience; The Religion of the Dinka;* and *Annak Village Headmen.*

Lipset, Seymour M. Contemporary American sociologist, educator, and author. His works include *Revolution and Counterrevolution.* He is co-author of *Professors, Unions, and Higher Education; The Politics of Unreason;* and *Social Mobility in Industrial Society.*

Lowell, Robert. Twentieth-century American poet and translator. His works include *Lord Weary's Castle; Life Studies; For the Union Dead;* and *History.* He died in 1977.

Lynd, Robert. Twentieth-century American sociologist, educator, and author. His works include *Knowledge for What?* With his wife, Helen, he wrote *Middletown* and *Middletown in Transition.* He died in 1970.

Macdonald, Dwight. Contemporary American critic and essayist. His works include *The Root is Man; Against the American Grain; Discriminations;* and *The Responsibility of Peoples.*

Maddox, George. Contemporary American sociologist, educator, and author. He is the co-author of *Drinking among Teenagers; Behavioral Science;* and *Research and Development in Aging;* and editor of *The Domesticated Drug.*

Mailer, Norman. Contemporary American novelist, short-story writer, and essayist. His works include *The Naked and the Dead; An American Dream; The Armies of the Night;* and *Miami and the Siege of Chicago.*

Malinowski, Bronislaw. Twentieth-century Polish-born anthropologist, educator, and author, who taught in the United States and in England. His works include *The Family among the Australian Aborigines; Argonauts of the Western Pacific; Sex and Repression in a Savage Society;* and *The Dynamics of Culture Change.* He died in 1942.

Malraux, André. Twentieth-century French novelist, essayist, archaeologist, and government official. His works include *Man's Hope; Man's Fate; Anti-Memoirs;* and *The Metamorphosis of the Gods.* He died in 1976.

Mead, George Herbert. Twentieth-century American philosopher, social psychologist, and educator. His students edited four volumes of his papers: *The Philosophy of the Present; Mind, Self, and Society; Movements of*

*Thought in the Nineteenth Century;* and *The Philosophy of the Act.* He died in 1931.

Mead, Margaret. Contemporary American anthropologist, educator, and author. Her works include *Coming of Age in Samoa; Growing Up in New Guinea; Sex and Temperament in Three Primitive Societies;* and *Male and Female.*

Metzger, Walter. Contemporary American historian, educator, and author. His works include *Freedom and Order in the University.* He is co-author of *Dimensions of Academic Freedom* and *The Development of Academic Freedom in the United States.*

Miller, Henry. Contemporary American novelist, essayist, and critic. His works include *Tropic of Cancer; The Cosmological Eye; The Colossus of Maroussi;* and *The Air-Conditioned Nightmare.*

Mills, C. Wright. Twentieth-century American sociologist, educator, and author. His works include *The Power Elite; White Collar; The Sociological Imagination;* and *The Causes of World War Three.* He died in 1962.

Newman, Edwin. Contemporary American news correspondent, interviewer, and author. His works include *Strictly Speaking: Will America Be the Death of English?* and *A Civil Tongue.*

Nin, Anaïs. Twentieth-century American novelist, short-story writer, and essayist, born in Paris. Her works include *Under a Glass Bell; The Four-Chambered Heart; Seduction of the Minotaur;* and *Diary of Anaïs Nin* (6 vols.). She died in 1977.

Nisbet, Robert A. Contemporary American sociologist, educator, and author. His works include *The Quest for Community; Twilight of Authority; Social Change and History;* and *Sociology as an Art Form.*

O'Connor, Frank. Twentieth-century Irish short-story writer, novelist, and playwright. His works include *Bones of Contention; Lords and Commons; The Common Chord;* and *The Mirror in the Roadway.* He died in 1966.

Oppenheimer, Joel. Contemporary American poet, essayist, and short-story writer. His works include *In Time; On Occasion; The Great American Desert;* and *The Wrong Season.*

Orwell, George. Twentieth-century English novelist, essayist, and critic. His works include *Animal Farm; Nineteen Eighty-Four; Down and Out in Paris and London;* and *Homage to Catalonia.* He died in 1950.

Pessen, Edward. Contemporary American historian, educator, and author. His works include *Most Uncommon Jacksonians; Jacksonian America;* and *New Perspectives on Jacksonian Parties and Politics.* He is editor of *Three Centuries of Social Mobility in America.*

Pierce, Kenneth. Contemporary American journalist and author. He was editor of the *Columbia Journalism Review,* and wrote for many publications on the civil rights movement in the 1960s.

Porter, Katherine Anne. Contemporary American novelist, short-story writer, essayist, and translator. Her works include *Pale Horse, Pale Rider; Ship of Fools; The Leaning Tower, and Other Stories;* and *The Days Before.*

Powdermaker, Hortense. Contemporary American anthropologist, educator, and author. Her works include *Life in Lesu: The Study of a Melanesian Society in New Ireland; Stranger and Friend: The Way of an Anthropologist; Hollywood, the Dream Factory;* and *Copper Town, Changing Africa.*

Powys, John Cowper. Twentieth-century English novelist, poet, and essayist. His works include *The Pleasures of Literature; The Meaning of Culture; A Glastonbury Romance;* and *Wolf Solent.* He died in 1963.

Price, Martin. Contemporary American educator, critic, and author. His works include *Swift's Rhetorical Art* and *To the Palace of Wisdom.* He is co-editor of *Literary Theory and Structure.*

Radin, Paul. Twentieth-century Polish-born anthropologist, educator, and author who lived in the United States. His works include *The Winnebago Tribe; Crashing Thunder; Primitive Man as Philosopher;* and *Primitive Religion.* He died in 1959.

Rainwater, Lee. Contemporary American sociologist, educator, and author. His works include *And The Poor Get Children; Behind Ghetto Walls;* and *Social Problems and Public Policy.* He is co-author of *Workingman's Wife.*

Rich, Adrienne. Contemporary American poet and translator. Her works include *A Change of World; Necessities of Life: Poems 1962-65; The Will to Change;* and *Diving into the Wreck.*

Richards, I. A. Contemporary English critic, educator, poet, and playwright. His works include *Principles of Literary Criticism; Science and Poetry; Coleridge on Imagination;* and *Goodbye Earth, and Other Poems.*

Rilke, Rainer Maria. Twentieth-century German poet. Born in Prague, he lived in Austria and Germany. His works include *Poems; Sonnets to Orpheus; Duino Elegies;* and *Stories of God.* He died in 1926.

Roethke, Theodore. Twentieth-century American poet, essayist, and educator. His works include *Open House; The Lost Son; Words for the Wind;* and *The Poet and His Craft.* He died in 1963.

Roth, Philip. Contemporary American novelist, short-story writer, and essayist. His works include *Goodbye, Columbus; Letting Go; Portnoy's Complaint;* and *My Life as a Man.*

Schumacher, E. F. Twentieth-century German-born economist and author who lived in England. His works include *Export Policy and Full Employment; Roots of Economic Growth;* and *Small Is Beautiful: Economics as if People Mattered.* He died in 1977.

Simmel, Georg. Nineteenth- and twentieth-century German philosopher, educator, and author. His works include *Soziologie; Philosophie des*

*Geldes; Sociology of Religion;* and *The Conflict in Modern Culture, and Other Essays.* He died in 1918.

Snow, C. P. Contemporary English scientist, novelist, and administrator. His works include *The Search; Strangers and Brothers; The Masters;* and *The Two Cultures and the Scientific Revolution.*

Sontag, Susan. Contemporary American novelist, short-story writer, dramatist, essayist, and film director. Her works include *The Benefactor; Death Kit; Against Interpretation and Other Essays;* and *Styles of Radical Will.*

Staël-Holstein, Anne L. G. (Mme de Staël). Eighteenth- and nineteenth-century French novelist and critic. Her works include *Lettres sur Jean-Jacques Rousseau; De la Littérature, Considerée dans ses Rapports avec les Institutions Sociales; Delphine;* and *Corinne.* She died in 1817.

Starkie, Walter. Twentieth-century English educator, translator, critic, and author. His works include *The Road to Santiago; The Waveless Plain; A Musician's Journey through Time and Space;* and *Scholars and Gypsies.* He died in 1976.

Steiner, George. Contemporary American critic, educator, and author. His works include *The Death of Tragedy; Language and Silence; Extraterritorial;* and *After Babel: Aspects of Language and Translation.*

Stott, William. Contemporary American cultural historian, educator, and author. His major work is *Documentary Expression and Thirties America.*

Szarkowski, John. Contemporary American photographer and author. His works include *The Idea of Louis Sullivan; Looking at Photographs;* and *The Photographer's Eye.* He is editor of *The Photographer and the American Landscape.*

Taine, Hyppolyte A. Nineteenth-century French historian, literary and art critic, and author. His works include *Les Origenes de la France Contemporaine; Histoire de la Littérature Anglaise;* and *Les Philosophes Classiques du XIX$^e$ Siècle en France.* He died in 1893.

Terkel, Studs. Contemporary American interviewer and author. His works include *Division Street: America; Hard Times; Working;*and *Giants of Jazz.*

Theroux, Paul. Contemporary American novelist, poet, and educator residing in England. His works include *Waldo; Girls at Play; The Black House;* and *V. S. Naipaul: An Introduction to His Work.*

Thomas, W. I. Nineteenth-and twentieth-century American social psychologist, educator, and author. His works include *Sex and Society; Source Book for Social Origins;* and *The Unadjusted Girl.* He is co-author of *The Polish Peasant in Europe and America* (5 vols.). He died in 1947.

Tönnies, Ferdinand. Nineteenth- and twentieth-century German sociologist, educator, and author. His works include *Community and Society; Custom: An Essay on Social Codes; Kritik der Öffentlichen Meinung;* and *Soziologische Studien und Kritiken.* He died in 1936.

Trilling, Lionel. Twentieth-century American critic, educator, and short-story writer. His works include *The Liberal Imagination; A Gathering of Fugitives; Beyond Culture: Essays on Learning and Literature;* and *Mind in the Modern World.* He died in 1975.

Unamuno, Miguel de. Twentieth-century Spanish poet, novelist, short-story writer, philosopher, essayist, and educator. His works include *The Life of Don Quixote and Sancho; [The] Tragic Sense of Life in Men and in Peoples; Mist;* and *Abel Sanchez.* He died in 1936.

Vendler, Helen. Contemporary American critic, educator, and author. Her works include *Yeats' Vision and the Later Plays; The Poetry of George Herbert;* and *On Extended Wings.*

Warner, W. Lloyd. Twentieth-century American anthropologist, educator, and author. His works include *A Black Civilization: A Social Study of an Australian Tribe.* He is co-author of *The Social Life of a Modern Community; Social Class in America;* and *American Life: Dream and Reality.* He died in 1970.

Warren, Robert Penn. Contemporary American poet, novelist, critic, and educator. His works include *All the King's Men; World Enough and Time; Segregation;* and *Selected Poems.*

Watt, Ian. Contemporary English critic and bibliographer residing in the United States. His works include *The Rise of the Novel* and *The British Novel.* He is the compiler of *The Victorian Novel: Modern Essays in Criticism* and editor of *Jane Austen.*

Wattenberg, Ben J. Contemporary American political administrator and author. His works include *The Real America: A Surprising Examination of the State of the Union.* He is co-author of *This U.S.A.* and *The Real Majority.*

Waugh, Evelyn. Twentieth-century English novelist. His works include *Decline and Fall; Brideshead Revisited; The Loved One;* and *Officers and Gentlemen.* He died in 1966.

Weber, Max. Nineteenth- and twentieth-century German sociologist, educator, and author. His works include *The Protestant Ethic and the Spirit of Capitalism; General Economic History; The Theory of Social and Economic Organization;* and *Ancient Judaism.* He died in 1920.

Weil, Simone. Twentieth-century French writer. Her works include *Gravity and Grace; The Need for Roots; Waiting on God;* and *Oppression and Liberty.* She died in 1943.

Whyte, William Foote. Contemporary American sociologist, educator, and author. His works include *Street Corner Society; Pattern for Industrial Peace; Men at Work;* and *Organizational Behavior.*

Williams, William Carlos. Twentieth-century American poet, novelist, short-story writer, and essayist. His works include *Spring and All; Adam and Eve and the City; Paterson;* and *The Build-up.* He died in 1963.

Wilson, Edmund. Twentieth-century American critic, novelist, and short-story writer. His works include *I Thought of Daisy; Memoirs of Hecate County; A Piece of My Mind;* and *Upstate.* He died in 1972.

Wilson, Robert N. Contemporary American sociologist, educator, and author. His works include *Man Made Plain.* He is co-author of *Community Structure and Health Action* and co-editor of *Explorations in Social Psychiatry.* He is editor of *The Arts in Society.*

Withers, Carl. Contemporary American anthropologist, folklorist, and author. His works include *Plainville, U.S.A.,* which he wrote under the pseudonym James West. He is co-editor of *The Illustrated Book of American Folklore; Strange and Humorous Tales from Many Lands;* and *World of Nonsense.*

Wolfe, Tom. Contemporary American journalist, humorist, and essayist. His works include *The Kandy-Kolored Tangerine-Flake Streamline Baby; The Electric Kool-Aid Acid Test; Radical Chic and Mau-mauing the Flak Catchers;* and *The Painted Word.*

Wolin, Sheldon S. Contemporary American political scientist, educator, and author. His works include *Politics and Vision: Continuity and Innovation in Western Political Thought.* He is co-author of *The Berkeley Rebellion and Beyond* and co-editor of *The Berkeley Student Revolt.*

Wood, Michael. Contemporary American critic, educator, and author. His works include *Stendahl* and *America in the Movies.*

Woolf, Virginia. Twentieth-century English novelist and essayist. Her works include *Jacob's Room; To the Lighthouse; The Waves;* and *Orlando.* She committed suicide in 1941.

Znaniecki, Florian. Twentieth-century Polish-born sociologist, educator, and author who lived in the United States. His works include *Social Actions; Cultural Sciences;* and *The Social Role of the Man of Knowledge.* He is co-author of *The Polish Peasant in Europe and America.* He died in 1958.

# NOTES

## Introduction

1. Hermann Hesse, *Magister Ludi (The Bead Game)*, trans. Mervyn Savill (New York: Frederick Ungar, 1967). In the introduction, Hesse tells the history of the Bead Game.
2. Elizabeth and Tom Burns, "Introduction," *Sociology of Literature and Drama*, Elizabeth and Tom Burns, eds. (Harmondsworth, Middlesex, England: Penguin Books, 1973), pp. 10-11.
3. Morroe Berger, *Real and Imagined Worlds: The Novel and Social Science* (Cambridge, Mass.: Harvard University Press, 1977), p. 153.
4. *Ibid.*, p.255.
5. *Ibid.*
6. Eric Larsen, "Notes on Emptiness: The State of Fiction," *South Dakota Review* (Autumn 1975), 13(3): 125-26.
7. Ian Watt, "*Robinson Crusoe* as a Myth," in *Sociology of Literature and Drama*, pp. 242-43.
8. Eric Larsen, "Notes on Emptiness: The State of Fiction," p. 128.
9. *Ibid.*
10. *Ibid.*, p. 134.
11. *Ibid.*
12. *Ibid.*, p. 127.
13. "Trashing the 50's," Hilton Kramer writes, in a review of Morris Dickstein's *Gates of Eden: American Culture in the Sixties*, "a 'radical' stance in the 60's, has become in the 70's something of an academic industry—a fixed item in the college curriculum, and a convenient refuge for conventional minds." Kramer says that one of the most distinctive features of the literary defense of the 1960s "is the impulse . . . to portray the 1950s as a period of unparalleled wickedness, repression and fear." A stereotype has emerged, as false as it is widely accepted, of the 1950s "as a time when an entire culture collapsed in a state of academic torpor and moral retreat, and an entire generation of writers and intellectuals succumbed to an atmosphere of blandness and sterility, guided solely by motives of cowardice and venality." Hilton Kramer, "Trashing the Fifties," *New York Times Book Review*, April 10, 1977, p. 3.
14. Morroe Berger, *Real and Imagined Worlds*, p. 153.
15. Michel Foucault, *The Order of Things: An Archaeology of the Human Sciences*, Vintage Books ed. (New York: Random House, 1973), p. xv.
16. Saul Bellow, in *Writers at Work: The Paris Review Interviews* (third series), George Plimpton, ed. (New York: Viking Press, Viking Compass ed., 1968), p. 181.

17. *Ibid.*, p. 189.

18. John Hollowell, *Fact and Fiction: The New Journalism and the Nonfiction Novel* (Chapel Hill: University of North Carolina Press, 1977), p. 125.

19. For a brilliantly drawn contrast between two great men, D. H. Lawrence and Max Weber, who took these separate paths, see Martin Green, *The von Richthofen Sisters: The Triumphant and the Tragic Modes of Love* (New York: Basic Books, 1974.)

20. "It is a human tendency," Bierstedt writes, "to believe what we want to believe and to disbelieve what displeases us. In seeking to prove a proposition, we find it easy to look for confirming evidence and to disregard or to avoid any evidence that seems to disprove it." Thus Darwin took care to record observations that did not fit into his theory, knowing that he would remember evidence that seemed to confirm it, and might too easily forget that which appeared to refute it. Robert Bierstedt, *The Social Order*, 4th ed. (New York: McGraw-Hill, 1974), p. 17.

21. Alvin W. Gouldner, *The Coming Crisis of Western Sociology* (New York: Basic Books, 1970), p. 41.

22. Raymond Aron, *Main Currents in Sociological Thought*, vol. II, trans. Richard Howard and Helen Weaver (New York: Basic Books, Anchor Books ed., 1970), p. 282.

23. Daniel J. Boorstin, *Democracy and Its Discontents: Reflections on Everyday America* (New York: Random House, 1974), pp. 47, 45.

24. Ruth Benedict, "Anthropology and the Humanities," in Margaret Mead, ed., *Ruth Benedict* (New York: Columbia University Press, 1974), p. 168. The issue of anthropology as a science and anthropology as a humanistic discipline is far from dormant. See the item by G. B. K., "Social Anthropologists Learn to Be Scientific" in *Science* (February 25, 1977), 195 (4280): 770, and the letters written in response to this in *Science* (April 22, 1977), 196(4288): 372, 374, 378, and 380.

25. E. F. Schumacher, *Small Is Beautiful: Economics as if People Mattered* (New York: Harper & Row, 1973), p. 49.

26. *Ibid.*, p. 94.

27. Robert Bierstedt, "Sociology and Humane Learning," in *Power and Progress: Essays on Sociological Theory* (New York: McGraw-Hill, 1974), pp. 312-13.

28. *Ibid.*, p. 317.

## 1. On the Sin of Social Science

1. Edmund Wilson, *Axel's Castle* (New York: Scribner's, 1931), p. 41.

2. *Ibid.*, pp. 59-60.

3. Robert N. Wilson, *Man Made Plain* (Cleveland: Howard Allen, 1958), p. xlv.

4. Henry Murray, "Foreword," *Man Made Plain*, p. xx.

5. Peter L. Berger, *Invitation to Sociology: A Humanistic Perspective* (Garden City, N.Y.: Doubleday Anchor Books, 1963), p. 2.

6. Robert Bierstedt, *The Social Order*, 4th ed. (New York: McGraw-Hill, 1974), p. 6.

7. Elizabeth and Tom Burns, "Introduction," *Sociology of Literature and Drama*, Elizabeth and Tom Burns, eds. (Harmondsworth, Middlesex, England: Penguin Books, 1973), pp. 16-17.

8. *Ibid.*, p. 18.

9. *Ibid.*, p. 9.

10. Alvin W. Gouldner, *The Coming Crisis of Western Sociology* (New York: Basic Books, 1970), p.57.

11. Edwin Newman, *Strictly Speaking: Will America Be the Death of English?* (New York: Warner Books, 1975), p.174.

12. Edward Pessen, "Current Historiographical Modes, Obfuscatory in Nature,

Manifest an Indifference to Quintessential Elements of Meaningfulness," *New York Times*, March 27, 1976, p. 25.

13. *Ibid.*

14. After nearly twenty years of service in the classroom, listening to students of diverse backgrounds, ages, and persuasions, I have come to think of "opinion" as meaning what one does not want to believe, and of "fact" as what one does. Students who do not accept an idea will demand a "study" that supports it. And once this is provided them, they will attack it relentlessly. But if they hear of an idea of which they approve, no "study" is requested; whoever advocated it is praised as a person of extraordinary insight.

15. Max Weber, "Science as a Vocation," in *From Max Weber: Essays in Sociology*, trans., ed., and with an introduction by H. H. Gerth and C. Wright Mills (New York: Oxford University Press, 1946), p. 150.

16. Frank Kermode, *The Sense of an Ending: Studies in the Theory of Fiction* (New York: Oxford University Press, 1967), pp. 140-41.

17. Saul Bellow, *Humboldt's Gift* (New York: Viking Press, 1975), p. 404.

18. As quoted in A. Alvarez, *The Savage God: A Study of Suicide* (New York: Random House, Bantam Books ed., 1973), p.272.

19. C. Wright Mills, *The Sociological Imagination* (New York: Grove Press, Evergreen ed., 1961), p. 6.

20. See Peter Berger, *Invitation to Sociology*, chap. 7.

21. Herbert Blumer, "Sociological Analysis and the 'Variable,'" in *Symbolic Interaction: A Reader in Social Psychology*, 2d ed., Jerome G. Manis and Bernard N. Meltzer, eds. (Boston: Allyn and Bacon, 1972), pp. 95-96.

22. *Ibid.*, p. 101. Although Blumer stated that variable analysis is an appropriate procedure for areas of social life and formation that are not mediated by interpretation, he did not specify what those areas might be.

23. Amitai Etzioni, "Effects of Small Computers on Scientists," *Science* (July 11, 1975), 189(4197): 93. Etzioni suggests that one way to benefit from the use of miniaturized computers without succumbing to them is to train graduate students in the dangers of yielding to computers, allowing them to set the pace and direction of their research, and also teaching them of "the need to protect time for reflection."

24. George Maddox, "Age as Explanation," *Science* (October 20, 1972), 178(4058): 294-95.

25. John A. Clausen, "The Young as Outsiders," *Science* (February 21, 1975), 187(4177): 637.

26. Edwin Newman, *Strictly Speaking*, p. 100. Classification, Newman goes on to say, "tends to destroy the privacy and secrecy of the voting booth." One consequence of knowing how a person is likely to vote "is the promotion of excessive calculation among politicians." (pp. 100-1).

27. Dorothy D. Bromley and Florence H. Britten, *Youth and Sex: A Study of 1300 College Students* (New York: Harper, 1938).

28. Suzanne Reichard, Florine Livson, and Paul G. Petersen, *Aging and Personality* (New York: John Wiley, 1962), pp. 170-72.

29. Walter P. Metzger, "Leanings of the Professoriate," *Science* (January 23, 1976), 191(4224): 279.

30. "Not to realize that democratic politics may be a world rather than a degree removed from extremist politics," Metzger observes, "is either to foreshorten the range of existing options or to give the rabid fringes an unwarranted gift of near-allies." "Leanings of the Professoriate," p. 280.

31. Metzger, "Leanings of the Professoriate," p. 280.

32. Robert N. Wilson, *Man Made Plain*, p. 19.

## 1. On the Sin of Social Science

33. Studs Terkel, "A Steel Worker Speaks: Interview with Mike Fitzgerald," *Dissent* (Winter 1972), 19(1): 15.
34. *Ibid.*, p. 17.
35. Kenneth M. Pierce, "Copping Out on Civil Rights: The Case against Racial Quotas," *The Village Voice* (February 9, 1976), 21(6): 43.
36. *Ibid.*, p. 44.
37. Sheila K. Johnson, "It's Action, but Is It Affirmative?" *The New York Times Magazine*, May 11, 1975, p. 33.
38. *Ibid.*, p. 30. Many people throughout the United States have written letters to the editor of the *New York Times* expressing their dismay at the collection of racial and ethnic identification data. In a letter appearing in the *Times* on March 6, 1977, Lucille Natkins writes that she was asked to identify Indian children in her high school homeroom class in order that the New York City Board of Education could apply for a grant under the Indian Education Act. Referring to ethnic surveys and the quota systems and the preferential treatment they have spawned as "abominations" that "ought to be obliterated from American life," Natkins finds it all but inevitable that ethnic surveys invoke the language of the Nuremberg Laws, "which designated as Jews those with at least one Jewish grandparent." She wonders if the day on which children are asked to identify themselves as Indians if they have at least one Indian grandparent will not soon be followed by the day when they will be asked to make a public declaration that they have a grandparent who is Jewish or black or white. Lucille G. Natkins, "On Ethnic Surveys," *New York Times*, March 6, 1977, p. 16E.
39. Sheila K. Johnson, "It's Action, but Is It Affirmative?" pp. 30-31.
40. "American Poetry Review Is Charged with Racism," *New York Times*, January 31, 1977, p. 28.
41. Lucien Goldmann, "'Genetic Structuralism' in the Sociology of Literature," in *Sociology of Literature and Drama*, p. 112.
42. Harry Levin, "Literature as an Institution," *Accent* (Spring 1946), 6(3): 167.
43. Joel Oppenheimer, "In the Dark Month," *The Village Voice* (January 20, 1975), 20(3): 48.
44. As quoted in Ernest Becker, *The Denial of Death* (New York: Free Press, 1973), p. 144.
45. Martin Price, "The Other Self: Thoughts about Character in the Novel," in *Imagined Worlds: Essays on some English Novels and Novelists in Honour of John Butt*, Maynard Mack and Ian Gregor, eds. (London: Methuen, 1968), p. 281.
46. Jacqueline Johnson Jackson, "NCBA, Black Aged and Politics," *The Annals of the American Academy of Political and Social Science* (September 1974), 415(5): 138.
47. Marlene Dixon, "On Liberation: For Women, For All," in *Seeing Ourselves: Introductory Readings in Sociology*, Peter I. Rose, ed. (New York: Knopf, 1972), p. 294.
48. Martin Price, "The Other Self: Thoughts about Character in the Novel," p. 283.
49. Daniel J. Boorstin, *Democracy and Its Discontents: Reflections on Everyday America* (New York: Random House, 1974), p. 58.
50. Elizabeth Hardwick, *Seduction and Betrayal: Women and Literature* (New York: Random House, 1974), p. 134.
51. Annette Duffy, "Esalen: Slow Death," *The Village Voice* (June 2, 1975), 20(22): 10.
52. Martin Price, "The Other Self: Thoughts about Character in the Novel," p. 283.
53. Edward C. Whitmont, *The Symbolic Quest: Basic Concepts of Analytical Psychology* (New York: Putnam, 1969), p. 158.
54. *Ibid.*, p. 159.
55. Jorge Luis Borges, *The Book of Imaginary Beings*, rev., enlarged, and trans. Norman Thomas di Giovanni in collaboration with the author (New York: Dutton, 1969), pp. 204-5.

## 2. On The Search For Reality

1. John Hollowell, *Fact and Fiction: The New Journalism and the Nonfiction Novel* (Chapel Hill: University of North Carolina Press, 1977), p. 3.
2. *Ibid.*, p. 4.
3. *Ibid.*, p. 5.
4. *Ibid.*, p. 6.
5. *Ibid.*, p. 7.
6. *Ibid.*, p. 8.
7. *Ibid.*, pp. 11-12.
8. H. E. F. Donohue, *Conversations with Nelson Algren* (New York: Berkley Medallion, 1965), p. 27.
9. *Ibid.*, p. 28.
10. William Foote Whyte, *Street Corner Society*, enlarged ed. (Chicago: University of Chicago Press, 1955), pp. 280-81.
11. *Ibid.*, p. 281.
12. Godfrey Lienhardt, *Social Anthropology*, 2d ed. (London: Oxford University Press, Oxford Paperbacks University Series Opus 15, 1966), p. 1.
13. Peter L. Berger, *Invitation to Sociology: A Humanistic Perspective*, Anchor Books ed. (Garden City, N.Y.: Doubleday, 1963), p. 20.
14. *Ibid.*, p. 24.
15. Lienhardt, *Social Anthropology*, p. 17.
16. Edmund Carpenter, "Ohnainewk, Eskimo Hunter," in *In the Company of Man: Twenty Portraits of Anthropological Informants*, Joseph B. Casagrande, ed., (New York: Harper & Row, Harper Torchbooks, 1964), pp. 425-26.
17. Whyte, *Street Corner Society*, p. 321.
18. *Ibid.*, p. 303.
19. Robert Penn Warren, *Writers at Work: The Paris Review Interviews*, (first series), Malcolm Cowley, ed. (New York: Viking Press, Viking Compass ed., 1959), pp. 197-98.
20. *Ibid.*, p. 190.
21. Lienhardt, *Social Anthropology*, p. 7.
22. Sheldon S. Wolin, "Looking for 'Reality,'" *The New York Review of Books* (February 6, 1975), 22(1): 18.
23. *Ibid.*
24. Robert Reinhold, "Polling Encounters Public Resistance; Decision-Making Process Is Threatened," *New York Times*, October 26, 1975, p. 58.
25. Kai T. Erikson, *Everything in Its Path: Destruction of Community in the Buffalo Creek Flood* (New York: Simon and Schuster, 1976), p. 15. A statement, perhaps definitive, about the problem of establishing evidence in social science research is to be found in Harold Garfinkel, "Common Sense Knowledge of Social Structures: The Documentary Method of Interpretation," in *Symbolic Interaction: A Reader in Social Psychology*, 2d ed., Jerome G. Manis and Bernard N. Meltzer, eds. (Boston: Allyn and Bacon, 1972), pp. 356-78.
26. Erikson, *Everything in Its Path*, p. 187.
27. *Ibid.*, p. 197.
28. Michael Harrington, "Everything in Its Path," *New York Times Book Review*, February 20, 1977, pp. 3, 14.
29. Erikson, *Everything in Its Path*, pp. 257-58.
30. *Ibid.*, pp. 246-47.
31. *Ibid.*, p. 12.
32. *Ibid.*
33. *Ibid.*, p. 13.

34. *Ibid.*, p. 137.
35. *Ibid.*, p. 177.
36. *Ibid.*, p. 178.
37. *Ibid.*, p. 10.
38. Ulf Hannerz, *Soulside: Inquiries into Ghetto Culture and Community* (New York: Columbia University Press, 1969), p. 36.
39. *Ibid.*
40. *Ibid.*, p. 37.
41. *Ibid.*, p. 112.
42. *Ibid.*, p. 117.
43. *Ibid.*, p. 158.
44. *Ibid.*, p. 186.
45. *Ibid.*, pp. 190-91.
46. *Ibid.*, pp. 195-200.
47. *Ibid.*, p. 204.
48. *Ibid.*, p. 14.
49. Aldous Huxley, *Writers at Work: The Paris Review Interviews* (second series), George Plimpton, ed. (New York: Viking Press, Viking Compass ed., 1965), pp. 208-9.
50. Nelson Algren, *Writers at Work* (first series), p. 235. How very different writers are from one another in this as in other respects, can best be appreciated by reading through all the interviews. Aldous Huxley, for example, said that he never felt strongly that the place where he lived at the time he was writing was of very much importance for his work. Aldous Huxley, *Writers at Work* (second series), p. 208.
51. Nelson Algren, *Writers at Work* (first series), pp. 236-38.
52. *Ibid.*, p. 239.
53. *Ibid.*, pp. 240-41.
54. Katherine Anne Porter, *Writers at Work* (second series), pp. 150-51.
55. Erikson, *Everything in Its Path*, p. 219.
56. Hannerz, *Soulside*, p. 112.
57. Frank O'Connor, *Writers at Work* (first series), p. 181.
58. William Faulkner, *Writers at Work* (first series), p. 133.
59. *Ibid.*, p. 141.
60. Nelson Algren, *Writers at Work* (first series), pp. 245-46.
61. Joyce Cary, *Writers at Work* (first series), p. 55.
62. Aldous Huxley, *Writers at Work* (second series), p. 213.
63. *Ibid.*, p. 214.
64. Robert Lowell, *Writers at Work* (second series), p. 346.
65. *Ibid.*, p. 366.
66. Robert Penn Warren, *Writers at Work* (first series), pp. 196-97.
67. Hollowell, *Fact and Fiction*, p. 70.
68. *Ibid.*, p. 78.
69. Robert Penn Warren, *Writers at Work* (first series), p. 195.
70. Hollowell, *Fact and Fiction*, p. 77.
71. Elizabeth and Tom Burns, "Introduction," *Sociology of Literature and Drama*, Elizabeth and Tom Burns, eds. (Harmondsworth, England: Penguin, 1973), p. 10.
72. Learned by personal communication with Rudolf Heberle. Burns and Burns, too, make a reference to genitive sociology, and write that the "sociologies of . . ." can be meaningful in the long run only insofar as they contribute to the field of sociology in general. *Sociology of Literature and Drama*, p. 16.
73. Northrop Frye, "The Critical Path: An Essay on the Social Context of Literary Criticism," *Daedalus* (Spring 1970), 99(2): 271-72.
74. Robert Penn Warren, *Writers at Work* (first series), p. 199.

75. George Steiner, "Marxism and the Literary Critic," in *Sociology of Literature and Drama*, p. 176.
76. Joyce Cary, *Writers at Work* (first series), p. 57.
77. Aldous Huxley, *Writers at Work* (second series), p. 210.
78. Martin Price, "The Other Self: Thoughts about Character in the Novel," in *Imagined Worlds: Essays on some English Novels and Novelists in Honour of John Butt*, Maynard Mack and Ian Gregor, eds. (London: Methuen, 1968), p. 288.
79. Henry Miller, *Writers at Work* (second series), pp. 172-73.
80. Robert Escarpit, "'Creative Treason' as a Key to Literature," *Yearbook of Comparative and General Literature*, no. 10, (1961), p. 20.
81. Edward Robb Ellis, "A National Drawer for Dusty, Yellowing Diaries," *New York Times*, December 13, 1976, p. 35.
82. Loren Eiseley, *The Night Country* (New York: Scribner's, 1971), p. 81.
83. Erich Auerbach, "The Emergence of a Literary Public in Western Europe," in *Sociology of Literature and Drama*, p. 424, n. 26.

## 3. Satirist and Sociologist: Some Likenesses

1. Morroe Berger, *Real and Imagined Worlds: The Novel and Social Science* (Cambridge, Mass.: Harvard University Press, 1977), p. 231.
2. Peter L. Berger, *Invitation to Sociology: A Humanistic Perspective* (Garden City, N.Y.: Doubleday, Anchor Books ed., 1963), p. 20.
3. Leonard Feinberg, *Introduction to Satire* (Ames: Iowa State University Press, 1967), p. 238.
4. *Ibid.*, pp. 238-39.
5. *Ibid.*, p. 232.
6. *Ibid.*, p. 261.
7. *Ibid.*, p. 228.
8. Alvin W. Gouldner, *The Coming Crisis of Western Sociology* (New York: Basic Books, 1970), p. 24.
9. *Ibid.*
10. Leonard Feinberg, *The Satirist* (Ames: Iowa State University Press, 1963), pp. 101-2.
11. Robert Coles, "Understanding White Racists," *The New York Review of Books* (December 30, 1971), 17(11): 15.
12. Emile Durkheim, *Suicide: A Study in Sociology*, trans. John A. Spaulding and George Simpson, ed. with an introduction by George Simpson (New York: Free Press, 1951), p. 151.
13. A. Alvarez, *The Savage God: A Study of Suicide* (New York: Random House, Bantam Books, ed., 1973), p. 164.
14. *Ibid.*, p. 166.
15. *Ibid.*, pp. 198-99.
16. Durkheim, *Suicide*, p. 280.
17. Alvarez, *The Savage God*, p. 91.
18. Yet even the great bard himself succumbed to the classifying craze of our time when he made his proposals for a better world! In one of the last book reviews he wrote before his death, he recommended that the members of all govermnents should be "elected, like jurors, by lot,"' justifying this by suggesting that it would destroy party machines. Those who are elected, he wrote, "could vote according to their consciences, since there would be no question of re-election." But then he paid homage to the

sociological version of distributive justice, affirmative action, for, despite the commandments of "Under Which Lyre," he decreed that "the computers could work out the proper representation of minority groups." And he did not stop there. Women, he went on, "preferably wives and mothers," ought to "be in control of foreign policy," because, he suspected, males are possessed of "a strong Manichaean stress, an unacknowledged secret contempt for matter, both animate and inanimate"—high praise, indeed, for the social category "female," though no orthodox feminist would care to accept it. W. H. Auden, "Death at Random," *The New York Review of Books* (December 12, 1974), 21(20): 28.

19. Feinberg, *The Satirist*, p. 41.
20. Feinberg, *Introduction to Satire*, p. 12.
21. Feinberg, *The Satirist*, p. 37.
22. *Ibid.*, pp. 185-86.
23. Irvin Ehrenpreis, *The Personality of Jonathan Swift* (Cambridge, Mass.: Harvard University Press, 1958), p. 115.
24. Thomas Robert Malthus, *On Population*, ed. and introduced by Gertrude Himmelfarb (New York: Random House, 1960).
25. Jonathan Swift, *A Modest Proposal*, illustrated by Leonard Baskin (New York: Grossman, 1969), n. p.
26. Dom Moraes, *A Matter of People* (New York: Praeger, 1974), p. 60.
27. Miguel de Unamuno, *Tragic Sense of Life*, trans. J. E. Crawford Flitch (New York: Dover, 1954), p. 138.
28. See Aleksandr Nekrich, "Inside the Leviathan," *The New York Review of Books*. (April 14, 1977), 24(6): 8-10; and Grace Glueck, "Dissidence as a Way of Art," *The New York Times Magazine*, May 8, 1977, pp. 33-35.
29. Donella H. Meadows, Dennis L. Meadows et al., *The Limits to Growth* (New York: Universe, 1972).
30. Robert Heilbroner, *An Inquiry into the Human Prospect* (New York: Norton, 1974).
31. Eric Larsen, "Notes on Emptiness: The State of Fiction," *South Dakota Review* (Autumn 1975), 13(3): 132.
32. *Ibid.*, p. 133.
33. Berger, *Invitation to Sociology*, p. 165.
34. Simone de Beauvoir, *The Coming of Age*, trans. Patrick O'Brian (New York: Warner Paperback Library, 1973). In this exhaustive work, which exhibits an impressive erudition and command of facts, the view of old age is unrelieved by humor; the tone is stark and, in certain passages, strongly militant.
35. Florida Scott-Maxwell, *The Measure of My Days* (New York: Knopf, 1969), pp. 13-14.
36. Jonathan Swift, *A Tale of a Tub* (Oxford: Clarendon Press, 1958), p. 173.
37. Feinberg, *Introduction to Satire*, p. 81.
38. The choice of singing in the evening was deliberate here. The figure of the poet-singer is familiar. What is not so well known is that some social scientists, as well as some fiction writers, had thought of a career in singing at one time, or had made an avocation of singing. Among the former are Oscar Lewis, who was said to have been in possession of a beautiful voice, and to have taken great pleasure in singing opera. Among the latter are Agatha Christie who, according to one of her obituaries, had once set her cap on becoming a diva; and no less a literary figure than James Joyce, who thought of becoming a singer in his youth, and who was said to have been crushed when he was told he would not make the grade. W. R. Rodgers, ed., *Irish Literary Portraits* (New York: Taplinger, 1973), p. 30.
39. Beauvoir, *The Coming of Age*, p. 604.

## 4. On Compassion

1. Jules Henry, *Pathways to Madness* (New York: Random House, Vintage Books ed., 1973), p. 197.
2. Lewis A. Coser, "Some Social Functions of Violence," in *Societal Guidance: A New Approach to Social Problems*, Sarajane Heidt and Amitai Etzioni, eds. (New York: Thomas Y. Crowell, 1969), p. 214.
3. Daniel J. Boorstin, *Democracy and Its Discontents: Reflections on Everyday America* (New York: Random House, 1974), p. 89.
4. Robert Nisbet, "The Study of Social Problems," *Contemporary Social Problems*, 3d ed., Robert K. Merton and Robert Nisbet, eds. (New York: Harcourt Brace Jovanovich, 1971), p. 6.
5. *Ibid.*, p. 5.
6. *Ibid.*, p. 7. Tocqueville provided both a positive and a negative demonstration of this thesis, Nisbet writes, the former drawn from the treatment of prisoners in the United States in the early nineteenth century, and the latter drawn from the treatment of black slaves by southern whites. "The Study of Social Problems," pp. 8-9.
7. Theodore Isaac Rubin, *Compassion and Self-Hate* (New York: David McKay, 1975), p. 298.
8. Nisbet, "The Study of Social Problems," p. 3.
9. See Alvin W. Gouldner, *The Coming Crisis of Western Sociology* (New York: Basic Books, 1970), pp. 40-45.
10. Miguel de Unamuno, *Tragic Sense of Life*, trans. J. E. Crawford Flitch (New York: Dover Publications, 1954), p. 138.
11. *Ibid.*, p. 141.
12. Margaret Mead, *Blackberry Winter: My Earlier Years* (New York: William Morrow, Pocket Book ed., 1975), p. 98.
13. *Ibid.*, p. 99.
14. Simone de Beauvoir, *The Coming of Age*, trans. Patrick O'Brian (New York: Warner Paperback Library, 1973), p. 7.
15. Jack Bass and Walter DeVries, *The Transformation of Southern Politics: Social Change and Political Consequence since 1945* (New York: Basic Books, 1976), p. 49.
16. *Ibid.*, p. 50.
17. Nisbet, "The Study of Social Problems," pp. 18-19.
18. *Ibid.*, pp. 19-20.
19. *Ibid.*, pp. 20-21.
20. *Ibid.*, pp. 21-25.
21. Unamuno, *Tragic Sense of Life*, p. 140.
22. Robert Knox Dentan, *The Semai: A Nonviolent People of Malaya* (New York: Holt, Rinehart and Winston, 1968), p. 64.
23. James Agee and Walker Evans, *Let Us Now Praise Famous Men* (New York: Ballantine Books, published by arrangement with Houghton Mifflin, 1974), p. 292.
24. *Ibid.*, p. 98.
25. Jules Henry, *Pathways to Madness*, p. 96.
26. George Steiner, *The Death of Tragedy* (New York: Hill and Wang, 1961), p. 4.
27. *Ibid.*, p. 5.
28. *Ibid.*, pp. 8-9.
29. Nicola Chiaromonte, *The Worm of Consciousness and Other Essays*, ed. Miriam Chiaromonte (New York: Harcourt Brace Jovanovich, 1976), p. 189.
30. Henry, *Pathways to Madness*, p. xi.
31. John Cowper Powys, *A Philosophy of Solitude* (New York: Simon and Schuster, 1933), p. 48.

## 4. On Compassion

32. John Dos Passos, "A Novelist of Disintegration," *The Freeman* (October 20, 1920), 2:133. This essay is reprinted in a slightly different form in John Dos Passos, *Rosinante to the Road Again* (New York: George H. Doran, 1922.)

33. Konrad Lorenz, *On Aggression*, trans. Marjorie Latzke (London: Methuen, 1966), p. 197.

34. Loren Eiseley, *The Night Country* (New York: Scribner's, 1971), p. 85.

35. Bruno Bettelheim, *The Children of the Dream: Communal Child-Rearing and American Education* (Toronto, Canada: Macmillan, 1969), pp. 169-71.

36. *Ibid.*, p. 171.

37. *Ibid.*, pp. 171-72.

38. *Ibid.*, p. 173.

39. Amitai Etzioni, "Collective Violence," in *Contemporary Social Problems*, 4th ed., Robert K. Merton and Robert Nisbet, eds. (New York: Harcourt Brace Jovanovich, 1976), p. 678.

40. Christopher Lasch, "The Narcissist Society," *The New York Review of Books* (September 30, 1976), 23(15):13.

41. Geoffrey Gorer, "Man Has No 'Killer' Instinct," in *Man and Aggression*, M. F. Ashley Montagu, ed. (New York: Oxford University Press, 1968), p. 34.

42. *Ibid.*, pp. 34-36.

43. Anaïs Nin, *The Diary of Anaïs Nin*, Vol. 1, 1931-34 (New York: Harcourt Brace and World, 1966), p. 116.

44. Paul Theroux, "Minamata," *The New York Times Book Review*, June 8, 1975, p. 2.

45. Hilton Kramer, "Smith's Terrifying Photos Cry Out against Pollution," *New York Times*, April 17, 1975, p. 46.

46. James Agee and Walker Evans, *Let Us Now Praise Famous Men*, p. 211.

47. Alfred Kazin, "Can Today's Movies Tell the Truth about Fascism?" *New York Times*, January 12, 1975, pp. 1D, 13D.

48. John Szarkowski, "A Different Kind of Art," *The New York Times Magazine*, April 13, 1975, p. 64.

49. Margaret Mead, "The Mass Consists of 1 and 1 and 1 and 1 and . . . ." *New York Times*, August 4, 1976, p. 31M.

50. Susan Sontag, "Photography: The Beauty Treatment," *The New York Review of Books* (November 28, 1974), 21(19): 38-39.

51. As quoted in James R. Mellow, "Walker Evans Captures the Unvarnished Truth," *New York Times*, December 1, 1974, p. 38D. No statement, of course, on Evans' or on any critic's part can be taken as definitive; Evans' vision was too wide and complex for that. For a sensitive and perceptive discussion of Evans' work, see William Stott, *Documentary Expression and Thirties America* (New York: Oxford University Press, 1973), chap. 14.

52. Hilton Kramer, "Walker Evans: A Devious Giant of Photography," *New York Times*, April 20, 1975, p. 33D.

53. John Cowper Powys, *A Philosophy of Solitude*, p. 161.

54. Walter Starkie, "Introduction," in Miguel de Unamuno, *Our Lord Don Quixote*, trans. Anthony Kerrigan (Princeton: Princeton University Press, 1967), p. xv. Unamuno's critics attacked him as being "paradoxical," Starkie wrote, but "paradoxes are necessary as weapons against routine of thought, and Unamuno's function in modern Spain had been to make men probe and sift ideas."

55. Hilton Kramer, "Visions of the Surrogate Eye," *New York Times*, December 1, 1974, p. 37D.

56. Paul Radin, *Primitive Man as Philosopher* (New York: Appleton, 1927), p. 287.

## 5. Witnessing

1. George Orwell, "Politics and the English Language," in *Identity and Anxiety: Survival of the Person in Mass Society*, Maurice R. Stein, Arthur J. Vidich, and David Manning White, eds. (New York: Free Press of Glencoe, 1960), p. 311.
2. *Ibid.*, pp. 318-19.
3. J. M. Cameron, "Sex in the Head," *The New York Review of Books* (May 13, 1976), 23(8):21.
4. J. Bronowski, *The Ascent of Man* (Boston: Little, Brown, 1973), p. 332.
5. David Rothman, *The Discovery of the Asylum* (Boston: Little, Brown, 1971).
6. Erving Goffman, *Asylums* (Garden City, N. Y.: Doubleday Anchor Books, 1961).
7. Ken Kesey, *One Flew Over the Cuckoo's Nest* (New York: Viking Press, 1968).
8. Bronislaw Malinowski, *Argonauts of the Western Pacific: An Account of Native Enterprise and Adventure in the Archipelagoes of Melanesian New Guinea* (New York: Dutton, 1950), pp. 18-19.
9. Hortense Powdermaker, *Stranger and Friend: The Way of an Anthropologist* (New York: Norton, 1967), p. 9.
10. Clyde Kluckhohn, "The Personal Document in Anthropological Science," in *The Use of Personal Documents in History, Anthropology, and Sociology* by Louis Gottschalk, Clyde Kluckhohn, and Robert Angell (New York: Social Science Research Council, 1947), pp. 162-63.
11. *Ibid.*, p. 155.
12. Jeremy Larner, "Introduction," *The Addict in the Street* by Jeremy Larner and Ralph Tefferteller (New York: Grove Press, Zebra ed., 1966), p. 16.
13. *Ibid.*, pp. 20-21.
14. *Ibid.*, p. 23.
15. W. Edson Richmond, "'Just Sing It Yourself': The American Lyric Tradition," in *Our Living Traditions: An Introduction to American Folklore*, Tristram Potter Coffin, ed. (New York: Basic Books, 1968), p. 94.
16. Harold Garfinkel, "Common Sense Knowledge of Social Structures: The Documentary Method of Interpretation," in *Symbolic Interaction: A Reader in Social Psychology*, 2d ed., Jerome G. Manis and Bernard N. Meltzer, eds. (Boston: Allyn and Bacon, 1972), pp. 356-78.
17. Oscar Lewis, *The Children of Sanchez: Autobiography of a Mexican Family* (New York: Random House, Vintage Books, 1961), p. xxi.
18. C. Wright Mills, *The Sociological Imagination* (New York: Grove Press, Evergreen ed., 1961), p. 6.
19. Jan Kott, "Introduction," in Tadeusz Borowski, *This Way for the Gas, Ladies and Gentlemen* (New York: Penguin Books, published by arrangement with the Viking Press, 1976), p. 12.
20. Kluckhohn, "The Personal Document in Anthropological Science," pp. 117-118.
21. Robert N. Butler, M.D., *Why Survive? Being Old in America* (New York: Harper & Row, 1975), pp. 82-83.
22. John Stewart, "Oral History Is beyond the Stage of Talking," *New York Times*, May 22, 1977, p. 9E.
23. *Ibid.*
24. Robert Coles, "Understanding White Racists," *The New York Review of Books* (December 30, 1971), 17(11):14.
25. Theodore Roethke, "The Waking," *The Collected Verse of Theodore Roethke: Words for the Wind* (Bloomington: Indiana University Press, by arrangement with Doubleday, 1961), p. 124.
26. Herbert Blumer, "Society as Symbolic Interaction," in *Symbolic Interaction*, p. 149, 151-52.

## 5. Witnessing

27. Robert Coles, *Farewell to the South* (Boston: Little, Brown, 1972), p. 276.
28. Helen Vendler, "Art, Life and Dr. Williams," *The New York Review of Books* (November 13, 1975) 22(18): 17-18.
29. Richard Gilman, "Pauline Kael Lost It All at the Movies," *The Village Voice* (June 7, 1976), 21(23):41.
30. Sir James George Frazer, "Preface," *Argonauts of the Western Pacific*, p. ix.
31. Joseph B. Casagrande, "Preface," *In the Company of Man: Twenty Portraits of Anthropological Informants* (New York: Harper & Row, Harper Torchbooks, 1964), p. x.
32. Kluckhohn, "The Personal Document in Anthropological Science," p. 118.
33. David L. Gutmann, "Aging among the Highland Maya: A Comparative Study," in *Middle Age and Aging: A Reader in Social Psychology*, Bernice L. Neugarten, ed. (Chicago: University of Chicago Press, 1968), p. 445.
34. The account given in West's *Plainville* might properly be called a classic. See the introduction to James West, *Plainville, U.S.A.* (New York: Columbia University Press, 1961), and the appendix in William Foote Whyte, *Street Corner Society*, enlarged ed. (Chicago: University of Chicago Press, 1955.)
35. Kluckhohn, "The Personal Document in Anthropological Science," p. 119. Whyte wrote in the appendix to *Street Corner Society* that the social scientist ought to keep in mind that one of the differences between him and an anthropologist working in a remote corner of the world is that the former is working with a literate people. He knew, Whyte acknowledged, that there was the possibility that certain persons might suffer because of the publication of his book. Whyte, *Street Corner Society*, p. 342.
36. Elisabeth Kübler-Ross, *On Death and Dying* (New York: Macmillan, 1969), p. 261.
37. In very meticulous research reports, the social scientist usually discusses this issue. For example, in his study of ghetto culture, Ulf Hannerz wrote that, although his exposure to many aspects of ghetto life had been very strong, it could not be complete. For one thing, "people everywhere tend to keep some parts of their lives private." For another, a field worker, in following what Hannerz calls "natural networks," may not obtain access to a representative sample of the community, especially in one as heterogeneous and subdivided as the ghetto. Ulf Hannerz, *Soulside: Inquiries into Ghetto Culture and Community* (New York: Columbia University Press, 1969), p. 207.
38. Jules Henry, *Pathways to Madness* (New York: Random House, Vintage Books ed., 1973), p. xv.
39. *Ibid.*, p. 91. (Italics added. He is referring here to Mrs. Jones' relationship to her son, Bobby.)
40. *Ibid.*, p. 217.
41. *Ibid.*, p. 90.
42. Erving Goffman, *Interaction Ritual* (New York: Doubleday, 1967), pp. 79-80.
43. Lee Rainwater, "Crucible of Identity: The Negro Lower-Class Family," in *Marriage and the Family: A Comparative Analysis of Contemporary Problems*, Meyer Barash and Alice Scourby, eds. (New York: Random House, 1970), p. 244.
44. *Ibid.*, pp. 246-47.
45. E. E. Le Masters, *Blue-Collar Aristocrats* (Madison: University of Wisconsin Press, 1975), pp. 14-15.
46. B. D. Colen, "'Living with the Dying,'" *Poughkeepsie Journal*, October 31, 1976, p. 22C. It is stated in this article that the results of Buckingham's research are contained in a paper to be published by the Canadian Medical Association Journal.
47. Coles, *Farewell to the South*, p. 395.
48. *Ibid.*, p. 380.
49. *Ibid.*, p. 383.

## 5. Witnessing

50. Oscar Lewis, *La Vida: A Puerto Rican Family in the Culture of Poverty—San Juan and New York* (New York: Random House, 1965), p. xxiii.

51. In his paper on "Marxism and the Literary Critic," George Steiner refers to the fine distinction drawn between "realism" and "naturalism" in Marxist theory. It may be traced, Steiner says, to Hegel's finding that, whereas in the Homeric epics the depictions of objects did not interfere with the movement and life of the poem, modern descriptive writing seemed to be without life. Hegel suggested that, because of the Industrial Revolution and the division of labor that it necessitated, people had become estranged from the material world. Hegel's ideas, Steiner notes, were a strong influence on Marx and Engels when they developed their own theory about the alienation of modern man under the capitalist mode of production. They came to believe, Steiner writes, that the problem of estrangement was directly related to the problem of realism in art. Whereas the "classical realists" and the poets of antiquity had created an organic relationship between objective reality and imaginative life, the naturalists' view of the material world is that of a warehouse, the contents of which were there to be inventoried. Steiner discusses the vast implications of this distinction for literature. George Steiner, "Marxism and the Literary Critic," in *Sociology of Literature and Drama*, Elizabeth and Tom Burns, eds. (Harmondsworth, Middlesex, England: Penguin Books, 1973), pp. 175-76.

52. Rainer Maria Rilke, letter of November 13, 1925 to his Polish translator, Witold von Hulewicz, *Duino Elegies*, trans. J. B. Leishman and Stephen Spender (New York: Norton, 1939), Appendix 4, p. 129.

53. Butler, *Why Survive? Being Old in America*, pp. ix-x.

54. Le Masters, *Blue-Collar Aristocrats*, p. 18.

55. Margaret Mead, *Blackberry Winter: My Earlier Years* (New York: William Morrow, Pocket Book ed., 1975), pp. 224-25. The effect of the personality of the witness upon the nature of the findings should never be underestimated. Le Masters writes that one of his students served in Dobu during World War II and claimed that he did not find the paranoid attitude that Reo Fortune had reported to be characteristic of the Dobuans. Le Masters, *Blue-Collar Aristocrats*, p. 9.

56. James Agee and Walker Evans, *Let Us Now Praise Famous Men* (New York: Ballantine Books, published by arrangement with Houghton Mifflin, 1974), pp. xiv-xv.

57. *Ibid.*, p. 7.

58. *Ibid.*, pp. 376-77.

59. *Ibid.*, p. xi.

60. Robert Fitzgerald, "A Memoir," in *Remembering James Agee*, David Madden, ed. (Baton Rouge: Louisiana State University Press, 1974), p. 86.

61. Agee and Evans, *Let Us Now Praise Famous Men*, p. 11.

62. *Ibid.*, p. 12.

63. *Ibid.*, pp. 12-13.

64. *Ibid.*, p. 91.

65. Coles, "Understanding White Racists," p. 14.

66. Roberta Hellman and Marvin Hoshino, "Anthropologist with a Camera," *The Village Voice* (June 9, 1975), 20(23):100.

67. Agee and Evans, *Let Us Now Praise Famous Men*, p. 11.

68. *Ibid.*, p. 37.

69. *Ibid.*, pp. 66-68.

70. *Ibid.*, p. 147. The excerpts quoted here are taken from pages 142-64, the sections on "The Front Bedroom," "The Rear Bedroom," and "The Kitchen."

71. *Ibid.*, p. 140.

72. *Ibid.*, p. 256.

73. *Ibid.*, p. 165.

74. *Ibid.*, p. 330.

75. *Ibid.*, pp. 331-32.

76. Coles, "Understanding White Racists," p. 14.
77. Agee and Evans, *Let Us Now Praise Famous Men*, pp. 73-77.
78. Fitzgerald, "A Memoir," p. 92.
79. Agee and Evans, *Let Us Now Praise Famous Men*, p. 344.
80. Dwight Macdonald, "Jim Agee: A Memoir," in *Remembering James Agee*, p. 142.
81. As quoted in A. Alvarez, *The Savage God: A Study of Suicide*, Bantam Books (New York: Random House, 1973), p. 236.
82. William Stott, *Documentary Expression and Thirties America* (New York: Oxford University Press, 1973), p. 302.
83. *Ibid.*, pp. 304-5.
84. *Ibid.*, pp. 310-11.
85. *Ibid.*, p. 153.
86. *Ibid.*, pp. 154-55.
87. *Ibid.*, p. 163.
88. *Ibid.*, pp. 157-58.
89. *Ibid.*, p. 166.
90. *Ibid.*, p. 30.
91. *Ibid.*, p. 170.
92. "Confession literature" was so popular during the later thirties and early forties, Stott reports, that many prominent social scientists wrote monographs which attempted "to legitimate 'the human or personal document' as source material." However, when social scientists used first-person narrative, the testimony became "over-directed"; it was used "merely to confirm their theories, not to let informants voice their essential characters." Sutherland's *The Professional Thief* is, in Stott's judgment, "neither the autobiography nor the confession" that it is purported to be. "Ninety-nine per cent of the text," Stott finds, "is straight sociology." Even though *The Professional Thief* was presented in documentary form, it "was too rigid a piece of social science to let an individual come alive." Stott, *Documentary Expression*, pp. 200-1.
93. Oscar Lewis, *The Children of Sanchez*, p. xii.
94. *Ibid.*, pp. xxiii-xxiv.
95. Lewis, *La Vida*, p. xxxiii.
96. Hannerz, *Soulside*, pp. 55, 70.
97. Le Masters, *Blue-Collar Aristocrats*, p. 12.
98. Elliot Liebow, *Tally's Corner: A Study of Negro Streetcorner Men* (Boston: Little, Brown, 1967), p. 22.
99. *Ibid.*, pp. viii-ix.
100. Oliver La Farge, "Foreword," in Oscar Lewis, *Five Families: Mexican Case Studies in the Culture of Poverty* (New York: Basic Books, 1959), pp. vii-ix.
101. Louis Gottschalk, "The Historian and the Historical Document," in *The Use of Personal Documents in History, Anthropology, and Sociology*, p. 23.
102. *Ibid.*, p. 66. J. M. Cameron complains of this, in reviewing Eugene Bianchi and Rosemary Radford Ruether's *From Machismo to Mutuality: Essays on Sexism and Woman-Man Liberation*. Remarking that history is "a difficult matter" and that "the balance of truth is hard to come by," Cameron says that "Ruether's chapter on women during the rise of industrial society is a model of how not to write a historical sketch." Her generalizations, he reports, are loose, and often very misleading, and he comments, "What a *mean* view of the past Ruether gives us!" J. M. Cameron, "Sex in the Head," p. 26.
103. Gottschalk, "The Historian and the Historical Document," p. 27.
104. Vendler, "Art, Life and Dr. Williams," p. 17.
105. I. A. Richards, "The Future of the Humanities in General Education," in *Identity and Anxiety*, p. 388.

106. *Ibid.*, p. 390.

107. J. M. Cameron recalls that Lionel Trilling published a comment on the Kinsey Report in *Partisan Review* in 1948—"a classic statement, calm, judicious, prescient," in which he remarked on the "bland assurance" that the title of the report implies, that is, that a sample of males in the United States was to be taken as a basis for making generalizations about men everywhere and in all times. Trilling took exception to the implication that what social scientists find to be the case may not be judged, except at the peril of being accused of being "undemocratic." He also saw that the report was a powerful agent of sexual revolution: "Its scientism, its half-concealed complacency toward mechanical models of the life of feeling and action, the bad faith which presented as a purely technical work what it was foreknown would be widely read by an audience quite unable to weigh its claims, all these gave it a unique authority wherever it was read." J. M. Cameron, "Sex in the Head," pp. 19-20.

108. Stott, *Documentary Expression and Thirties America*, p. 132.

109. Simone de Beauvoir, *The Coming of Age*, trans. Patrick O'Brian (New York: Warner Paperback Library, 1973), pp. 317-18.

110. Nicola Chiaromonte, "History, Freedom, and Utopia," *Dissent* (Spring 1976), 23(2):197-203.

111. James Agee, "A Note on This Book," *Agee on Film: Reviews and Comments by James Agee* (Boston: Beacon Press, 1964), n. p.

## 6. On the Uses of the Imagination

1. C. Wright Mills, *The Sociological Imagination* (New York: Grove Press, Evergreen ed., 1961), p. 17.

2. Hortense Calisher, "World Violence and the Verbal Arts," *New York Times*, September 30, 1975, p. 37C.

3. *Ibid.*

4. William Stott, *Documentary Expression and Thirties America* (New York: Oxford University Press, 1973), pp. 119-20.

5. Morroe Berger, *Real and Imagined Worlds: The Novel and Social Science* (Cambridge, Mass.: Harvard University Press, 1977), pp. 171-72.

6. John Hollowell, *Fact and Fiction: The New Journalism and the Nonfiction Novel* (Chapel Hill: University of North Carolina Press, 1977), p. 147.

7. Robert Bierstedt, *The Social Order*, 4th ed. (New York: McGraw-Hill, 1974), pp. 183-84.

8. Mills, *The Sociological Imagination*, p. 146.

9. As quoted by Lawrence Graver in his review of Henry James' letters in *The New York Times Book Review*, January 19, 1975, p. 2.

10. Robert Nisbet, *Sociology as an Art Form* (New York: Oxford University Press, 1976), p. 16.

11. *Ibid.*, p. 69.

12. *Ibid.*, pp. 70-71.

13. See "The World of the Brain," a *Wraparound* in *Harper's Magazine* (December 1975), 251(1507):3-10, 117-24.

14. J. Bronowski, *The Ascent of Man* (Boston: Little, Brown, 1973), p. 332.

15. *Ibid.*, pp. 334-36.

16. Bennett M. Berger, "Sociology and Stereotypes," in *Seeing Ourselves: Introductory Readings in Sociology*, Peter I. Rose, ed. (New York: Knopf, 1972), p. 26.

17. *Ibid.*, pp. 27-28.

18. *Ibid.*, p. 23. Auden appears once more. Berger is referring here to the remark

246   6. On the Uses of the Imagination

made by Auden at a forum on "The Role of the Intellectual in Modern Society" held at New York's Museum of Modern Art, to the effect that most of the panelists of such a forum held in the Middle Ages would have been clergymen, that most of them would have been natural scientists in the sixteenth and seventeenth centuries, and most of them, in the twentieth century, literary people. Auden implied that he believed that the image of the intellectual at the present time is "essentially a literary one."

19. Berger, "Sociology and Stereotypes," p. 23. Very few literary people enjoy the freedom Berger imputes to them. He says that there is a "large market for fiction in the U.S.," which is actually not the case. He also says that, because of the opportunities for selling "critical and interpretative articles" to the "high- and middle-brow magazines," which he maintains are flourishing in this country, free-lance writers can support themselves without having to depend upon a salary from a university or other large organization. Thus, he claims, writers are more free than others to be critics of contemporary life ("Sociology and Stereotypes," p. 24.) Unfortunately, the number of free-lance writers of either fiction or nonfiction who can support themselves wholly by their income from writing is extremely small indeed. For a recent discussion, see "Fiction Writers: Can They Make a Living?" in the *Coda: Newsletter* of Poets and Writers (September-October 1976), 4(1).

20. In *The Sense of an Ending*, Burns writes, Kermode distinguishes between the expectation that poets will help us to make sense of the lives we live, and the expectation that critics (and, by implication, sociologists of literature) will help us to make sense of the ways in which we try to make sense of our lives. Elizabeth and Tom Burns, "Introduction," *Sociology of Literature and Drama*, Elizabeth and Tom Burns, eds. (Harmondsworth, Middlesex, England: Penguin Books, 1973), p. 9.

21. Emile Durkheim, *Suicide: A Study in Sociology*, trans. John A. Spaulding and George Simpson, ed. with an introduction by George Simpson (New York: Free Press, 1951), p. 315.

22. Saul Bellow, in Joseph Epstein, "A Talk with Saul Bellow," *New York Times Book Review*, December 5, 1976, p. 92.

23. Nisbet, *Sociology as an Art Form*, p. 13.

24. *Ibid.*, p. 20.

25. Max Weber, "Science as a Vocation," *From Max Weber: Essays in Sociolgy*, trans., ed., and with an introduction by H. H. Gerth and C. Wright Mills (New York: Oxford University Press, 1946), p. 155.

26. Margaret Mead, *Blackberry Winter: My Earlier Years* (New York: William Morrow, Pocket Book ed., 1975), pp. 119-21.

27. Margaret Mead, *An Anthropologist at Work: Writings of Ruth Benedict* (Boston: Houghton Mifflin, 1959), p. xv.

28. *Ibid.*, p. 83.

29. Audrey F. Borenstein, "The Ethical Ideal of the Professions: A Sociological Analysis of the Academic and Medical Professions," Dissertation, Louisiana State University, 1958.

30. Hollowell, *Fact and Fiction*, p. 79.

31. Michael Wood, "Unhappy Dictators," *New York Review of Books* (December 9, 1976) 23(20): 57.

32. Benjamin De Mott, "Once More in Academe, Purists vs. Utilitarians," *New York Times*, March 28, 1976, p. 16E.

33. Benjamin De Mott, "Are the Humanities Really Out of Style?" *New York Times*, October 26, 1975, p. 9E. De Mott mentions other factors that may account for the demoralization of those in the humanistic professions today—"The continuing inability of the humanities to present themselves as indispensable to contemporary problem-solvers," the "decline of the academic job market," and the "refusal of the humanistic

professions to temper their enthusiasm for ever more abstract, involuted, over-professionalized modes of approach to arts and letters."

34. See Bernard Weinraub, "Today's Writers Failing Mankind, Bellow Contends," *New York Times*, December 13, 1976, pp. 1, 9; and "Bellow Talk in Excerpts," *New York Times*, December 13, 1976, p. 8.

35. Michael Wood, "Fiction in Extremis," *New York Review of Books* (November 28, 1974) 21(19):31.

36. Stuart Hampshire, "The Future of Knowledge," *New York Review of Books* (March 31, 1977), 24(5):14-15.

37. *Ibid.*, p. 17.

38. Clyde Kluckhohn, *Mirror for Man* (New York: McGraw-Hill, A Premier Book, 1965), p. 19.

# Bibliography

Agee, James. "A Note on This Book." *Agee on Film: Reviews and Comments by James Agee*. Boston: Beacon Press, 1964.

Agee, James and Walker Evans. *Let Us Now Praise Famous Men*. New York: Ballantine Books, published by arrangement with Houghton Mifflin, 1974.

Algren, Nelson. *Writers at Work: The Paris Review Interviews* (first series), pp. 231-49, Malcolm Cowley, ed. New York: Viking Press, Viking Compass ed., 1959.

Alvarez, A. *The Savage God: A Study of Suicide*. New York: Random House, Bantam Books ed. 1973.

"American Poetry Review Is Charged With Racism." *New York Times*, January 31, 1977, p. 28.

Aron, Raymond. *Main Currents in Sociological Thought II*. Richard Howard and Helen Weaver, trans. Garden City, N.Y.: Doubleday Anchor Books, 1970.

Auden, W. H. "Death at Random." *The New York Review of Books* (December 12, 1974), 21(20):28-29.

Auerbach, Erich. "The Emergence of a Literary Public in Western Europe." In *Sociology of Literature and Drama*, pp. 418-32, Elizabeth and Tom Burns, eds. Middlesex, England: Harmondsworth, Penguin, 1973.

Bass, Jack and Walter DeVries. *The Transformation of Southern Politics: Social Change and Political Consequence Since 1945*. New York: Basic Books, 1976.

Beauvoir, Simone de. *The Coming of Age*. Patrick O'Brian, trans. New York: Warner Paperback Library, 1973.

Becker, Ernest. *The Denial of Death*. New York: Free Press, 1973.

Bellow, Saul. "Bellow Talk in Excerpts." *New York Times*, December 13, 1976, p. 8.

——*Humboldt's Gift*. New York: Viking Press, 1975.

——"A Talk with Saul Bellow." Joseph Epstein, interviewer. *The New York Times Book Review*, December 5, 1976, pp. 3, 92-3.
——In *Writers at Work: The Paris Review Interviews* (third series), pp. 175-96, George Plimpton, ed. New York: Viking Press, Viking Compass ed., 1968.
Benedict, Ruth. "Anthropology and the Humanities." In *Ruth Benedict*, pp. 165-76, Margaret Mead, ed. New York: Columbia University Press, 1974.
Berger, Bennett M. "Sociology and Stereotypes." In *Seeing Ourselves: Introductory Readings in Sociology*, pp. 19-28, Peter I. Rose, ed. New York: Knopf, 1972.
Berger, Morroe. *Real and Imagined Worlds: The Novel and Social Science*. Cambridge, Mass.: Harvard University Press, 1977.
Berger, Peter L. *Invitation to Sociology: A Humanistic Perspective*. Garden City, N.Y.: Doubleday Anchor Books, 1963.
Bettelheim, Bruno. *The Children of the Dream: Communal Child-Rearing and American Education*. Toronto, Canada: Macmillan, 1969.
Bierstedt, Robert. *The Social Order*. 4th ed. New York: McGraw-Hill, 1974.
——"Sociology and Humane Learning." *Power and Progress: Essays on Sociological Theory*, pp. 309-21. New York: McGraw-Hill, 1974.
Blumer, Herbert. "Society as Symbolic Interaction" and "Sociological Analysis and the 'Variable.'" In *Symbolic Interaction: A Reader in Social Psychology* (2d ed.), pp. 145-54 and 92-102, respectively, Jerome G. Manis and Bernard N. Meltzer, eds. Boston: Allyn and Bacon, 1972.
Boorstin, Daniel J. *Democracy and Its Discontents: Reflections on Everyday America*. New York: Random House, 1974.
Borenstein, Audrey F. "The Ethical Ideal of the Professions: A Sociological Analysis of the Academic and Medical Professions." Doctoral dissertation, Louisiana State University, 1958.
Borges, Jorge Luis. *The Book of Imaginary Beings*. Norman Thomas di Giovanni, trans., in collaboration with the author. New York: Dutton, 1969.
Bromley, Dorothy D. and Florence H. Britten. *Youth and Sex: A Study of 1300 College Students*. New York: Harper, 1938.
Bronowski, J. *The Ascent of Man*. Boston: Little, Brown, 1973.
Burns, Elizabeth and Tom. "Introduction." In *Sociology of Literature and Drama*, pp. 9-30, Elizabeth and Tom Burns, eds. Harmondsworth, Middlesex, England: Penguin, 1973.
Butler, Robert N., MD *Why Survive? Being Old in America*. New York: Harper and Row, 1975.
Calisher, Hortense. "World Violence and the Verbal Arts." *New York Times*, September 30, 1975, p. 37C.
Cameron, J. M. "Sex in the Head." *The New York Review of Books* (May 13, 1976), 23(8):19-28.
Carpenter, Edmund. "Ohnainewk, Eskimo Hunter." In *In the Company of*

*Man: Twenty Portraits of Anthropological Informants*, pp. 417-26, Joseph B. Casagrande, ed. New York: Harper and Row, Harper Torchbooks, 1964.

Cary, Joyce. In *Writers at Work: The Paris Review Interviews* (first series), pp. 51-67, Malcolm Cowley, ed. New York: Viking Press, Viking Compass ed., 1959.

Casagrande, Joseph B. "Preface." In *In the Company of Man: Twenty Portraits of Anthropological Informants*, pp. ix-xvi, Joseph B. Casagrande, ed. New York: Harper and Row, Harper Torchbooks, 1964.

Chiaromonte, Nicola. "History, Freedom, and Utopia." *Dissent* (Spring 1976), 23(2): 197-203.

——*The Worm of Consciousness and Other Essays*. Miriam Chiaromonte, ed. New York: Harcourt Brace Jovanovich, 1976.

Clausen, John A. "The Young as Outsiders." *Science* (February 21, 1975), 187(4177):637-38.

Colen, B. D. "Living with the Dying." *Poughkeepsie Journal*, October 31, 1976, p. 22C.

Coles, Robert. *Farewell to the South*. Boston: Little, Brown, 1972.

——"Understanding White Racists." *The New York Review of Books* (December 30, 1971), 17(11):12-15.

Coser, Lewis A. "Some Social Functions of Violence." In *Societal Guidance: A New Approach to Social Problems*, pp. 204-19, Sarajane Heidt and Amitai Etzioni, eds. New York: Thomas Y. Crowell, 1969.

De Mott, Benjamin. "Are the Humanities Really Out of Style?" *New York Times*, October 26, 1975, p. 9E.

——"Once More in Academe, Purists vs. Utilitarians." *New York Times*, March 28, 1976, p. 16E.

Dentan, Robert Knox. *The Semai: A Nonviolent People of Malaya*. New York: Holt, Rinehart and Winston, 1968.

Dixon, Marlene. "On Liberation: For Women, For All." In *Seeing Ourselves: Introductory Readings in Sociology*, pp. 282-98, Peter I. Rose, ed. New York: Knopf, 1972.

Donohue, H. E. F. *Conversations with Nelson Algren*. New York: Berkley, Medallion ed., 1965.

Dos Passos, John. "A Novelist of Disintegration." *The Freeman* (October 20, 1920), 2: 32-34.

Duffy, Annette. "Esalen: Slow Death." *The Village Voice* (June 2, 1975), 20(22):8-10.

Durkheim, Emile. *Suicide: A Study in Sociology*. Trans. John A. Spaulding and George Simpson. George Simpson, ed. New York: Free Press, 1951.

Ehrenpreis, Irvin. *The Personality of Jonathan Swift*. Cambridge, Mass.: Harvard University Press, 1958.

Eiseley, Loren. *The Night Country*. New York: Scribner's, 1971.

Ellis, Edward Robb. "A National Drawer for Dusty, Yellowing Diaries." *New York Times*, December 13, 1976, p. 35.
Erikson, Kai T. *Everything in Its Path: Destruction of Community in the Buffalo Creek Flood*. New York: Simon and Schuster, 1976.
Escarpit, Robert. "'Creative Treason' as a Key to Literature." *Yearbook of Comparative and General Literature* (1961), no. 10:16-21.
Etzioni, Amitai. "Collective Violence." In *Contemporary Social Problems* (4th ed.), pp. 675-724, Robert K. Merton and Robert Nisbet, eds. New York: Harcourt Brace Jovanovich, 1976.
——"Effects of Small Computers on Scientists." *Science* (July 11, 1975), 189(4197):93.
Faulkner, William. In *Writers at Work: The Paris Review Interviews* (first series), pp. 119-41, Malcolm Cowley, ed. New York: Viking Press, Viking Compass ed., 1959.
Feinberg, Leonard. *Introduction to Satire*. Ames: Iowa State University Press, 1967.
——*The Satirist*. Ames: Iowa State University Press, 1963.
"Fiction Writers: Can They Make a Living?" *Coda: Poets and Writers Newsletter* (September-October 1976), 4(1):3-7.
Fitzgerald, Robert. "A Memoir." In *Remembering James Agee*, pp. 35-94, David Madden, ed. Baton Rouge: Louisiana State University Press, 1974.
Foucault, Michel. *The Order of Things: An Archaeology of the Human Sciences*. New York: Random House, Vintage Books, 1970, 1973.
Frazer, Sir James George. "Preface." Bronislaw Malinowski, *Argonauts of the Western Pacific: An Account of Native Enterprise and Adventure in the Archipelagoes of Melanesian New Guinea*, pp. vii-xiv. New York: Dutton, 1950.
Frye, Northrop. "The Critical Path: An Essay on the Social Context of Literary Criticism." *Daedalus* (Spring 1970), 99(2):268-342.
Garfinkel, Harold. "Common Sense Knowledge of Social Structures: The Documentary Method of Interpretation." In *Symbolic Interaction: A Reader in Social Psychology* (2d ed.), pp. 356-78, Jerome G. Manis and Bernard N. Meltzer, eds. Boston: Allyn and Bacon, 1972.
Gilman, Richard. "Pauline Kael Lost It All at the Movies." *The Village Voice* (June 7, 1976), 21(23):40-41.
Glueck, Grace. "Dissidence as a Way of Art." *The New York Times Magazine*, May 8, 1977, pp. 33-5.
Goffman, Erving. *Asylums*. Garden City, N. Y.: Doubleday Anchor Books, 1961.
——*Interaction Ritual*. Garden City, N. Y.: Doubleday, 1967.
Goldmann, Lucien. "'Genetic Structuralism' in the Sociology of Literature." In *Sociology of Literature and Drama*, pp. 109-23, Elizabeth and Tom Burns, eds. Harmondsworth, Middlesex, England: Penguin, 1973.

Gorer, Geoffrey. "Man Has No 'Killer' Instinct." In *Man and Aggression*, pp. 27-36, M. F. Ashley Montagu, ed. New York: Oxford University Press, 1968.

Gottschalk, Louis. "The Historian and the Historical Document." In *The Use of Personal Documents in History, Anthropology, and Sociology*, pp. 3-75, Louis Gottschalk, Clyde Kluckhohn, and Robert Angell. New York: Social Science Research Council, 1947.

Gouldner, Alvin W. *The Coming Crisis of Western Sociology*. New York: Basic Books, 1970.

Graver, Lawrence. "Henry James Letters." *The New York Times Book Review*, January 19, 1975, pp. 1-2.

Green, Martin. *The von Richthofen Sisters: The Triumphant and the Tragic Modes of Love*. New York: Basic Books, 1974.

Gutmann, David L. "Aging among the Highland Maya: A Comparative Study." In *Middle Age and Aging: A Reader in Social Psychology*, pp. 444-52, Bernice L. Neugarten, ed. Chicago: University of Chicago Press, 1968.

Hampshire, Stuart. "The Future of Knowledge." *The New York Review of Books* (March 31, 1977), 24(5):14-18.

Hannerz, Ulf. *Soulside: Inquiries into Ghetto Culture and Community*. New York: Columbia University Press, 1969.

Hardwick, Elizabeth. *Seduction and Betrayal: Women and Literature*. New York: Random House, 1974.

Harrington, Michael. "Everything in Its Path." *The New York Times Book Review*, February 20, 1977, pp. 3, 14.

Heilbroner, Robert. *An Inquiry into the Human Prospect*. New York: Norton, 1974.

Hellman, Roberta and Marvin Hoshino. "Anthropologist with a Camera." *The Village Voice* (June 9, 1975), 20(23):99-100.

Henry, Jules. *Pathways to Madness*. New York: Random House, Vintage Books ed., 1973.

Hesse, Hermann. *Magister Ludi (The Bead Game.)* Trans. Mervyn Savill. New York: Frederick Ungar, 1967.

Hollowell, John. *Fact and Fiction: The New Journalism and the Nonfiction Novel*. Chapel Hill: University of North Carolina Press, 1977.

Huxley, Aldous. In *Writers at Work: The Paris Review Interviews* (second series), pp. 193-214, George Plimpton, ed. New York: Viking Press, Viking Compass ed., 1965.

Jackson, Jacqueline Johnson. "NCBA, Black Aged and Politics." *The Annals of the American Academy of Political and Social Science* (September 1974), 415(5):138-59.

Johnson, Sheila K. "It's Action, but Is It Affirmative?" *The New York Times Magazine*, May 11, 1975, pp. 18-20, 22, 24, 26, 30, 33.

Kazin, Alfred. "Can Today's Movies Tell the Truth about Fascism?" *New York Times*, January 12, 1975, pp. 1D, 13D.

Kermode, Frank. *The Sense of an Ending: Studies in the Theory of Fiction.* New York: Oxford University Press, 1967.

Kesey, Ken. *One Flew Over the Cuckoo's Nest.* New York: Viking Press, 1968.

Kluckhohn, Clyde. *Mirror for Man*, New York: McGraw-Hill, A Premier Book, 1965.

——"The Personal Document in Anthropological Science." In *The Use of Personal Documents in History, Anthropology, and Sociology*, pp. 79-173, Louis Gottschalk, Clyde Kluckhohn, and Robert Angell. New York: Social Science Research Council, 1947.

Kott, Jan. "Introduction." In *Tadeusz Borowski, This Way for the Gas, Ladies and Gentlemen*, pp. 11-26. New York: Penguin Books, published by arrangement with Viking Press, 1976.

Kramer, Hilton. "Smith's Terrifying Photos Cry Out against Pollution." *New York Times*, April 17, 1975, p. 46.

——"Trashing the Fifties." *The New York Times Book Review*, April 10, 1977, pp. 3, 31.

——"Visions of the Surrogate Eye." *New York Times*, December 1, 1974, p. 37D.

——"Walker Evans: A Devious Giant of Photography." *New York Times*, April 20, 1975, pp. 1D, 33D.

Kübler-Ross, Elisabeth. *On Death and Dying.* New York: Macmillan, 1969.

La Farge, Oliver. "Foreword." In Oscar Lewis, *Five Families: Mexican Case Studies in the Culture of Poverty*, pp. vii-x. New York: Basic Books, 1959.

Larner, Jeremy. "Introduction." *The Addict in the Street*, pp. 11-24, Jeremy Larner and Ralph Tefferteller, eds. New York: Grove Press, Zebra ed., 1966.

Larsen, Eric. "Notes on Emptiness: The State of Fiction." *South Dakota Review* (Autumn 1975), 13(3):121-38.

Lasch, Christopher. "The Narcissist Society." *The New York Review of Books* (September 30, 1976), 23(15)5, 8-13.

Le Masters, E. E. *Blue-Collar Aristocrats.* Madison: University of Wisconsin Press, 1975.

Levin, Harry. "Literature as an Institution." *Accent* (Spring 1946), 6(3):159-68.

Lewis, Oscar. *The Children of Sanchez: Autobiography of a Mexican Family.* New York: Random House, 1961.

——*La Vida: A Puerto Rican Family in the Culture of Poverty—San Juan and New York.* New York: Random House, 1965.

Liebow, Elliot. *Tally's Corner: A Study of Negro Streetcorner Men.* Boston: Little, Brown, 1967.

Lienhardt, Godfrey. *Social Anthropology.* 2d ed. London: Oxford University Press, Oxford Paperbacks University Series Opus 15, 1966.
Lorenz, Konrad. *On Aggression.* Marjorie Latzke, trans. London: Methuen, 1966.
Lowell, Robert. In *Writers at Work: The Paris Review Interviews* (second series), pp. 335-68, George Plimpton, ed. New York: Viking Press, Viking Compass ed., 1963.
Macdonald, Dwight. "Jim Agee: A Memoir." In *Remembering James Agee,* pp. 119-44, David Madden, ed. Baton Rouge: Louisiana State University Press, 1974.
Maddox, George. "Age as Explanation." *Science* (October 20, 1972), 178(4058):294-95.
Malinowski, Bronislaw. *Argonauts of the Western Pacific: An Account of Native Enterprise and Adventure in the Archipelagoes of Melanesian New Guinea.* New York: Dutton, 1950.
Malthus, Thomas Robert. *On Population.* Gertrude Himmelfarb, ed. New York: Random House, 1960.
Mead, Margaret. *An Anthropologist at Work: Writings of Ruth Benedict.* Boston: Houghton Mifflin, 1959.
——*Blackberry Winter: My Earlier Years.* New York: William Morrow, Pocket Books, 1975.
——"The Mass Consists of 1 and 1 and 1 and 1 and . . . ." *New York Times,* August 4, 1976, p. 31M.
Meadows, Donella H. and Dennis L. Meadows, et al. *The Limits to Growth.* New York: Universe, 1972.
Mellow, James R. "Walker Evans Captures the Unvarnished Truth." *New York Times,* December 1, 1974, pp. 37D-38D.
Metzger, Walter P. "Leanings of the Professoriate." *Science* (January 23, 1976), 191(4224):279-80.
Miller, Henry. In *Writers at Work: The Paris Review Interviews* (second series), pp. 165-91, George Plimpton, ed. New York: Viking Press, Viking Compass ed., 1965.
Mills, C. Wright. *The Sociological Imagination.* New York: Grove Press, Evergreen ed., 1961.
Moraes, Dom. *A Matter of People.* New York: Praeger, 1974.
Murray, Henry. "Foreword." In Robert N. Wilson, *Man Made Plain,* pp. xi-xxxiii. Cleveland: Howard Allen, 1958.
Natkins, Lucille G. "On Ethnic Surveys." *New York Times,* March 6, 1977, p. 16E.
Nekrich, Aleksandr. "Inside the Leviathan." *The New York Review of Books* (April 14, 1977), 24(6):8-10.

Newman, Edwin. *Strictly Speaking: Will America Be the Death of English?* New York: Warner Books, 1975.

Nin, Anaïs. *The Diary of Anaïs Nin*, vol. I, 1931-34. New York: Harcourt Brace and World, 1966.

Nisbet, Robert. *Sociology as an Art Form*. New York: Oxford University Press, 1976.

——"The Study of Social Problems." In *Contemporary Social Problems* (3d ed.), pp. 1-25, Robert K. Merton and Robert Nisbet, eds. New York: Harcourt Brace Jovanovich, 1971.

O'Connor, Frank. In *Writers at Work: The Paris Review Interviews* (first series), pp 161-82, Malcolm Cowley, ed. New York: Viking Press, Viking Compass ed., 1959.

Oppenheimer, Joel. "In the Dark Month." *The Village Voice* (January 20, 1975), 20(3):48.

Orwell, George. "Politics and the English Language." In *Identity and Anxiety: Survival of the Person in Mass Society*, pp. 308-19, Maurice R. Stein, Arthur J. Vidich, and David Manning White, eds. New York: Free Press of Glencoe, 1960.

Pessen, Edward. "Current Historiographical Modes, Obfuscatory in Nature, Manifest an Indifference to Quintessential Elements of Meaningfulness." *New York Times*, March 27, 1976, p. 25.

Pierce, Kenneth M. "Copping Out on Civil Rights: The Case against Racial Quotas." *The Village Voice* (February 9, 1976), 21(6):43-44.

Porter, Katherine Anne. In *Writers at Work: The Paris Review Interviews* (second series), pp. 137-63, George Plimpton, ed. New York: Viking Press, Viking Compass ed., 1965.

Powdermaker, Hortense. *Stranger and Friend: The Way of an Anthropologist*. New York: Norton, 1967.

Powys, John Cowper. *A Philosophy of Solitude*. New York: Simon and Schuster, 1933.

Price, Martin. "The Other Self: Thoughts about Character in the Novel." In *Imagined Worlds: Essays on some English Novels and Novelists in Honour of John Butt*, pp. 279-99, Maynard Mack and Ian Gregor, eds. London: Methuen, 1968.

Radin, Paul. *Primitive Man as Philosopher*. New York: D. Appleton, 1927.

Rainwater, Lee. "Crucible of Identity: The Negro Lower-Class Family." In *Marriage and the Family: A Comparative Analysis of Contemporary Problems*, pp. 215-60, Meyer Barash and Alice Scourby, eds. New York: Random House, 1970.

Reichard, Suzanne, Florine Livson, and Paul G. Peterson. *Aging and Personality*. New York: Wiley, 1962.

Reinhold, Robert. "Polling Encounters Public Resistance; Decision-Making Process Is Threatened." *New York Times*, October 26, 1975, pp. 1, 58.

Richards, I. A. "The Future of the Humanities in General Education." In *Identity and Anxiety: Survival of the Person in Mass Society*, pp. 383-90, Maurice R. Stein, Arthur J. Vidich, and David Manning White, eds. New York: Free Press of Glencoe, 1960.

Richmond, W. Edson. "'Just Sing It Yourself': The American Lyric Tradition." In *Our Living Traditions: An Introduction to American Folklore*, pp. 94-107, Tristram Potter Coffin, ed. New York: Basic Books, 1968.

Rilke, Rainer Maria. Letter of November 13, 1925 to his Polish translator, Witold von Hulewicz. In *Duino Elegies*, Appendix 4, J. B. Leishman and Stephen Spender, trans. New York: Norton, 1939.

Rodgers, W. R., ed. *Irish Literary Portraits*. New York: Taplinger, 1973.

Roethke, Theodore. "The Waking." *The Collected Verse of Theodore Roethke: Words for the Wind*. Bloomington: Indiana University Press, by arrangement with Doubleday, 1961.

Rothman, David. *The Discovery of the Asylum*. Boston: Little, Brown, 1971.

Rubin, Theodore Isaac. *Compassion and Self-Hate*. New York: David McKay, 1975.

Schumacher, E. F. *Small Is Beautiful: Economics as If People Mattered*. New York: Harper & Row, 1973.

Scott-Maxwell, Florida. *The Measure of My Days*. New York: Knopf, 1969.

Smith, W. Eugene and Aileen M. Smith. *Minamata*. New York: Holt, Rinehart and Winston, 1975.

"Social Anthropologists Learn to Be Scientific" by G. B. K. *Science* (February 25, 1977), 195(4280):770.

Sontag, Susan. "Photography: The Beauty Treatment." *The New York Review of Books* (November 28, 1974), 21(19):35-39.

Starkie, Walter. "Introduction." In Miguel de Unamuno, *Our Lord Don Quixote*, pp. ix-xxxv, Anthony Kerrigan, trans. Princeton: Princeton University Press, 1967.

Steiner, George. *The Death of Tragedy*. New York: Hill and Wang, 1961.

——"Marxism and the Literary Critic." In *Sociology of Literature and Drama*, pp. 159-78, Elizabeth and Tom Burns, eds. Harmondsworth, Middlesex, England: Penguin, 1973.

Stewart, John. "Oral History Is Beyond the Stage of Talking." *New York Times*, May 22, 1977, p. 9E.

Stott, William. *Documentary Expression and Thirties America*. New York: Oxford University Press, 1973.

Swift, Jonathan. *A Modest Proposal*. Leonard Baskin (illus.). New York: Grossman Publishers, 1969.

——*A Tale of a Tub*. Oxford: Clarendon Press, 1958.

Szarkowski, John. "A Different Kind of Art." *The New York Times Magazine*, April 13, 1975, pp. 16-19, 64-68.

Terkel, Studs. "A Steel Worker Speaks: Interview with Mike Fitzgerald." *Dissent* (Winter 1972), 19(1):9-20.
Theroux, Paul. "Minamata." *The New York Times Book Review*, June 8, 1975, pp. 2-3.
Unamuno, Miguel de. *Tragic Sense of Life*. J. E. Crawford Flitch (trans.). New York: Dover, 1954.
Vendler, Helen. "Art, Life and Dr. Williams." *The New York Review of Books* (November 13, 1975), 22(18):17-20.
Warren, Robert Penn. In *Writers at Work: The Paris Review Interviews* (first series), pp. 183-207, Malcolm Cowley, ed. New York: Viking Press, Viking Compass ed., 1959.
Watt, Ian. "*Robinson Crusoe* as a Myth." In *Sociology of Literature and Drama*, pp. 402-17, Elizabeth and Tom Burns, eds., Harmondsworth, Middlesex, England: Penguin, 1973.
Weber, Max. "Science as a Vocation." In *From Max Weber: Essays in Sociology*, pp. 129-56, H. H. Gerth and C. Wright Mills, trans. and eds. New York: Oxford University Press, 1946.
Weinraub, Bernard. "Today's Writers Failing Mankind, Bellow Contends." *New York Times*, December 13, 1976, pp. 1, 9.
West, James. *Plainville, U.S.A.* New York: Columbia University Press, 1961.
Whitmont, Edward C. *The Symbolic Quest: Basic Concepts of Analytical Psychology*. New York: Putnam, 1969.
Whyte, William Foote. *Street Corner Society*. Chicago: University of Chicago Press, 1955.
Wilson, Edmund, *Axel's Castle*. New York: Scribner's, 1931.
Wilson, Robert N. *Man Made Plain*. Cleveland: Howard Allen, 1958.
Wolin, Sheldon S. "Looking for 'Reality.'" *The New York Review of Books* (February 6, 1975), 22(1):15-20.
Wood, Michael. "Fiction in Extremis." *The New York Review of Books* (November 28, 1974), 21(19):29-31.
——"Unhappy Dictators." *The New York Review of Books* (December 9, 1976), 23(20):57-58.
"The World of the Brain." Wraparound in *Harper's Magazine* (December 1975), 251(1507):3-10, 117-24.

# Name Index

Aaron, Daniel, 178
Agee, James, xix, 105, 115, 121, 142, 153-62, 166, 169, 175, 238, 242, 243, 244
Algren, Nelson, 37-38, 55-56, 59, 235
Alvarez, Alfred, 48, 81, 232, 236, 243
Anderson, Alston, 55
Angell, Robert C., 137, 163, 240
Aristophanes, 77
Arnold, Matthew, 66
Aron, Raymond, xxii, 34, 78, 231
Auden, W. H., 1, 42, 83, 188, 237, 245
Auerbach, Erich, 236
Austen, Jane, xv

Bagehot, Walter, 34, 181
Bakke, E. Wight, 163
Balzac, Honoré de, 182
Barash, Meyer, 241
Bass, Jack, 238
Baudelaire, Charles, 117
Beauvoir, Simone de, 67, 89, 91, 99-100, 173, 237, 238, 244
Becker, Ernest, 233
Behan, Brendan, 67
Bellamy, Edward, 78
Bellow, Saul, xviii-xx, 9, 11, 66, 91-92, 187, 212, 230, 232, 245, 246
Benedict, Ruth, xxiii, 91, 192-93, 231, 245
Berg, Stephen, 25
Berger, Bennett, 184-86, 244, 245
Berger, Morroe, xiv-xv, 75, 179, 230, 236, 244
Berger, Peter, 4, 40, 76, 88-90, 231, 232, 234, 236, 237

Bergson, Henri, 79
Bernanos, Georges, 142
Bettelheim, Bruno, 110-11, 239
Bianchi, Eugene, 243
Bierstedt, Robert, xxiv, 4, 180, 231, 244
Blake, William, 4, 65, 115
Blumer, Herbert, 13-14, 19, 23, 140, 173, 232, 240
Boas, Franz, 91, 192
Bohannan, Laura, 91
Bohr, Niels, 183
Boorstin, Daniel, xxiii, 29, 94, 231, 233, 238
Borenstein, Audrey F., 245
Borges, Jorge Luis, xviii, 33, 233
Borowski, Tadeusz, 136, 240
Britten, Florence H., 232
Bromley, Dorothy D., 232
Bronowski, Jacob, 129, 168, 183, 240, 244
Browning, Robert, 61
Buckingham, Robert, 150, 241
Burns, Tom and Elizabeth, xiv, 5, 64, 230, 231, 235, 242, 245
Butler, Robert, 137, 152, 171, 240, 242
Butler, Samuel, 101
Byron, George Gordon, Lord, 54

Cadalso, José, 91
Caesar, Julius, 96
Caffi, Andrea, 174
Calhoun, John C., 206
Calisher, Hortense, 177-78, 244
Cameron, J. M., 128, 240, 243, 244
Capote, Truman, 34, 36, 62-63, 180, 210

Carpenter, Edmund, 41, 152, 234
Carpentier, Alejo, 210
Carter, James (President), xix
Cary, Joyce, 60, 66, 235, 236
Casagrande, Joseph, 143, 234, 241
Cavan, Ruth, 169
Cervantes, Miguel de, 143
Chateaubriand, Francois-René de, 89
Chekhov, Anton, 168
Chiaromonte, Miriam, 238
Chiaromonte, Nicola, 106, 174, 238, 244
Christie, Agatha, 237
Cicero, 173
Clark, Kenneth, 168
Clausen, John, 15, 232
Coffin, Tristram P., 240
Colen, B. D., 241
Coleridge Samuel T., 61, 81
Coles, Robert, 46, 79, 90, 139, 141-42, 150, 155, 159, 168-69, 236, 240, 241, 242, 243
Comte, Auguste, 22, 78, 109
Condorcet, Marquis de, 84
Cooley, Charles Horton, 64, 162
Cooper, James Fenimore, 35
Cortázar, Julio, 213
Coser, Lewis, 94, 238
Cowley, Malcolm, 234

Daguerre, Louis J., 178
Darwin, Charles, 231
Davis, Allison, 163
Defoe, Daniel, 68-69
DeMott, Benjamin, 211-12, 245
Densmore, Francis, 122
Dentan, Robert K., 104, 238
Des Pres, Terrence, 48
DeVries, Walter, 238
Dewey, John, 140
Dickens, Charles, xv, 101, 182
Dickstein, Morris, 230
Dilthey, Wilhelm, 186
Dixon, Marlene, 233
Dollard, John, 162
Donohue, H. E. F., 234
Dos Passos, John, 108, 239

Dostoevski, Feodor M., 47, 61, 182, 212
Dreiser, Theodore, 178
Dubos, René, 168
Duffy, Annette, 30, 233
Durkheim, Emile, 5, 20, 80-82, 84, 88, 90, 102, 109, 186, 236, 245

Eastman, Max, xiv
Ehrenpreis, Irvin, 83, 237
Eichmann, Adolf, 32
Eiseley, Loren, 70, 110, 168, 236, 239
Eisenhower, Dwight D., 208
Eliot, George, xiv, 77, 187
Ellis, Edward R., 236
Ellison, Ralph, 42, 52-53, 142, 168
Engels, Friedrich, 90, 242
Epstein, Joseph, 187, 245
Erikson, Erik, 90
Erikson, Kai T., 44-48, 57-58, 63, 72, 234, 235
Escarpit, Robert, xiv, 68-69, 236
Etzioni, Amitai, 14, 112, 232, 238, 239
Evans, Walker, xix, 117-18, 153-56, 159-62, 238, 239, 242, 243

Farid-al-Din Attar, 33
Faulkner, William, 59, 142, 235
Feinberg, Leonard, 76-78, 83, 90, 236, 237
Fichte, Johann G., 81-82
Fiedler, Leslie, 35
Firdausi (Abul Qasim Mansur), 33
Firth, Raymond, 152
Fischer, Louis, 93
Fitzgerald, Robert, 154, 160, 242, 243
Flaubert, Gustav, 117
Fortune, Reo, 153, 242
Foucault, Michel, xviii, 230
Frankel, Lester, 44
Frazer, James, 143, 241
Frazer, Ray, 54
Freuchen, Peter, 152
Freud, Sigmund, xviii, 90, 122
Frost, Robert, 61
Frye, Northrup, 65, 235
Fuentes, Carlos, 214

## Name Index

Galsworthy, John, 101
Gandhi, Mahatma, 116
Gans, Herbert, 167
García Márquez, Gabriel, 210-11
Garfinkel, Harold, 135, 234, 240
Gerth, Hans H., 232, 245
Gide, André, 89
Gilman, Richard, 142-43, 241
Ginzberg, Eli, 163
Glazer, Nathan, 22-23
Glueck, Grace, 237
Godwin, William, 84
Goethe, Johann Wolfgang von, 201
Goffman, Erving, 20, 129, 148, 167, 240, 241
Goldmann, Lucien, 25, 233
Goldsmith, Oliver, 91
Gorer, Geoffrey, 112-13, 239
Gottschalk, Louis, 137, 169-70, 240, 243
Gouldner, Alvin, xxi-xxii, 6, 78, 231, 236, 238
Graver, Lawrence, 244
Green, Martin, 231
Gregor, Ian, 233, 236
Griffin, John H., 99
Gris, Juan, 183
Gutmann, David, 144, 241

Haley, Alex, xix
Hampshire, Stuart, 27, 213-14, 246
Hannerz, Ulf, 49-54, 57-58, 63, 72, 167, 235, 241, 243
Hardwick, Elizabeth, 30, 233
Hardy, Thomas, xiv, xx
Harper, Gordon L., xviii
Harrington, Michael, 45-46, 234
Havighurst, Robert J., 172
Hawthorne, Nathaniel, 35
Heberle, Rudolf, 204, 235
Hegel, Georg W. F., 33, 242
Heidt, Sarajane, 238
Heilbroner, Robert, 237
Hellman, Roberta, 155-56, 242
Henry, Jules, 93, 105, 107, 146-47, 152, 155, 167, 238, 241
Herodotus, 104

Herskovits, Melville J., xix-xx
Hesse, Hermann, xiii, xvii, 30, 168, 215, 230
Himmelfarb, Gertrude, 237
Hine, Lewis, 164
Hitler, Adolf, 24
Hobbes, Thomas, 114
Hollowell, John, xix, 34-36, 62-63, 179, 210, 231, 234, 235, 244, 245
Horace, 96
Hoshino, Marvin, 155-56, 242
Hughes, Everett, 90-91
Hugo, Victor, 173
Hulewicz, Witold von, 242
Hume, David, 81
Huston, John, 175
Huxley, Aldous, 54, 61, 67, 235, 236

Ibsen, Henrik, 101
Ignatow, David, 25

Jackson, Jacqueline J., 233
James, Henry, 9, 30, 135, 181, 244
James, William, 140
Johnson, Lyndon B., 23
Johnson, Robert, 41
Johnson, Samuel, 100
Johnson, Sheila, 23-24, 233
Johnson, Virginia E., 128
Jones, Ernest, xviii
Jordan, June, 25
Joyce, James, 237
Jung, Carl G., 12, 27, 68, 71, 90, 173, 190

Kael, Pauline, 142, 241
Kafka, Franz, 161
Kant, Immanuel, 81-82
Kazin, Alfred, 116, 239
Keats, John, 64
Kermode, Frank, 5, 8, 232, 245
Kesey, Ken, 129, 240
Kierkegaard, Søren, 33, 61, 105, 211
King, Martin Luther, 122
Kinsey, Alfred, 138, 244
Kluckhohn, Clyde, 131-32, 136-37, 144-45, 215, 240, 241, 246

Komarovsky, Mirra, 163
Kott, Jan, 136, 240
Kramer, Hilton, 115, 117-18, 121-22, 230, 239
Kroeber, Alfred, 91
Kübler-Ross, Elisabeth, 144-45, 241

La Bruyère, Jean de, 7
Ladd, Everett C., 17-19
La Farge, Oliver, 168, 243
Lamartine, Alphonse de, 82
Landesco, John, 163
Larner, Jeremy, 132-33, 164, 240
La Rochefoucauld, François, duc de, 21
Larsen, Eric, xv-xvii, 87-88, 230, 237
Lasch, Christopher, 239
Lawrence, D. H., 54, 231
Lazarsfeld, Paul, 163, 173
Le Masters, E. E., 149, 152, 167, 241, 242, 243
Lenin, Nicolai, 120
Le Play, P. G. Frédéric, 102
Levin, Harry, xiv, 26, 233
Lévi-Strauss, Claude, 91, 155, 191
Lewis, Hylan, 168
Lewis, Oscar, 36, 135, 151-52, 165-66, 168, 237, 240, 242, 243
Lewis, Sinclair, 171
Liebow, Elliot, 167-68, 243
Lienhardt, Godfrey, 39-40, 42, 234
Lindeman, Edward, 162
Lipset, Seymour M., 17-19
Livson, Florine, 232
Lorenz, Konrad, 110, 239
Lowell, Robert, 61, 235
Lowes, Livingston, 187
Lunt, Paul S., 171
Lynd, Robert and Helen, 58, 171

Macaulay, Thomas B., 75, 190
Macdonald, Dwight, 160-61, 243
Machiavelli, Niccolò, xxii, 143
MacIver, Robert, xiv
Mack, Maynard, 233, 236
Madden, David, 242
Maddox, George, 15, 232
Mailer, Norman, xix, 36, 180

Malinowski, Bronislaw, 91, 130, 143, 152, 240
Malraux, André, 93, 103, 108, 122
Malthus, Thomas Robert, 78, 84-86, 94, 109, 237
Manis, Jerome G., 232, 234, 240
Mann, Sir Horace, 73
Mannheim, Karl, 135
Marquand, J. P., 171
Martial, 71
Marx, Karl, xvi, 4, 27, 88, 90, 106-7, 120, 174, 242
Masters, William H., 128
Mead, George Herbert, 29, 111, 121, 140
Mead, Margaret, 91, 99, 116, 153, 191-93, 238, 239, 242, 245
Meadows, Donella and Dennis L., 237
Mellow, James R., 239
Meltzer, Bernard N., 232, 234, 240
Melville, Herman, 35
Mencken, H. L., 138
Merton, Robert, 94, 238, 239
Metzger, Walter, 17-19, 232
Michelangelo, Buonarroti, 89, 173
Michels, Robert, xiv
Miller, Henry, 67, 236
Mills, C. Wright, 12, 47, 88, 136, 176-82, 185, 188-89, 210, 212, 232, 240, 244, 245
Milton, John, 65
Minehan, Thomas, 162-64
Molière, 143
Montagu, M. F. Ashley, 239
Montaigne, Michel de, 3, 89, 173
Montesquieu, 91
Moraes, Dom, 86, 237
More, Hannah, 81
More, Sir Thomas, 78
Morgan, Lewis H., 91
Mouton, Edgar, 100-1
Mozart, Wolfgang A., 177
Mumford, Lewis, 168
Murdoch, Iris, 31
Murdock, George P., 91
Murray, Gilbert, 108
Murray, Henry, 4, 231
Myrdal, Gunnar, 55

## Name Index

Nader, Ralph, 43, 114
Natkins, Lucille, 233
Nekrich, Aleksandr, 237
Ness, Frederick, 212
Neugarten, Bernice L., 241
Nevins, Allan, 137
Newman, Edwin, 6, 16, 231, 232
Newton, Isaac, 183, 213
Nin, Anaïs, 27, 113, 239
Nisbet, Robert, 94-96, 101-3, 181-82, 187-88, 238, 239, 244, 245

Oates, Joyce Carol, 135
O'Connor, Flannery, 142
O'Connor, Frank, 58-59, 235
Odum, Howard, 134
Olson, Charles, 26
O'Neill, Eugene, 168
Oppenheimer, Joel, 26, 233
Ortega y Gasset, José, 8-9
Orwell, George, 128, 142, 159, 240

Pareto, Vilfredo, 90, 109
Percy, Walker, 142
Pessen, Edward, 6-7, 232
Peterson, Paul G., 232
Pierce, Kenneth, 22-23, 233
Plath, Sylvia, 193
Plato, xiv, 77-78
Plimpton, George, 231, 235
Pollack, Oscar, 161
Polt, John, 24
Pope, Alexander, 90
Porter, Katherine Anne, 57, 59, 235
Powdermaker, Hortense, 52, 131, 153, 240
Powys, John Cowper, 108, 120, 238, 239
Price, Martin, 27-29, 67, 233, 236
Proust, Marcel, 141, 213

Quetelet, Ernest, 136

Radin, Paul, 122, 239
Rainwater, Lee, 149, 168, 241
Rank, Otto, 90
Redfield, Robert, 91
Reichard, Suzanne, 232

Reinhold, Robert, 43-44, 234
Rich, Adrienne, 25-26
Richards, I. A., 171-72, 243
Richmond, W. Edson, 134, 240
Riis, Jacob, 164
Riley, Matilda, 15
Rilke, Rainer Maria, 29, 151-52, 156, 242
Rimbaud, Arthur, 81
Robinson, Paul, 128
Rodgers, W. R., 237
Röntgen, Wilhelm K., 183
Roethke, Theodore, 140, 240
Roosevelt, Franklin D., 205
Rose, Peter I., 233, 244
Rosenthal, M. L., 26
Roth, Philip, 35
Rothman, David, 129, 240
Rousseau, Jean Jacques, 114
Rubin, Theodore I., 96, 238
Ruether, Rosemary R., 243

Santayana, George, 47
Sapir, Edward, 91
Sartre, Jean Paul, 8-9, 87
Schopenhauer, Arthur, 89, 173
Schuetz, Alfred, 40, 130
Schumacher, E. F., xxiii-xxiv, 231
Scott, John C., 43
Scott-Maxwell, Florida, 237
Scourby, Alice, 241
Shakespeare, William, 38, 127, 143
Shaw, Clifford, 164
Shaw, George Bernard, 3-4, 101
Shelley, Percy B., 54
Sherrington, Charles, Sir, 182
Simmel, Georg, xxv, 88
Simpson, George, 236, 245
Singer, June, 90
Smith, W. Eugene and Aileen, 114-17, 239
Snow, C. P., xiv
Socrates, 172
Solzhenitsyn, Aleksandr I., 108
Sontag, Susan, 117, 239
Southern, Terry, 55
Sprehe, Timothy, 78
Staël, Madame de, xiv

Starkie, Walter, 120, 239
Stein, Gertrude, 193
Stein, Maurice R., 240
Steiner, George, 66, 106, 236, 238, 242
Stevens, Wallace, 178
Stewart, John, 137, 240
Stott, William, 161-64, 173, 178, 239, 243, 244
Stouffer, Samuel, 78
Sumner, William Graham, xxiv, 18
Sutherland, Edwin H., 243
Swados, Harvey, 171
Sweezy, Paul, 181
Swift, Jonathan, 68-69, 83, 85-86, 89, 94, 125, 237
Szarkowski, John, 116, 239

Taft, Donald R., 38
Taine, Hyppolite, xiv
Tanner, Tony, 210
Tawney, R. H., xvi
Tefferteller, Ralph, 132, 164, 240
Tennyson, Alfred, Lord, 188
Terkel, Studs, 21, 164, 233
Theroux, Paul, 115, 239
Thomas, Piri, 171
Thomas, W. I., 9, 102, 163, 169
Thoreau, Henry D., 210
Thrasher, Frederick, 167
Thurber, James, 90
Tocqueville, Count Alexis de, xxiv, 67, 95, 238
Tönnies, Ferdinand, 64
Tolstoy, Count Leo N., 89, 142, 182, 212
Trilling, Lionel, 36, 66, 244
Trollope, Anthony, 54
Truman, Harry S., 205
Twain, Mark, 90
Tylor, Edward, 91

Unamuno, Miguel de, 86, 97-98, 101, 104, 107-9, 113, 120, 237, 238, 239
Updike, John, 171

Veblen, Thorstein, xiv, xxiv
Vendler, Helen, 142, 171, 241, 243

Vidich, Arthur J., 240
Voltaire, 90

Wakefield, Dan, 171
Walpole, Horace, 73, 81-82
Walter, Eugene, 42
Warhol, Andy, 71
Warner, W. Lloyd, 58, 162, 171-72
Warren, Robert Penn, 42, 62-63, 66, 142, 234, 235
Watson, John B., 121
Watt, Ian, xvi, 230
Wattenberg, Ben, 43
Waugh, Evelyn, 76
Weber, Max, xvi, xviii, xxii, 5, 8, 33, 39, 88, 90, 109, 184, 188, 209-10, 213, 231, 232, 245
Weil, Simone, 106, 142, 159
Weinraub, Bernard, 246
Weirich, Bruce, 38
Wells, H. G., 101
Welty, Eudora, 142
Wesley, John, 76
West, James, 48, 58, 241
White, David M., 240
Whitman, Walt, 21
Whitmont, Edward C., 31-32, 233
Whyte, William Foote, 38, 41-42, 48, 58, 63, 164, 167-68, 234, 241
Wickes, George, 54
Williams, William Carlos, 142, 241, 243
Wilson, Edmund, 3-4, 231
Wilson, Robert N., 4, 19, 231, 232
Wirth, Louis, 163
Wister, Sarah, 181
Wolfe, Thomas, 180
Wolin, Sheldon, 43-44, 234
Wollstonecraft, Mary, 84
Wood, Michael, 210-11, 213, 245, 246
Woolf, Virginia, 11, 30, 176
Wright, Richard, 142

Yeats, William Butler, 3-4, 89, 127

Znaniecki, Florian, 102, 163
Zola, Emile, 101, 168
Zorbaugh, Harvey, 163

# Subject Index

*Addict in the Street, The,* 132-33, 164, 240
Affirmative action, xxii, 8, 22-23, 25, 233, 237
American Association of University Professors, 193
American Diary Repository, 70; *see also* Diaries
American Medical Association, 193, 209
*American Poetry Review,* 24-26, 233; *see also* Poetry
American Sociological Association, 13
Anthropology, 6, 37, 39, 66, 91, 168, 192-93; and humanism, xxiii, 41, 214, 231; and sociology, 39, 150; perspective, 49, 52-54, 94, 138-39, 147, 214-15; and poetry, 91, 151-52, 192-93; method, 112, 119, 131-32, 144-45, 151-58, 163, 167-68, 170-71, 240, 241; *The Children of Sanchez,* 135, 165-66, 168; medical anthropology, 150; *Let Us Now Praise Famous Men,* 155-58, 160, 168, 242
*Argonauts of the Western Pacific,* 130, 143, 240, 241
*Ascent of Man, The,* 129, 183, 240, 244
Association of American Colleges, 212
Autobiography, 36, 89, 99, 135, 169, 243; *see also* First-person story; Life history; Memoirs; Oral history

"Bad faith," 12, 244
Bead Game, xiii, xx, xxv, 168, 215, 230
"Bees of the invisible," 152, 156
Biography, 61, 101, 121, 136, 192

*Blackberry Winter,* 99, 153, 191-92, 238, 242, 245
Buffalo Creek, 44-46, 48, 57-58, 63, 72
Bureau of American Ethnology, 122

Carnegie Commission on Higher Education, 17
Case study, xv, 138, 147, 163-64, 173
Chicago school of sociology, 163
*Children of Sanchez, The,* 36, 135, 165-6, 168, 240, 243
Comedy, xxi, 73, 161
*Coming of Age, The,* 89, 91, 99, 173, 238, 244
Compassion, xxii, 78, 86, 93-123, 174, 191, 238
Confessions, 35-36, 62, 69, 71, 121, 127, 243
"Creative treason," 69, 236
Criticism, literary, xiv, 5, 26, 35, 65-66, 90, 235, 236, 242
"Culture of poverty," 51-52, 135

Data processing, 14-15
Determinism, 9-10, 105-6, 139-41, 173
Diaries, 62, 69-70, 89, 137, 169, 173, 236; *see also* American Diary Repository
Disasters, 45-46, 48, 57-58, 72, 145
Documentary, 35, 42, 65, 117, 134, 161-64, 178
*Documentary Expression and Thirties America,* 161-64, 178, 239, 243, 244
"Documentary method of interpretation," 134-35, 240
Dreams, 7, 10, 12, 46, 57, 119, 122, 174, 190, 205

"Ecology of the interview," 209
Economics, xxiii-xxiv, 3, 6, 37-38, 87, 138, 214
Editing, 56, 134-35
Empathy, 68, 110-12, 117, 153, 164; see also Sympathetic introspection
Encyclopedists, 65
Enlightenment, 22, 95, 103, 109, 213-14; see also Philosophes
Erklärende method, 5, 186
Essay on the Principle of Population, 84, 94, 237
Ethnomethodology, 135
Everything in Its Path, 45, 47, 54, 63, 234
Existentialism, 29, 146-47, 152, 155

Fact and Fiction: The New Journalism and the Nonfiction Novel, 34-36, 62-63, 179, 210, 231, 234, 235, 244, 245
"Faction," xv, 181
"Failure of nerve," 108, 211
Farm Security Administration, 118
Fiction writing, 139; and social science xiv-xx, xxii-xxiii, 34-72, 88, 90-92, 128-31, 141-43, 147-49, 164-65, 167-69, 171, 176-215, 245; satire, 87-88; social novel, 95, 101-2; and nonfiction, 121; and symbolic interactionism, 141, 148; and Let Us Now Praise Famous Men, 155
Film, 37, 69, 71, 104, 115-16, 118-19, 122, 131-32, 142-43, 156, 175, 239, 241, 242; see also Photography; Photojournalism
First-person story, 132, 135, 146, 164-66, 173, 243; see also Autobiography; Life history; Memoirs; Oral history

"Genitive sociology," 64, 235
Ghetto, 28, 49-53, 58, 141, 241; see also Soulside

Henry Street Settlement, 132
History, 6-8, 10, 12, 72, 77, 92, 101, 129, 136, 141, 168, 174, 189, 197; and literature, xix, 46, 61, 65, 121, 136, 171, 179, 214; a sense of the past, xxiii, 72, 110, 112; future historians, 46, 69-71, 180, 188; historical perspective, 96, 180; historical reality, 105-6, 176, 213; and films, 116; historical method, 129, 169-70, 232, 240, 243, 244; and sociology, 180-81, 185-86; see also Oral history
Humanism, 23, 34, 41, 47, 54, 83, 87-89, 97, 162, 168, 171-75, 181, 185-86, 211, 214, 231, 245-46; antihumanism, 4, 7
Humanitarianism, 84-85, 95-96, 103, 109, 114, 120-21, 174
Humanities, xiv, xxiii-xxv, 65, 122, 171-75, 184, 211-12, 214, 231, 243, 245

Ideal Type, 49-50, 77, 82
Imagination, xv, xviii-xx, xxiii, 8-10, 15; literary, 35, 59, 63-64, 66, 72, 81, 83, 86, 130-31, 139, 141-42, 155, 158-60, 176-215; social scientific, 37, 46, 54, 59, 63-64, 72, 88-89, 127-28, 130-31, 161, 173; romantic, 80; and compassion, 98-99, 101, 107, 110, 114, 120-22; and photography, 115; and behaviorism, 120-21; and films, 142-43
Inner conversation, 111
Inner life, 6, 10, 12, 20, 28, 30-31, 34, 46, 77, 91, 97-98, 120-21, 130, 138, 152, 163-65
Interdisciplinary study, xx, 142, 162
"Interposition," 206
Interpretation, 15, 119, 196; and variable analysis, 13, 19, 232; social scientific, 32, 37, 44, 127, 133, 138; literary, 59, 68, 140-41; "documentary method of interpretation," 134-35; in symbolic interaction, 140; and the tape recorder, 164
Introject, 110-11
Invitation to Sociology, 76, 88, 231, 232, 234, 236

John F. Kennedy Library, 137
Journalism, 3, 31, 130, 133, 176; and

fiction writing, xvii, 35, 56, 66; and documentary, xviii, 165, 178; "new journalism," xix, 34, 36, 62-63, 179-80; and social problems, 101-2, 165; and violation of privacy, 118; and *Let Us Now Praise Famous Men*, 153, 161, 168; and social science writing, 162; *see also* Photojournalism

Kibbutz, 110-11

*La Vida*, 36, 151, 166-68, 242, 243
*Let Us Now Praise Famous Men*, xix, 153-62, 166, 168-69, 171, 238, 239, 242, 243
Life history; 30, 135, 147, 152, 162-63; *see also* Autobiography; First-person story; Memoirs; Oral history
Lilliputians, 86-87

Macrosociology, 112
Marxism, 11-12, 65-66, 106, 236, 242
Memoirs, 69, 137, 160, 169; *see also* Autobiography; First-person story; Life history; Oral history
*Minamata*, 114-17, 239
*Modest Proposal, A*, 85-86, 94, 237
Morals, morality, and satire, xxi, 76, 79, 83, 90, 92; and social science, xxi, 36, 46, 76, 80, 83, 88-90, 92, 132, 164, 186, 188; and ideology, 18, 80, 174; moral responsibility, 32; and literature, 36-37, 188; in the ghetto, 49-51; and suicide, 81-82; in *Essay on the Principle of Population*, 84; in *A Modest Proposal*, 86; and compassion, 94-96, 99-103, 109-10, 114, 116, 118-21; moral law, 128, 186; and first-person stories, 132; in *Let Us Now Praise Famous Men*, 161; of physicians and professors, 193-210, 245; in the 1950s, 230

"New journalism," xix, 34, 36, 62-63, 179-80; *see also* Journalism; Photojournalism
"Nonfiction novel," xix, 34, 36, 62-63, 179-80

Nonviolence, 112, 238
Norm, 8, 24, 83, 92, 102, 104, 196

Oral history, 69, 137, 146, 164-65; *see also* Autobiography; First-person story; Life history; Memoirs
Oral History Association, 137
Organization for Economic Cooperation and Development, 14

Participant observation, 41-42, 56, 61, 79-80, 127-75, 202
*Persona*, xviii, 9-10, 12-13, 16, 20-21, 23-25, 27-28, 30, 32-33, 96, 99, 107
"Personal realities," xxi-xxii, 96
*Philosophes*, 22, 81-82, 92, 213; *see also* Enlightenment
Philosophy, xiv, 68, 189, 204; and fiction writing, 60-61, 171, 212; and suicide, 81-82; and aging, 89; and social science, 109, 172-73; of Oglala Dakota, 122; of George Herbert Mead, 140; and determinism, 141; in *Let Us Now Praise Famous Men*, 160-61; and the future of knowledge, 213-14, 239
Photography, 61, 69, 72, 114-119, 121, 129, 153-56, 159-61, 164, 239
Photojournalism, 114-15, 117-19, 153, 170; *see also* Film; Photography
Physicians, 193-210
Poetry, xiv, 87; and social science, 3-4, 10, 91, 129-30, 151-52, 157, 160-61, 167-68, 189-90, 192-93, 208, 215; and sociology, 4, 6; *American Poetry Review*, 24-26, 233; and ideology, 24-27; and *Everything in Its Path*, 45-46; and fiction writing, 61; and documentary criticism, 65; and generalization, 75; of Coleridge, 81-82; and anthropology, 91, 151-52, 192-93; and nonfiction, 121; and *Let Us Now Praise Famous Men*, 155-57, 160-61, 168-69; and historical study, 170, 186; in the 1950s, 177-79; and the future of knowledge, 214
Political science, 3, 6, 17-19, 37, 71, 128, 138, 169-70, 197, 212, 240

Positivism, 80, 103, 109, 172
"Principle of noninterference," 104
Professors, xxiv-xxv, 8, 17-19, 119, 193-210, 232
Psychoanalysis, psychiatry, psychology, 6, 7, 37, 90, 133, 138, 141-42, 168, 171, 204

*Real and Imagined Worlds*, 179, 230, 236, 244
Reality—cultural, historical, social, xviii-xix, xxv, 5, 8-9, 25, 30-31, 34-72, 79, 88, 105-6, 120, 139, 145, 162, 173-74, 176-80, 186-88, 210, 213, 234, 242; and films, 116, 121-22
Religion of humanity, 78, 96, 103
Role, 9-10, 20, 28-29, 31-32, 51, 182

Satire, xxi, 75-92, 160-61, 236, 237
*Savage God, The*, 81, 232, 236, 243
Scientific method, xiv, 3-4, 7, 14-15, 92, 102, 115-16, 128-32, 162, 170, 182-86, 202, 212-13, 244
Simurgh, 33
Social fact, xv, xvii, xix, 14, 32, 37, 42, 44, 66, 70-71, 76, 176-79, 186-87, 210-13
Social problem, xx, xxii, 20-21, 52-53, 60, 82-84, 86, 89, 94-96, 101-3, 119, 160, 171-73, 238, 239
Social science and fiction writing, xiv-xx, xxii-xxiii, 34-72, 88, 90-92, 128-31, 141-43, 147-49, 164-65, 167-69, 171, 176-215, 245; and humanism, xxiii-xxv, 162, 168, 171-75, 212-15; perspective, 3-4, 9-10, 31, 39-41, 51, 79-80, 87, 181-83; and poetry, 3-4, 10, 91, 129-30, 151-52, 157, 160-61, 167-68, 189-90, 192-93, 208, 215; use of language, 6, 128; and ideology, 7, 34, 42, 80, 105-6, 128; method, 15-17, 28, 34-72, 90, 127-75, 243, 244; as advisers to the prince, 22, 107; and compassion, 97, 101, 103, 107, 109-10, 112, 116, 119-20, 122; and determinism, 105-6, 140-41, 173; "consensus social science," 163; in the 1950s and 1960s, 165-66; social-science-become-art, 161; and the future of knowledge, 213-15
Sociobiology, 110, 170
*The Sociological Imagination*, 176, 180, 232, 240, 244
Sociology and fiction writing, xiv, 34-72, 90-91, 213; of literature, xiv, xx, 64-65, 88, 170-71, 233; and satire, xxi, 75-92; perspective, 3-5, 10-12, 39-41, 87-92, 106-7, 110, 136, 138-39, 180; and poetry, 4, 6; cultural interests, 6; use of language, 6, 128, 133; and ideology, 7-9, 12, 16, 34; method, 39, 45-49, 101-3, 127-75, 240, 244; and anthropology, 39, 150; priesthood of sociologists, 78, 109; of conflict, 93-94; of social perception, 94; as a Science of Minorities, 94; of everyday life, 112; and specialization, 119; Chicago school, 163; in the 1950s and 1960s, 165-66, 189; sociological imagination, 176-215; as *"upstart,"* 184
*Sociology as an Art Form*, 187-88, 244, 245
*Soulside*, 49-55, 57, 167, 235, 241, 243; see also Ghetto
Statistics, xv, 6-7, 17-19, 22, 32, 37, 42, 77-79, 83, 89, 107, 114, 116-17, 119, 127-28, 146-47, 162-63, 168, 170, 211
Status, 9-10, 29, 140, 148, 151, 166
*Street Corner Society*, 38, 168, 234, 241
Suicide, 20, 186, 236, 245
Survey, 17-18, 28, 43-44, 127, 132, 161, 170, 172
Symbolic interaction, 76, 89, 140-41, 148, 194-95, 232, 234, 240
Sympathetic introspection, 64; see also Empathy

Tape recorder, 69, 72, 127, 132, 152, 164-65, 193
Temporocentrism, 180
Tragedy, xxi, 57, 73, 82, 86, 97, 105-7, 115, 142, 237, 238; tragic sense of life, 80, 95, 104-06

Triage, 84-85
*Tristes Tropiques*, 155-56

Utopia, 77-79, 90, 109, 116

Variable, 10, 12-16, 19, 23, 28-30, 33, 173, 232; variable analysis, 13-15, 173, 232
*Verstehende* method, 5, 13, 23, 214
Vietnam, 118